Sustainable Tourism

Sustainable Tourism

driving green investment and shared
prosperity in developing countries.

Federico Vignati • Don Hawkins • Bruce Priedeaux

Federico Vignati Scarpati (author)

Fvignati@cnventures.org

Federico is an economist and sustainable development practitioner, with over 16 years of experience working in Asia, Africa and Latin America. While writing this book, he worked for SNV- Netherlands Development Organization (Mozambique), as Regional Tourism Sector Leader for East and Southern Africa. Between 2010-2013, he acted as country representative for the United Nations World Tourism Organization/Fund for Poverty Alleviation. In 2012 Ford Foundation and the International Institute of Education, through the recognition of his work, granted him funds for the publication of "Sustainable Tourism". Federico holds a Ph.D. in Applied Economics, is author of several scientific articles, papers and books. Through his career, he has provided consulting for EU, WB, CAF, IFC, ILO, UNESCO and lectured to graduate students at Wharton School of Business, Florida University, Barcelona University, PUC-Rio and Getulio Vargas Foundation. Federico is currently working for the Development Bank of Latin America (CAF).

Don Hawkins - Co-author (Chapter 7)

Dhawk@gwu.edu

Don is the Dwight D. Eisenhower Professor of Tourism Policy and Professor of Management and Tourism Studies in the School of Business and Professor of International Affairs in the Elliott School of Foreign Affairs at the George Washington University. He is engaged in tourism and hospitality management education and conducts policy-related research for the past 42 years. In 1988, he founded the International Institute of Tourism Studies as a collaborative initiative of GW and the World Tourism Organization. In 1994, he was appointed as the Dwight D. Eisenhower Professor of Tourism Policy (an endowed chair) in the GW School of Business. For detailed information, go to http://business.gwu.edu/tourism

In 2003, he received the first United Nations World Tourism Organization (UNWTO) Ulysses Prize for individual accomplishments in the creation and dissemination of knowledge in the area of tourism policy and strategic management. He received the UNWTO Themis Foundation Science Fellow Award, in April, 2005 in Andorra. Currently he is Vice Chairman of the Committee of Affiliate Members. In 2012, he was appointed as Special Advisor to the Secretary General of the United Nations World Tourism Organization to oversee the UNWTO Knowledge Network, which includes 135 universities and research centres worldwide.

Bruce Prideaux - Co-author (Chapter 2)
B.prideaux@cqu.edu.au

Bruce holds the position of Head of the Tourism Research Centre at the Central Queensland University, Australia. He is actively engaged in climatic change research with a particular interest in its impacts on coral reef systems and rainforests. Other active areas of research include a range of environmental issues related to sustainable development in developing countries, agro-tourism, military heritage, tourism transport, tourism aviation, crisis management, heritage and ecotourism. He holds Visiting Professorships at Bournemouth University in the UK and Taylors University Malaysia and has authored over 250 journal articles, book chapters and conference papers on a range tourism related issues.

To Luciana, Gael and Luca, my inspiration.

If you want to go fast, go alone,
If you want to go far, go together.

African Proverb.

Introduction.

Tourism is the largest growing industry on earth, It already represents 7 trillion USD annual turnover or 9.5 % of global GDP and is rising with 4% every year. Tourism has created directly 100 million jobs (3.4% of global employment) and supports 270 million jobs indirectly. If Global Tourism would be a country, its economy would rank third (between China, nr 2 and Japan, nr 3).

Tourism moves people from one place to another, be it from abroad, from within the same region, from within the same country or closer by but always impacts somewhere at the local level. Tourism has cultural and environmental interfaces, which can create new better situations, or it can influence negatively on both sides.

Tourism normally has an important multiplier effect for local or national economies. Therefore, tourism can be practised in a sustainable inclusive manner whereby it contributes to the wellbeing of the tourists and of the local people it employs and who live in the areas tourists go. So if we want to develop social and economic impacts we need to think about sustainability.

Tourism is done by people, the tourists. They decide *where* to go, for *how long, how much* to spend and *on what* to spend their money.

Sustainability is not the first thing people are concerned about. Yet it will determine the future of many of the attractions people come for and the experiences tourists take home with them. Sustainable tourism will have to impact the choices people make. If we want to maintain the attractions, which drive the tourism industry the sector has to improve the sustainability of its operations.

Let us think about the various angles of this sustainability:

Environmental sustainability: Tourists like clean beautiful places and nature with lots of big and fluffy or rare animals that should not be too difficult to spot. So tourism should contribute to waste and garbage collection, landscape cleaning and diminishing environmental pollution. Sustainable tourism not only will minimize its own environmental footprint but also actively contribute to habitat and species conservation.

Global warming is a concern and the high emissions from global increased flying should be addressed, as the destruction of rainforests and coral reefs – both ecosystems of incredible biodiversity.

Economic and financial sustainability.
One operator of rainforest trips in the amazon told me once: "The Eco in Ecotourism stands for economic." His point was that ecological tourism is only sustainable if it is economically and financially worth it and competitive. So we must not have red ocean race to the bottom strategies to compete for the last tourist Yen, Dollar or Real. Instead, competitive collaboration must enhance the attraction of a destination and bring in good returns for all actors in the tourism subsector. The local economy must benefit from jobs created, and local goods procured and consumed.

This will generate local supply chains and create jobs and income. Active inclusive business strategies can be pursued and implemented as well as value chain development approaches towards local produce.

Social and cultural sustainability.
Is tourism having an altering effect on the local customs and traditions, or does it contribute to local culture in preserving and supporting it. Are tourists knowledgeable about local customs and culture, can they learn about it and do they show respect towards the culture and its inhabitants supporting cultural tolerance. Can this interface enhance our mutual understanding and diminish tensions and envy – or will it only create a wider gap between the global Haves and Have-nots and stimulate economic refugees. Tourism should be developmental oriented and respecting human rights. Does tourism respect human dignities, voice and democracy, or does it support dictatorial regimes not concerned with basic rights. Basic access to water & sanitation, nutrition and dignified labour respecting minimum wages. Does it contribute to involuntary prostitution or not.

SNV as a development organisation has worked for many years in promoting and supporting Sustainable Tourism. The organisation had various programs in several countries promoting community tourism, local value chain development for inclusive tourism, destination management and branding like the Great Himalayan trail programme, and vocational skills training through the High Impact Tourism Training Programme.

Taking measures to enhance sustainability are paramount to foster and grow the tourism sector.

All actors have their role to play. The future workforce in tourism and higher learning institutions of students in tourism sciences are the ones to contribute to this, perhaps mostly towards a sustainable mind-shift.

If we do not make tourism more sustainable, we will create our own demise. The coming generation of tourism operators, managers and policy makers have the obligation to include sustainability in their plans and operations. The industry has moved already great strides but still more can be done. I hope that this book will inspire many to think about tourism sustainability and act upon it.

Rik Overmars
Country Director SNV Mozambique.

Acknowledgements

There are several contributors to the intellectual production and pub-lication of this book. The most important are Rik Overmars from the Netherlands Development Organization (SNV), Paula Nimpumo from Ford Foundation and Helen Mantell from the International Institute of Education, who supported the development of this publication, which started as a translation of my previous book, which focused on tourism development issues in Africa.

In addition to this early contributors, the book also counts as key con-tributors, Dr. Don Hawkins, Dwight D. Eisenhower Professor of Tourism Policy of the George Washington University and Dr. Bruce Prideaux, Professor of Marketing and Tourism Management of James Cook University. However, the list of colleagues who have kindly share their insights and contributions to this book has grown to include many other colleagues located in Central and South East Africa, where the initial pilot edition was published. Later, we received important contributions and new case studies from the Middle East, Eastern Europe, South East Asia and Latin America.

I greatly appreciate the assistance provided by Marcos Vaena, se-nior executive at the International Trade Centre who provided feedback and who encouraged the publication of the book. One of the major contributions of this book is the rich diversity of perspective that the publication provides, including illustrations and case studies that where elaborated by the following contributors: Ada Ogunkeye, Andrey Rylance, Anna Spenceley, Arjun Limbu, Boko Hermione, Chola Mfula, Chris Thouless, Fadi Shraideh, Gautier Amoussou, Gerrit Bosman, Hristov Hristomic, Jim Barborak, Knut Gerber, Matilde Cordoba, Manuel Bollmann, Mohammed Zaarour, Peter Burns, Rinus van Klinken, Sue Snyman, Van Truong, José Koechlin, Gabriel Meseth and Monica Oliveros. A special thanks is due to Ligia Castro, Miguel Baca, Erik Ricaurte, Julio Vignati, Alfredo Paino, Bruno Paino, René Gómez-García, Jon Hoekstra, Ann-Kathrin Zotz, Carlos Quintella, David Vivas, Fabio Scala, Marcello Notarianni, Marisela Vega, Gordon Sillence, Kelly Vaena, Oliver Hillel, Lorena Jaramillo, Luis Sarmento, Mariona Cusi, Monica Kobayashi, Quessanias Matsombe, Boris Olivas, Freddy Puente, Ronald Sanabria, Quirin Laumans, Emiliano Chimorich Caceres, and Alexander Kraul for their significant support. Finally my most sincere thanks for Sean Lothrop who seized the moment, revised texts, checked the references, and made a timely production of this edition possible.

Federico Vignati

Table of Contents

One

An Introduction to Sustainable Tourism Development

A society develops and solves its problems through its collective capacities. No matter how knowledgeable and skilled individuals or single groups are, if this type of capability cannot be coordinated for the common good, progress is improbable.

– SNV NETHERLANDS DEVELOPMENT ORGANISATION[1]

OBJECTIVES OF THE CHAPTER:

- Introduce some of the essential concepts of sustainable tourism and describe its relevance to developing countries.
- Set forth the structure of the book, its target audience and its main messages.
- Provide a starting point for understanding the nature and purpose of sustainable development and its potential contributions to the project of international development.

---

1 SNV Netherlands Development Organisation (2010) Capacity Development in Practice Jan Ubels, Naa-Aku Acquaye-Baddoo and Alan Fowler (Eds.) London: Earthscan.

INTRODUCTION

In recent decades international tourism has become an increasingly important driver of economic, social, cultural and environmental change in countries throughout the developing world—sometimes positive, too-often negative. Since the mid-20th Century the on-going process of globalisation has greatly accelerated this trend, extending tourism's reach and deepening its impact. Due to its unparalleled ability to transcend economic sectors, social classes and regional divisions, impacting lives and livelihoods from the most cosmopolitan city to the most isolated hinterland, tourism presents unique opportunities for marginalised communities that ironically live along the most bio diverse and rich natural areas. And yet the manifold contributions of tourism to economic growth and social development, as well as to cultural preservation and environmental protection, often remain poorly understood among development professionals, policymakers, and local communities in established, emerging and potential tourism destinations alike.

The unique characteristics of the tourism industry present extraordinary advantages, but they also limit the applicability of traditional development models. The success of tourism is exceptionally dependent on non-traditional forms of capital; social, cultural and environmental assets are as essential to the profitability of tourism as are more conventional economic and financial resources. While in most standard competitive markets the beneficiaries of economic capital have clear incentives to preserve it and to build their assets over time, the tourism industry is frequently characterised by the unsustainable exploitation of social, cultural and environmental resources, often with adverse effects on the economic competitiveness of tourism destinations, as well as disastrous consequences for local communities and irreplaceable ecosystems.

The failures and inadequacies of tourism in the developing world have contributed to the view that tourism is ancillary, inconsequential, or even counterproductive to the broader project of international economic development. This view is entirely incorrect. Tourism has enormous potential to advance critical development objectives by conferring concrete economic value—with all the attendant incentives for conservation and accumulation—on social organisations, cultural forms and environments both natural and manmade. In the absence of a tourism industry capable of capitalizing on these resources many rare and valuable forms of social, cultural and environmental capital may be regarded only as exploitable abstractions, or even discarded as 'worthless' by an economy that cannot derive any monetary returns from them. Yet within the context of international tourism cultural authenticity, social integrity, historical continuity, environmental uniqueness and irreproducible experience all have real, practical economic value; the challenge is to determine whether that value is preserved and progressively increased over time, or if it will be destroyed, often by the very people who benefit from it most.

The manifest damage done by uncoordinated, reckless tourism development, as well as its vast, still largely untapped potential to spur positive change, are the reasons this book was written. The history of tourism offers as many success stories as it does cautionary tales, and the lessons learned from this experience provide critical insights to inform more comprehensive, more conscientious, and more economically efficient practices, allowing destination stakeholders to achieve greater outcomes as a group than they could achieve as individuals.

Sustainable Tourism is not a product of simple idealism or good intentions; it is a pragmatic guide to understanding how economic sustainability functions in the unusual world of international tourism and how the public, private and civil society sectors can work together to establish a viable, resilient, equitable, broad-based and, above all, sustainable tourism industry. There is no way to separate the competitiveness of tourism enterprises from the local reality. A tourism industry that fails to sustain its local social, cultural and environmental capital undermines its own foundation.

Federico Vignati • Don Hawkins • Bruce Priedeaux

WHAT IS SUSTAINABLE TOURISM?

The concept of sustainability is increasingly used to inform economic and social development policy across a wide range of disciplines and subject areas. Its origin, meaning and evolving role in the discourse of development are described in Chapter 2. For our purposes, sustainable tourism may be defined as the creation and maintenance of a tourism industry in which growth does not deplete but rather preserves or enhances local stocks of economic, social, cultural or environmental capital. Because of the peculiar market characteristics of the tourism industry, and its unusually strong economic reliance on "non-traditional" forms of social, cultural and environmental capital in particular, sustainability can be understood either from a communal or an entirely private perspective.

A tourism industry is sustainable if it does not inflict net damage on the economic, social, cultural and environmental capital of the local community, enabling tourism firms to derive economic benefits that do not come at the expense of local livelihoods, environmental quality or social wellbeing. Alternatively, a tourism industry is sustainable if it does not undermine the foundations of its own economic viability by degrading the capital assets, both traditional and non-traditional, on which is profitability is based. The viability of the tourism industry depends on the economic, social, cultural and environmental capital of the local community; and the preservation and growth of these capital assets in turn depend on the viability of the tourism industry. Sustainable tourism development hinges on the ability of numerous, diverse stakeholders to recognize the mutually dependent nature of their interests and to align their actions to achieve common objectives. The role of the development practitioner is to facilitate this understanding and promote a collaborative, participatory approach to the development of tourism destinations.

The private sector plays a key role is this process, but it is not solely responsible for establishing a sustainable tourism industry. Indeed, even an unusually well-coordinated private sector would not be capable of guaranteeing sustainability on its own. Private firms cannot ensure responsible land management, sound infrastructure investment, the quality of public spaces, reliable law enforcement, efficient regulations and conscientious legislation, or the efficacy of public institutions. As individual actors private firms have a limited ability to influence public perceptions of tourism among the local community, to establish a brand identity for the destination as a whole, or to resolve conflicts over shared resources and other microeconomic market failures. Moreover, the experience of the tourist as a consumer—the utility value of the service that he or she is consuming—is rarely dependent on a single firm. In the vast majority of cases[2] a tourist's experience of a destination is influenced by the multiple firms that he or she patronizes, as well as by countless interactions with local institutions, community members, and other tourists, as well as with an ambient social, cultural and natural environment that is at least partially beyond the control of any individual firm or industry group.

This leads us to the heart of the matter, and the reason this book was written. Due to the unusually interconnected nature of tourism firms and their extraordinary dependence on local social, cultural and environmental capital, a healthy business and investment climate is not sufficient to ensure the development of an economically sustainable tourism industry. Uncoordinated development by private-sector actors will inevitably lead to conflicts over shared resources. And these conflicts, complicated by the often intangible nature of the resources at stake, will lead to the depletion of local capital stocks and degrade the quality of tourism services. Even a well-organised private sector that is capable of resolving some of these conflicts and market failures on its own will still be unable

---

2 The exception is all-inclusive package tours, in which the tourist purchases transportation, accommodation, food, drinks, activities and other services from a single firm or a formally organized group of firms. Although popular, these tours account for a minority share of global tourism, and often they are not entirely "all-inclusive", as tourists will typically have some limited interaction with firms outside of the primary service provider.

to provide the public goods and services that tourists consume and on which the quality of their overall experience at least partially depends. Finally, interactions between tourists and the destination community, yet another critical element of consumer satisfaction, are by nature spontaneous, unpredictable and difficult to control. In a diverse tourism sector no one firm can determine the relationship between the local community and the tourist community, as this depends on the perceptions, experiences and the costs and benefits, both physical and abstract, generated by the industry as a whole.

Sustainable tourism development, whether defined as the ability of the tourism industry to generate lasting economic and social benefits for the community or as its capacity to ensure its own long-run profitability, relies on intense and continuous collaboration at multiple levels. The first is collaboration with in the private sector, as tourism firms and firms in ancillary industries must be able to recognise and resolve conflicts and market failures swiftly and effectively. The second is collaboration between the private sector, the public sector and civil society, as the quality of tourism services depends not only on the firms from which they purchase those services, but also on their interactions with public institutions and the local community. In addition, there are countless instances in which multi-stakeholder collaboration is the only effective method to ensure the protection and preservation of the economic, social, cultural and human capital on which the tourism industry depends.

TOURISM GOVERNANCE: THE PRIVATE SECTOR, THE PUBLIC SECTOR AND CIVIL SOCIETY

Thus far we have concentrated primarily on describing sustainable tourism development from the standpoint of the private sector, as economic viability is the most basic, necessary condition for overall sustainability and because demonstrating the value of multi-stakeholder collaboration to private-sector actors is among the most critical challenges in sustainable tourism development. However, it is equally important to understand sustainable tourism from the perspective of the government, and to recognize the extent to which it can contribute to specific policy objectives at both the local and national level.

There are many reasons for the rapid expansion of tourism in developing countries, and destination governments are increasingly aware of its advantages as a tool for promoting economic growth. However, in many prospective and emerging tourism destinations the local and national authorities may not fully appreciate the benefits that sustainable tourism development offers. Governments are often focused on their existing industries and sectors, and in they may lack a specialised knowledge of tourism and its potential to advance key development policy objectives. Even in established destinations the government may not be aware of the distributive economic and welfare impacts of the tourism industry, and policymakers may tend to concentrate on maximising the industry's present value at the expense of its long-term sustainability. In cases such as these the role of the development practitioner is to raise awareness of sustainable tourism issues among the public sector and serve as a resource for information on the actual and potential impact of tourism on a given destination.

Among the many development-policy benefits of tourism is its ability to capitalise on non-traditional assets that might not otherwise generate strong economic returns. Tourism often thrives in remote areas, among small communities, minorities and indigenous groups, or in regions that are sparsely populated; as a result, tourism is often best suited to contexts that are structurally inhospitable to other industries and is capable of reaching populations that have few alternatives for income and employment growth. However, the income and employment effects of tourism depend largely on how it develops in any given destination, and this in turn is determined by the laws regulations and policies put in place by local and national governments.

Tourism can be relatively labour-intensive or relatively capital-intensive; the sector can be closely linked to the local economy or largely segregated from it; it can represent an important source of government revenue or a net drain on the public finances; it can have a strongly positive impact on poverty and smooth inequality, or it can prove irrelevant to poverty while exacerbating inequality. The character of a tourism industry and its effects on local social and economic conditions depends in large part on the legal, regulatory and policy framework in which the industry develops. In order to maximise its value as a tool of development policy, governments must have a thorough appreciation for the complexity, ambiguity and context-specific nature of the tourism industry. As always, the importance of collaboration is paramount. Policymakers must view the establishment of a sustainable tourism industry as process of continuous consultation, participation and coordination involving numerous stakeholders in both the private sector and civil society. The role of government in the development of a sustainable tourism industry is analysed in Chapter 3.

THE IMPACT OF TOURISM ON THE DESTINATION ECONOMY

Among the most remarkable features of the tourism industry is the way in which it shapes itself to its context. A tourism sector develops to fit the unique circumstances of the destination, and its growth is conditioned by its governing policy framework—the set of laws, regulations and government initiatives that affect the sector, both deliberately and incidentally. This framework has a major influence on the tourism industry's relationship with the broader destination economy, but it is not the sole determinant of how the industry develops. The character of the local economy, the types of goods and services available, the skills of the local labour force, the availability of private capital and the quality of public infrastructure each play a key role in the growth of the tourism industry.

In some destinations tourism firms are densely connected to local businesses in other sectors, purchasing inputs from domestic producers and encouraging direct spending by tourists in the local economy. In others they are essentially separate and self-contained, sourcing inputs from abroad and limiting direct tourists spending to a single firm or small group of firms in a tourism "enclave". The tourism industry's relationship with the local labour market is also highly variable. In some cases tourism firms are significant employers of skilled and semi-skilled labour, contributing to rising incomes and promoting the development of human resources in the local workforce. In others, however, they tend to hire only semi-skilled and unskilled workers locally, drawing on expatriate labour to fill the most highly skilled—and highly paid—positions. The input-purchasing and employment dynamics of the tourism industry reflect the extent to which tourism revenue enters the destination economy, and as a result they largely determine its impact on local economic development. The share of locally owned firms in the tourism industry is also an important component of this equation, both because the profits of foreign-owned firms will be "repatriated" abroad and because the accessibility of the sector to local firms offers a good indication of how well integrated it is with the destination economy.

Building a tourism industry that advances the government's employment, income, poverty-reduction and long-term growth objectives requires an intimate understanding of how the tourism sector shapes the broader destination economy and how it is shaped by it. Like all firms, tourism operators respond to economic incentives—they try to maximise profits and minimise risks. If sourcing inputs locally and hiring a large share of local workers helps them achieve these goals, they will do so, but if the destination's production capabilities and available labour pool are not suited to their needs, they will look to imports and foreign workers. Adopting policies that encourage domestic market linkages and promote employment and entrepreneurship in the tourism sector will boost the impact of tourism revenue on the local economy. Strategies for enhancing connectivity between the tourism sector and the destination's broader private sector are examined in Chapter 4.

In addition, some market models are especially suited to channelling revenue into the local economy, while others are prone to channelling revenue out of it. Large, all-inclusive resorts, for example, have been gaining prominence in international tourism, but basing a tourism industry on large, all-inclusive resorts can greatly diminish its benefits for the local economy. Knowing the advantages and liabilities of different models of tourism development can help destination managers to craft a policy framework that promotes positive outcomes well beyond the tourism sector itself.

Tourism development also has important implications for the government's fiscal stance, and in order to be sustainable the industry must be based on sustainable fiscal policies. Tourism can provide an important source of public revenue at both the local and national level, but capturing that revenue, and doing so efficiently and without creating unnecessary economic distortions, can present significant challenges. There are also fiscal costs to consider, especially in terms of building and maintaining sector-specific infrastructure. Finally, destination managers must consider the macroeconomic effects of tourism. International tourism is an export industry. It brings foreign currency into the destination country, which can influence its exchange rate, and tourist spending may affect prices both locally and nationally. In order to comprehensively account for the economic impact of the tourism sector these factors must be part of the analysis.

STRATEGIC PLANNING FOR SUSTAINABLE TOURISM DEVELOPMENT

Because of its complex influence on the domestic economy and its potential to unsustainably exploit the social, cultural and environmental capital on which its viability depends, tourism development must be carefully planned. As destination managers have come to appreciate the densely interconnected interests that make up the tourism sector and the importance of aligning those interests in order to maintain and build the productive capital of the destination, the principle of "territoriality" is increasingly used to inform the planning process. Territorial plans approach the destination from a holistic perspective, regarding the development of the destination as a whole—not the growth of individual firms or even the expansion of the tourism sector—as the basis and objective of strategic planning.

As discussed in Chapter 5, balancing the goals and aspirations of the numerous people, firms and organisations whose interests are affected by tourism development is the central challenge of the planning process. In order to be successful, tourism development plans must solicit and incorporate input from stakeholders from the public sector, the private sector and civil society, *inter alia*. Broadly participatory, consultative planning is essential to understanding and appreciating the complex dynamics at work it in the destination, and involving multiple, diverse stakeholders in the planning process can help to build consensus and bolster both popular and political support for the development plan.

Moreover, tourism planning is a continuous process that is not restricted to any one stage in a destination's development. Prospective, emerging and established destinations alike must form strategies to guide the development of the tourism sector, and these strategies must be frequently revised and updated to reflect the destination's constantly changing circumstances—economic, social, cultural and environmental. But ensuring long-term competitiveness is not just a matter of market research and positioning. International tourism is a complex and evolving global market based on exporting services with intensely subjective value. While price always plays an important role, destinations compete with one another across a range of dimensions that determine the aggregate quality of the services they offer. The relative advantages of different destinations are constantly shifting, and destination managers must carefully monitor the destination's place in a changing economic climate and adapt their strategy to exploit new opportunities and maintain their competitive edge.

THE VALUE OF COLLABORATION AND THE IMPORTANCE OF COMPETITION

Competitiveness at the destination level requires healthy competition with the tourism sector. A tourism industry that is dominated by a few large firms will be subject to a range of market imperfections, conditions that serve the interests of the dominant firms at the expense of the destination as a whole. In order to remain competitive and to ensure the widest, most equitable distribution of returns, a destination must work to develop a level playing field that encourages investment and entrepreneurship. New enterprises must be able to enter the market and compete with existing firms, and investors must be able to move swiftly in order to respond to changing market conditions and take advantage of emerging opportunities.

However, traditional market-based competition alone is not sufficient to guarantee the sustainability of the tourism industry. Tourism firms share a common basis for their competitiveness—the economic, social, cultural and environmental capital of the destination. Uncoordinated competition between individual firms can undermine the competitiveness of the destination as a whole, and consequently sustainable tourism development requires that competition by tempered by collaboration. In building collaboration between firms and other stakeholders, the first step is to cultivate an understanding of the ways in which a myopic focus on narrow self-interest can undermine the common interests that destination stakeholders share as members of a group. The complex relationship between individual interests and common interests in the tourism industry is a major theme of this book.

Although individual firms compete against one another in a competitive tourism marketplace, they also depend on the same capital stocks, both traditional and non-traditional. Tourism firms have a strong incentive to collaborate in a joint effort to build the competitiveness of the destination as a whole. Destination managers should strive to foster collaborative action between tourism firms, so long as it does not threaten competition between firms within the destination or promote excessive influence by the tourism industry over local policy and decision making. A collaborative environment must be grounded in a clear system of rules and regulations and prevent anticompetitive collusion or the exercise of undue influence.

Destination managers should also work to bring in other stakeholders from the public sector and civil society who share complementary objectives. Collaborative action can help to promote the development of shared infrastructure, build a strong destination brand identity, or provide information to prospective tourists about the destination and what it offers. Collaboration can help to increase joint competitiveness while at the same time serving broader development policy goals, for example, when tourism firms cooperate with local businesses to facilitate local sourcing. Enabling tourism firms to procure more inputs locally can reduce their operating costs while also extending the impact of tourism revenue on employment and income in the broader destination economy.

Organized collaboration between tourism firms and stakeholders outside the sector is a natural elaboration on the consultative, participatory process of tourism planning. Forums and associations including tourism councils, research organisations and industry groups can help to ensure that the interests of tourism firms are aligned with the destination's public, private and civil society stakeholders to produce mutually beneficial outcomes that support the sustainable management of the destination's economic, social, cultural and environmental capital. As in many other areas of destination management, fostering a view of the destination as a cohesive whole in which the needs, aspirations and goals of multiple actors are interdependent is a critical prerequisite for sustainable development. These issues are described in Chapter 6.

BUILDING AND MANAGING A TOURISM CLUSTER

In many ways the defining characteristic of tourism industries is their remarkable diversity. International tourism destinations cater to consumers from countries all over the world, from a wide range of income groups and with a dizzying array of interests, tastes and preferences. Different tourism firms specialise in different "segments" of the consumer market—some cruise lines cater specifically to families with children, some resorts do not allow children at all; some hotels focus on business travellers, while others specialise in leisure tourists. A five-star luxury hotel in which rooms start at US$350 per night and a one-star hostel with dorm beds for US$5 offer radically different services to completely different clientele, yet they both operate in the same sector, and by the nature of their coexistence they will generate both positive and negative effects for one another.

Managing these effects is a major challenge in sustainable tourism development, one which is discussed in detail in Chapter 7. The participatory planning systems and collaborative action forums described above can help to mitigate the costs that firms indirectly impose on one another, but the benefits they produce are best understood in the context of a "tourism cluster". While the first firm to establish itself in a new tourism destination enjoys certain advantages, it also faces serious obstacles. As other tourism firm move to the same area they help to alleviate these obstacles. New firms attract and train skilled workers, building the local labour pool. They help to popularise the destination in source markets, raising its international profile. And they offer complementary services and alternatives that increase the destination's appeal and the aggregate value of its services.

But a tourism cluster is more than just a private-sector phenomenon. As the tourism industry grows and expands, public agencies that operate in the tourism sector will gain important experience and the further development of the tourism industry will likely become an increasingly important priority for local policymakers. Meanwhile, local and international nongovernmental organisations will also increase their involvement in a growing tourism industry, as will local civil society groups involved in the sector. Research organisations will take a greater interest in analysing the sector and its impacts, and educational service providers will offer vocational training in sector-specific skills. Together the private firms, public agencies, civil society groups, academic institutions and other parties with a vested interest in the development of tourism will form a tourism cluster.

Leveraging the mutual benefits generated by the members of the tourism cluster to enhance the competitiveness of the sector as a whole is a major challenge for destination managers. Understanding the implications of cluster development, collectively known as "economic geography", and how they impact the comparative and competitive advantages of a destination can be difficult, and this is an area of economics which continues to evolve. At the intersection of cluster development and sustainability is the question of social, cultural and environmental externalities—the propensity of tourism firms and other actors in the tourism cluster to either positively or negatively impact the underlying stocks of non-traditional capital on which the tourism industry depends. Evaluating these dynamics and using them to inform development policy requires that destination managers be able to measure the impact of the tourism cluster on the social, cultural and environmental capital of the destination. This in turn presents complex challenges for data collection and analysis.

DATA COLLECTION AND ANALYSIS IN THE TOURISM SECTOR

In order to determine the long-term viability of tourism development destination managers must be able to accurately assess changes in the destination's underlying stock of productive capital. This is true for any economic sector, but in the tourism industry it poses a more complex challenge due

Federico Vignati • Don Hawkins • Bruce Priedeaux

to the non-traditional nature of tourism assets. Far more than any other industry tourism derives enormous economic value from the stability of the destination society, the richness of its culture and the beauty and integrity of tis natural environment. The long-term viability of the industry consequently hinges on the ability of destination mangers to conserve, protect and augment the value of these non-traditional capital assets. But before trends in the destination's non-traditional capital stocks can be assessed, the value of non-traditional forms of capital must be determined.

Despite their largely intangible nature social, cultural and environmental capital all have measurable value. Social capital reflects the strength of the bonds that hold a society together; it measures the extent to which individuals view themselves as members of a group with shared interests, goals and values, and whether or not they believe conflicts can be resolved through established social systems. Social cohesion and engagement are abstractions, but insights from both economics and sociology allow these factors to be quantified and compared over time. Cultural capital is even more nebulous, and cultural value is inherent subjective. Nevertheless, creative methodologies have been developed for identifying, valuating and monitoring cultural capital. Environmental capital is somewhat more straightforward, as ecosystems are more tangible than social cohesion or cultural authenticity, but assessing the integrity of a local environment and calculating its long-term economic value is still a complex process. Current systems for accounting the value of social, cultural and environmental capital are detailed in Chapter 8.

Complicating the process of assessing non-traditional capital stocks is the fact that different types of tourists value different destination assets. Tourists focused on "sun-and-sand" leisure activities may have limited interest in the destination's cultural traditions or local cuisine; ecotourists may value natural beauty and biodiversity, but pay less attention to the destination's architectural heritage or historical sites. Moreover, there may be any number of "special interest tourism" opportunities that

16

will prove highly attractive to tourists who share that special interest, but which will be largely ignored by those who do not. Unfortunately, social, cultural and environmental assets that are not currently generating economic returns may be judged as worthless and ignored or discarded, whatever their potential value might be. Consequently, how the destination is perceived by prospective consumers in tourism source markets will have a major impact on the mix of destination capital that may be profitably exploited and unsustainably depleted. In this context, the destination's marketing efforts and attempts to develop special interest tourism are vital to the industry's long-run sustainability.

MARKETING RESEARCH AND SPECIAL INTEREST TOURISM

Tourists travel for a wide range of reasons and seek an ever-expanding variety of experiences. In an international tourism market defined by its continuous growth and diversification new, emerging and even established tourist destinations must strive to build a distinctive identity. Creating this individual brand requires a careful accounting of the destination's assets, research into current trends in international tourism, and the identification of target consumers in distant source markets. In order to capitalise on a well-crafted brand identity destinations must communicate a clear and coherent vision to target tourist groups, requiring a high degree of coordination and multi-stakeholder collaboration.

Building consensus among the numerous firms, public agencies, civil society organisations and individuals with vested interests in the tourism sector is a difficult process, but it is necessary to ensure that the destination's identity reflects the aspirations, self-perceptions and resources of local actors. In some cases new and emerging destinations in the developing world have allowed themselves to be defined by international tourism firms, resulting in the development of market models that are neither optimal for destination stakeholders nor sustainable over the long term. Public agencies often take the lead in developing a destination brand identity, but a common vision for the development of tourism should be informed a diversity of opinion from a variety of stakeholders. This vision should be based on an accurate assessment of the destination's tourism capital—the economic, social, cultural and environmental assets on which the long-term viability of the tourism industry depends—and it should reflect the strain that a rising tourism sector will place on these assets.

Reaching potential customers in tourism source markets can be costly and difficult. Given the vast array of options available in the global tourism market, a new or expanding destination may have trouble being "heard" by its target audience. Organising stakeholders to sponsor common outreach efforts and consolidating information in easy-to-use formats, such as a destination-wide tourism web portal, can greatly reduce the cost of marketing and expand the scope of the audience. Understanding information and search costs is the key to effective outreach, and the savvy use of technology can greatly facilitate a destination's marketing efforts. In addition, it is important to consider the impact of independent media on the public perception of a destination. Although media messaging cannot be controlled as easily as a marketing outreach campaign it can have a major impact on the international reputation of an emerging tourism destination.

Outreach and marketing are even more crucial for a destination attempting to reach highly specific niche markets. As international tourism has diversified, destinations have increasingly sought to access particular segments of the consumer market and develop niches for their unique services. The rise of special interest tourism presents special opportunities for new destinations, allowing them to capitalise on non-traditional assets and advantages. While building a special interest tourism industry is a challenging objective, successfully cultivating a market niche can help an emerging destination in the developing world gain traction in an increasingly diverse and competitive international tourism market.

CONCLUSION

The growth of international tourism has given rise to exciting new possibilities for developing countries. More than at any time in modern history the abstract values of social cohesion, cultural authenticity, historical continuity, natural beauty and environmental diversity can be translated directly into material wealth. Through international tourism these non-traditional assets can be used to build the foundation for lasting economic growth and enduring human development.

However, this process is not automatic and positive outcomes cannot be taken for granted. No endowment of tourism capital, however rich or varied, will be sufficient to generate permanent improvements in income, employment and quality of life indicators if the local tourism industry is not itself sustainable. Tourism sectors that grow in haphazard, uncoordinated ways will generate conflicts, inhibit the formation of a coherent brand identity, generate uncontrolled and unpredictable costs, miss valuable opportunities for collaboration or otherwise compromise the competitiveness of the destination as a whole. By adhering to the good-practice principles described in this book, destination managers can help emerging tourism destinations to overcome these obstacles and build a sustainable tourism industry that conserves, protects and builds the underlying stocks of economic, social, cultural and environmental capital on which the tourism industry depends.

To be effective, destination managers must be leaders, advocates, advisors and informational resources. A destination manager should be able to manage complex and competing interests, support capacity building among public agencies, private firms and civil society organisations alike, and identify and address critical systemic obstacles to inclusive and sustainable development. Destination managers should draw upon their experience and expertise to assist in the formulation of tourism development plans and address new challenges as they arise. And destination managers should always work to broaden the concept of value among tourism stakeholders, building a mutual recognition of their intimately connected interests and fostering an accurate and compressive under-standing of sustainable development and its implications for the com-petitiveness, profitability, and long-term viability of a tourism destination.

Sustainable and tourism development is predicated on inclusive in-stitutions, participatory processes, sound governance structures and credible, effective policies. Destination managers must be able to build support for broad-based dialogue and encourage active participation in the policy debate. Ensuring sustainability is a continuous process, and destination managers must work to build local capacity for collaboration. This requires strengthening the connections between the public sector, the private sector and civil society and establishing forums in which a wide range of stakeholders may jointly develop the policies, strategies and in-stitutional arrangements that will guide the destination's development.

EXERCISES

In the context of what you now know about sustainable tourism develop-ment, analyse and discuss each of the following statements:

1. "If the clearing of tropical forests advances at the same pace of ten years ago, we will destroy much of the natural resource base on which humanity depends. As an involuntary result, we will extinguish half of all animal and plant species by the end of the 21st century."
   – E.O. Wilson, biologist and naturalist
2. "Our society will be defined not only by what we create but also by what we refuse to destroy."
   – John Sawhill, former CEO of The Nature Conservancy
3. "In general we do not know the benefits offered by intact ecosys-tems: clean air, pure water, partial climate regulation, the creation of fertile soils, control of pests and pathogens. Only when we begin to lose these services will we realize how valuable they are."
   – Jane Lubchenco, marine ecologist and former administrator of the US National Oceanic and Atmospheric Administration

CASE 1 - COMMUNITY-BASED ECOTOURISM IN THE NORTH OF BENIN

By Gautier Amoussou, Hermione Boko & Gerrit Bosman, SNV – Netherlands Development Organization.

1. Context and objectives

The Beninese architectural heritage is composed of a variety of dwelling types of which the most famous is the one commonly known as Tata Somba. As a matter of fact the Tata Somba regroups a number of dwellings with similar overall architectural features but specific details according to Somba ethnic subgroups. The Somba people are known for their particular methods of construction and their rich traditions. Their homes resemble small castles. They often have a variety of floors, a roof terrace and very thick walls, to protect the inhabitants from intruders in a not so long ago past. Their villages are constructed in contrast to what is considered a more typical way of building in Africa, as the houses are built far apart from each other spread out over the land, rather than close together in the form of a village.

Nowadays, Tata Somba dwellings are veritable witnesses of the past and the first identity of the Somba ethnic. Somba people however have begun to copy modern architecture and now the combed oblong slots of sheet metal leaves covered houses are changing in rapid tempo the appearance of the region. This has caused the traditional dwellings to be abandoned and which holds a high risk that these long-established techniques might be lost for ever. Growing poverty, as result of on-going destruction of the natural resources through farming and hunting activities, leading to rural exodus, was stated to be the main reason for increasing abandonment of the Tata Somba dwellings. To find appropriate answers to the continuing loss of this cultural heritage, ECO-BENIN conducted a survey in 2006 and the findings of this survey underscored the need to include Tata Somba dwellings as a central element of an ecotourism scheme.

In 2007, ECO-BENIN has set up a community-based organisation (CBO) called "la Perle de l'Atacora" in Koussou village in order to give lead to the development of ecotourism products owned and managed by villagers.

Being situated in the Atacora region, a region experiencing a growing interest by tour operators, and being located right on the border of the route from Togo to the renowned Pendjari National Park, Koussou has seen the number of its visitors increasing steadily.

When the ECO-BENIN team arrived in the village for the preliminary diagnostics, they noted three points more or less characteristic for the rural ecotourism planning context: 1) People overestimated the positive material and non material effects of tourism; 2) People underestimated the negative impacts on environment, society and culture of tourism; 3) Just one person among the villagers had experience in tourism and catering. This man later became the president of the CBO giving the association a professional foundation.

2. Intervention approaches and activities

In the diagnostic and planning phase of the project, ECO-BENIN team paid considerable attention to awareness raising and opinion building. First of all, population had to be made aware of the technical feasibility of ecotourism but also of the risks local realities were presenting: unique attraction in process of disappearance, poor living standards, low education level, no running water and electricity. Given those facts, the only realistic option seemed to be the development of small-scale and low-budget type of tourism based on catering and housing in families (home stay), short hiking trails within the village and in the surrounding nature and day-long handicraft workshops. The presentation of this model as the most suitable and also desirable model went along with numerous village meetings, explaining again and again the idea of community-based ecotourism and expected outcomes from it. The support team and the president of the CBO invested a lot of time and work in convincing the population that tourism is a high-risk business and that it can be highly volatile with its development often depending on external factors nobody can influence. With the capacities and means on the spot, big and quick money resulting from tourism wasn't realistic. However, as experience in Koussou showed, a little money can make a big difference for the poor rural people. To be on the safe side, the population agreed to set up tourism services as a complementary income source and with a minimum of investment and maintenance costs.

The preconditions for subsequent participatory planning and implementation steps were created by systematic community training and empowerment in close collaboration with the CBO. Originally composed of 18 men and 15 women from the village, the association now unites Tata Somba- and land-owners, eco-guides, caterers as well as craftspeople, being all interested in the development of eco-touristic products and services in the villages. After a first series of meeting and training workshop, further planning steps were discussed between support team and CBO to integrate aspects of sustainability, simplicity and adaptability in the products and services.

During the implementation phase in the beginning of 2007, it was decided that CBO should take charge of creating a visitor centre and should conceive hikes and villages tours. In the following period, while the technical implementation was rather in the hands of the CBO, the support team provided trainings (guiding, housekeeping, catering, first aids, hygiene, small business management, waste management) and some small material support (dry toilets, sheets of bed, covers, robust mats, mattresses, rechargeable lamps). After this the CBO became the official and only management and administration body for ecotourism in Koussoukoingou.

With the build-up of local planning and management capacities and its experience and lessons-learnt throughout the last years, the CBO members have developed a growing self-confidence and enlarged its intervention to the mobilization of resources for locally initiated micro projects.

3. Results and success factors

- ### *Broad effect*

There are direct and indirect economic benefits and nuisances that arise from community-based ecotourism in Koussoukoingou. A jointly setup and adapted revenue distribution scheme is therefore key in order to avoid conflicts. In that sense, individuals, households and the community should benefit from ecotourism according to their contribution to developed product and services.

An eco-guide taking a group of visitors on a Tata Somba tour in the village would therefore get 50% of the fees, whereas the Tata Somba-owners receive 20% as compensation and encouragement to maintain their buildings. Hence, with each guided tour a significant part of the revenues is shared between eco-guides and Tata Somba owners respectively. The latter can even maximise their benefits if visitors stay overnight in their dwellings. Eco-guides and Tata Somba owners reported in unison that living conditions of their families substantially improved with the additional income arising from tourism. With most of the population living from agriculture, the tourism-related revenues, helps them to balance losses and income gaps in the dry season (which is at the same time the high season for tourism in the region). The revenue gained from tourism is usually invested in food security, household and schooling equipment.

Other economic effects arise from the serving of meals in the Tata Somba. As most of the food ingredients are purchased on the spot, local retailers benefit from additional turnover visitors bring about. Moreover, local craftsmen and women benefit increasingly from the purchase of their products by visitors (such as bracelets, slingshots etc.).

Indirect economic benefits are created by the 20% revenue share from any ecotouristic service or product delivered (except catering) allocated to "Community Development Fund". The fund is administered by the CBO who also acts as a village development organization and whose functionality is assured by a separate 10% share of revenues from all guided tours. The money is saved for investments in a variety of local development initiatives like the help to the enrolment of kids to school through the financing of school supplies and homework support, the improvement of the access to water by the installation of an impounding device linking the village to a water source and the drilling of a well and by improving the sanitation through the construction of toilets. All these development initiatives and more were co-financed by tourism revenues.

A landmark step towards food security and livelihood stability is demonstrated by the garden project "les Jardins de Koussou", initiated in 2009. The idea for this project was advanced by the female CBO members, mostly working in catering services for visitors. They were looking for greater autonomy in the access to vegetables for their catering activities and for their proper families. The general shortage of vegetables in the village is worsened by the distance to local markets. The funding of the initiative was a joint action of the CBO and "La Via Natura", a French organization for sustainable camping-sites. On several plots, 29 participants organised in 11 groups are now cultivating peppers, potatoes, cauliflowers, tomatoes, onions, spinaches, green beans, carrots, salads and aubergines. Having achieved a remarkable 6.160 kg harvest in 2009, the project is being intensified.

The growing reputation that Koussoukoingou gained from its successful ecotourism scheme also facilitated other infrastructural improvements in the village such as electricity and ICT. In April 2010, a rural school electrification system is successfully providing photovoltaic electricity to the two boarding schools of the village. In addition, the CBO benefited of 10 computers and 2 printers in order to introduce the young village population to modern information and communication technologies.

Among the social and cultural effects of tourism in Koussoukoingou, it first of all has to be mentioned that villagers feel honoured by the visitors coming from far away only to experience their lifestyle and culture. Population reports that this significantly fostered their self-esteem. This is an important effect especially with regard to the younger generation who increasingly consider their culture and way of life as "primitive" or "backwards" compared to urban and Western culture. A "Youth Nature Club" has been founded, involving children and youths from the village. The members of Youth Nature Club in Koussoukoingou receive environmental education and awareness training and participate in environmental campaigns e.g. for proper waste disposal, re-forestation, targeting in particular the adult population.

- **Qualified jobs in tourism**

Without any touristic structures present, the project literally had to start from zero. With an emphasis on ecotourism as a complementary income source – although with a growing importance - service providers are only partly dependant on tourism activities, pursuing a variety of different other livelihood strategies. Eco-guides, home owners and caterers were all trained and eventually certified. Without a license, local people are not allowed to guide tours or host visitors, in order to assure service quality and fairness to those who had to make investments in terms of time and efforts to get their own license. In 2009, the Koussoukoingou-project lists the following trained and certified ecotourism service providers:

26

- 9 eco-guides trained in welcoming and guiding visitors ;
- 4 women specialized in catering and 1 professional cook;
- 6 Tata Somba owners trained in welcoming and hosting visitors;
- 4 Tata Somba owners who open their houses to visits;
- 5 craftsmen and women who offer their handicraft to tourists;
- 8 women for house-keeping and house maintenance services.

The revenue generated from different services exceeds by far the average agricultural income in the area, providing a financial buffer to compensate income shocks. Comparison between agricultural and tourist incomes shows that guides earn nearly twice the average annual income of agriculture households in the district, while the earnings of caterers and home-stay providers stay a little bit below. Figures confirm the importance of ecotourism activities to villages households and its important to stress that tourism is an additional income source and most of the villages working in tourism are still continuing their farming activities (see graph below). In addition, touristic service providers enjoy a high reputation as they interact with the generally well-respected visitors. With the Tata Somba ecolodge currently under construction, it is expected that an important number of additional tourism related jobs in management, marketing, guiding and catering will be created in near future.

- ***Increasing economic impacts***

Tourism revenues increased while the number of visitors saw a slight decrease in 2010, meaning visitors are spending more money through longer stays and/or the additional consumption of services and products, justifying the efforts put into the diversification of the touristic offer by Koussoukoingou CBO.

With the current ecotourism structures established in Koussoukoingou, all tourism-related services create a profit. There are no loans or investments to be paid back, and all services are carried out on demand.

4. Lessons Learned

- ### *Strengthen identity*

By welcoming visitors to experience local lifestyle and tradition, the Koussoukoingou population became more and more aware of their social and cultural richness. People report to recognize the value of their cultural heritage, all ahead the famous Tata Somba that serve as a prime example of how cultural identity can be enhanced by responsible tourism. With the steady increase of tourism from 2007 on, lodging options for visitors became scarce. This motivated community members to build two new Tata Somba houses in 2008 where none had been built for 30 years. The owners of these new Tata Somba have already joined the CBO to offer home-stays and signs are numerous that this project will continue to stimulate the conservation of local building traditions through the added value that can be gained by tourism.

- ### *Minimise damage and environmental compatibility*

In order to avoid begging and to facilitate a healthy relation between hosts and visitors, it is strictly forbidden to give money and small gifts to the village children. Instead, the latter are strictly advised to donate their gifts to the CBO who records all monetary and non-monetary donations from visitors and subsequently ensures a balanced distribution, primary to deprived families and schools. "Walking and watching" characterizes most the guided tours offered by the CBO. Concerning the housing of the visitors in the Tata Somba, comfort is kept very basic and natural. Visitors sleep open air on the roof, using robust mats, mattresses as well as oil- and rechargeable lamps. Environmental compatibility of sanitation is sought by combustible dry toilets for the visitors. For other tourism-related waste, a village waste agent is considered to supervise the established measures. Beyond the minimization of negative environmental impacts, the project in Koussoukoingou also aims to foster pro-actively

environmental reconstitution. As an ideal consequence, the usually negative ecological balance of tourism would not only be neutralized but even
turned into positive in Koussoukoingou. Since June 2008, the association
members have already planted about 1100 seedlings (local tree species)
on the land around the future Tata Somba ecolodge.

- ### *Deal with gender Justice*

45% of the CBO members are women. They are involved in all of the
activities. Two of them guide tourists. In addition they reported to have
gained more self-esteem and respect among family and community members. It is also worth noting that in the beginning, their husbands tried to
put their wives off from engaging in tourism. But with the first revenues
arising from their work, those women reported that now they become
even encouraged by their husbands to do some side-work in tourism! The
women who have already been in the village association from the beginning additionally reported to be considered by other women to be forerunners. As a consequence, those women are increasingly and seriously
asked by other women about the way their engagement in the CBO and
ecotourism works out and how to participate. This indicates that changes
are under way, enhancing the self-confidence and respect of the women
in the village, going along with an economic autonomy. A remarkable
change in the self-confidence and empowerment of the village women is
also illustrated by the successful garden project that has been initiated by
the female members of the CBO. Even if assistance is still necessary, the
prior self-mobilization of the women states a high degree of participation
and empowerment a development unthinkable a couple of years ago.

5. Overall context

SNV Benin started only recently (2010) its intervention in tourism sector
as part of a SNV West Africa Regional Tourism Program after an absence
of several years. In the framework of this program SNV Benin wants to

catch-up together with SNV Mali and Guinea Bissau on the experiences with Pro Poor Sustainable Tourism of other SNV countries (Ghana and several East African countries)

Following the SNV strategy to 'localize' interventions, much of the work in tourism sector – the shaping and execution of the intervention–is carried out in close collaboration with local services providers.

The following case is drawn from the experience of the NGO ECO-BENIN, our local service provider and partner with which we work on the development of the Atacora-Donga destination in the North of Benin. The destination is accommodating on of the best wildlife parks in West Africa, the Pendjari Park, and several sites of natural beauty (waterfalls) and of cultural value scattered in the beautiful landscape of the Atacora mountain range. The site, Koussoukoingou (shortly Koussou), from which the experience is drawn, has a number of well preserved traditional dwellings – Tata Sombas - renowned for their typical architecture.

The Koussoukoingou experience is also a good example of sustainability of SNV work since the site has benefited in the past from SNV interventions in the framework of a rural development programs located in the district and got some specific support in the framework of the SNV BATOB program.

The case study seeks to inform the reader on an experience with community-based ecotourism as a driver for local economic development.

6. Context and objectives

The Beninese architectural heritage is composed of a variety of dwelling types of which the most famous is the one commonly known as Tata Somba. As a matter of fact the Tata Somba regroups a number of dwellings with similar overall architectural features but specific details according to Somba ethnic subgroups. The Somba people are known for their particular methods of construction and their rich traditions. Their homes resemble small castles. They often have a variety of floors, a roof terrace and very thick walls, to protect the inhabitants from intruders in a not so long ago past. Their villages are constructed in contrast to what is considered a more typical way of building in Africa, as the houses are built far apart from each other spread out over the land, rather than close together in the form of a village.

Nowadays, Tata Somba dwellings are veritable witnesses of the past and the first identity of the Somba ethnic. Somba people however have begun to copy modern architecture and now the combed oblong slots of sheet metal leaves covered houses are changing  in rapid tempo the appearance of the region. This has caused the traditional dwellings to be abandoned and which holds a high risk that these long-established techniques might be lost for ever. Growing poverty, as result of ongoing destruction of the natural resources through farming and hunting activities, leading to rural exodus, was stated to be the main reason for increasing abandonment of the Tata Somba dwellings. To find appropriate answers to the continuing loss of this cultural heritage, ECO-BENIN conducted a survey in 2006 and the findings of this survey underscored the need to include Tata Somba dwellings as a central element of an ecotourism scheme.

In 2007, ECO-BENIN has set up a community-based organisation (CBO) called "la Perle de l'Atacora" in Koussou village in order to give lead to the development of ecotourism products owned and managed by villagers. The village of Koussoukoingou is part of the Commune of Boukombé, situated in the department of Atacora in the North-West of Benin. It is located on the overland route that links the district town of Natitingou (25 km) to the town of Boukombé (14 km) and further on to the border with Togo. The district of Koussoukoingou is composed of 10 villages with an approximate surface of 278 km² and counts approximately 5200 inhabitants. Population is very young in spite of massive emigration with less than the 49% of the population older of less than 40 years. Koussoukoingou village is composed of 45 households of which 35% are member of the CBO and involved in the community-based ecotourism project.

Being situated in the Atacora region, a region experiencing a growing interest by tour operators, and being located right on the border of the route from Togo to the renowned Pendjari National Parc, Koussou has seen the number of its visitors increasing steadily.

When the ECO-BENIN team arrived in the village for the preliminary diagnostics, they noted three points more or less characteristic for the rural ecotourism planning context: 1) People overestimated the positive material and non material effects of tourism; 2) People underestimated the negative impacts on environment, society and culture of tourism; 3) Just one person among the villagers had experience in tourism and catering. This man later became the president of the CBO giving the association a professional foundation.

7. Intervention approaches and activities

In the diagnostic and planning phase of the project, ECO-BENIN team paid considerable attention to awareness raising and opinion building. First of all, population had to be made aware of the technical feasibility of (eco)tourism but also of the risks local realities were presenting: unique attraction in process of disappearance, poor living standards, low education level, no running water and electricity. Given those facts, the only realistic option seemed to be the development of small-scale and low-budget type of tourism based on catering and housing in families (home stay), short hiking trails within the village and in the surrounding nature and day-long handicraft workshops. The presentation of this model as the most suitable and also desirable model went along with numerous village meetings, explaining again and again the idea of community-based ecotourism and expected outcomes from it. The support team and the president of the CBO invested a lot of time and work in convincing the population that tourism is a high-risk business, that it can highly volatile with its development often depending on external factors nobody can influence. With the capacities and means on the spot, big and quick money resulting from tourism wasn't realistic. However, as experience in Koussou showed, a little money can make a big difference for the rural people, living with less than 1US$ per day. To be on the safe side, the population agreed to set up tourism services as a complementary income source and with a minimum of investment and maintenance costs.

The preconditions for subsequent participatory planning and implementation steps were created by systematic community training and empowerment in close collaboration with the CBO. Originally composed of 18 men and 15 women from the village, the association now unites Tata Somba- and land-owners, eco-guides, caterers as well as craftspeople, being all interested in the development eco-touristic products and services in the villages. After a first series of meeting and training workshop, further planning steps were discussed between support team and CBO to integrate aspects of sustainability, simplicity and adaptability in the products and services.

During the implementation phase in the beginning of 2007, it was decided that CBO should take charge of creating a visitor centre and should conceive hikes and villages tours. In the following period, while the technical implementation was rather in the hands of the CBO, the support team provided trainings (guiding, housekeeping, catering, first aids, hygiene, small business management, waste management) and a some small material support (dry toilets, mattress, sheet of bed, covers, robust mats, mattresses, rechargeable lamps). After this the CBO became the official and only management and administration body for ecotourism in Koussoukoingou.

With the build-up of local planning and management capacities and its experience and lessons-learnt throughout the last years, the CBO members have developed a growing self-confidence and enlarged its intervention to the mobilization of resources for locally initiated micro projects.

8. Results and success factors

• *Broad effect*

There are direct and indirect economic benefits and nuisances that arise from community-based ecotourism in Koussoukoingou. A jointly setup and adapted revenue distribution scheme is therefore key in order to avoid conflicts. In that sense, individuals, house-

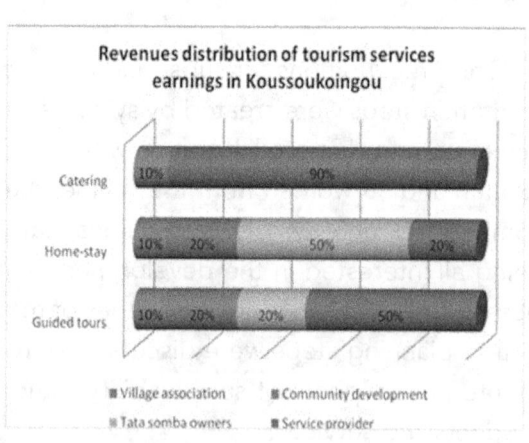

holds and the community should benefit from ecotourism according to their contribution to developed product and services. The opposite graph illustrates the current revenues distribution schemes.

An eco-guide taking a group of visitors on a Tata Somba tour in the village would therefore get 50% of the fees, whereas the Tata Somba-owners receive 20% as compensation and encouragement to maintain their buildings. Hence, with each guided tour a significant part of the revenues is shared between eco-guides and Tata Somba owners respectively. The latter can even maximise their benefits if visitors stay overnight in their dwellings. Eco-guides and Tata Somba owners reported in unison that living conditions of their families substantially improved with the additional income arising from tourism. With most of the population living from agriculture, the tourism-related revenues, helps them to balance losses and income gaps in the dry season (which is at the same time the high season for tourism in the region). The revenue gained from tourism is usually invested in food security, household and schooling equipment.

Other economic effects arise from the serving of meals in the Tata Somba. As most of the food ingredients are purchased on the spot, local retailers benefit from additional turnover visitors bring about. Moreover, local craftsmen and women benefit increasingly from the purchase of their products by visitors (such as bracelets, slingshots etc.).

Indirect economic benefits are created by the 20% revenue share from any ecotouristic service or product delivered (except catering) allocated to "Community Development Fund". The fund is administered by the CBO who also acts as a village development organization and whose functionality is assured by a separate 10% share of revenues from all guided tours. The money is saved for investments in a variety of local development initiatives like the help to the enrolment of kids to school through the financing of school supplies and homework support, the improvement of the access to water by the installation of an impounding device linking the village to a water source and the drilling of a well and by improving the sanitation through the construction of toilets. All these development initiatives and more were co-financed by tourism revenues.

A landmark step towards food security and livelihood stability is demonstrated by the garden project "les Jardins de Koussou", initiated in 2009. The idea for this project was advanced by the female CBO members, mostly working in catering services for visitors. They were looking for greater autonomy in the access to vegetables for their catering activities

Some members of the CBO working in their potato garden

and for their proper families. The general shortage of vegetables in the village is worsened by the distance to local markets. The funding of the initiative was a joint action of the CBO and "La Via Natura", a French organization for sustainable camping-sites. On several plots, 29 participants organised in 11 groups are now cultivating peppers, potatoes, cauliflowers, tomatoes, onions, spinaches, green beans, carrots, salads and aubergines. Having achieved a remarkable 6.160 kg harvest in 2009, the project is being intensified.

The growing reputation that Koussoukoingou gained from its successful ecotourism scheme also facilitated other infrastructural improvements in the village such as electricity and ICT. In April 2010, a rural school electrification system is successfully providing photovoltaic electricity to the two boarding schools of the village. In addition, the CBO benefited of 10 computers and 2 printers in order to introduce the young village population to modern information and communication technologies.

Among the social and cultural effects of tourism in Koussoukoingou, it first of all has to be mentioned that villagers feel honoured by the visitors coming from far away only to experience their lifestyle and culture. Population reports that this significantly fostered their self-esteem. This is an important effect especially with regard to the younger generation who increasingly consider their culture and way of life as "primitive" or "backwards" compared to urban and Western culture. A "Youth Nature Club" has been founded, involving children and youths from the village. The members of Youth Nature Club in Koussoukoingou receive environmental education and awareness training and participate in environmental campaigns e.g. for proper waste disposal, re-forestation, targeting in particular the adult population.

- ### *Qualified jobs in tourism*

Without any touristic structures present, the project literally had to start from zero. With an emphasis on ecotourism as a complementary income source – although with a growing importance - service providers are only partly dependant on tourism activities, pursuing a variety of different other livelihood strategies. Eco-guides, home owners

Certified eco-guides with their badges

and caterers were all trained and eventually certified. Without a license, local people are not allowed to guide tours or host visitors, in order to assure service quality and fairness to those who had to make investments in terms of time and efforts to get their own license.

In 2009, the Koussoukoingou-project lists the following trained and certified ecotourism service providers:

- 9 eco-guides trained in welcoming and guiding visitors ;
- 4 women specialized in catering and 1 professional cook;

- 6 Tata Somba owners trained in welcoming and hosting visitors;
- 4 Tata Somba owners who open their houses to visits;
- 5 craftsmen and women who offer their handicraft to tourists;
- 8 women for house-keeping and house maintenance services.

The revenue generated from different services exceeds by far the average agricultural income in the area, providing a financial buffer to compensate income shocks. Comparison between agricultural and tourist incomes shows that guides earn nearly twice the average annual income of agriculture HH in the district, while the earnings of caterers and home-stay providers stay a little bit below. Figures confirm the importance of ecotourism activities to villages HH and its important to stress that tourism is an additional income source and most of the villages working in tourism are still continuing their farming activities (see graph below). In addition, touristic service providers enjoy a high reputation as they interact with the generally well-respected visitors. With the Tata Somba ecolodge currently under construction, it is expected that an important number of additional tourism related jobs in management, marketing, guiding and catering will be created in near future.

- *Increasing economic impacts*

The opposite graph shows the development of the number of visitors and revenues. It is impressive to see that tourism revenues are increasing while the number of visitors has decreased in 2010, meaning visitors are spending more money through longer stays and/or the additional consumption of services and products, justifying the efforts put into the diversification of the touristic offer by Koussoukoingou CBO.

With the current ecotourism structures established in Koussoukoingou, all tourism-related services create a profit. There are no loans or investments to be paid back, and all services are carried out on demand.

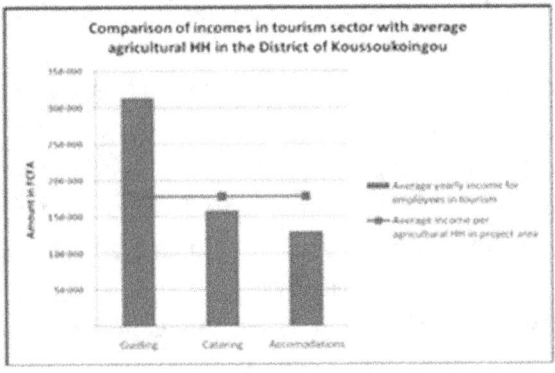

9. Lessons Learned

• Strengthen identity

By welcoming visitors to experience local lifestyle and tradition, the Koussoukoingou population became more and more aware of their social and cultural richness. People report to recognize the value of their cultural heritage, all ahead the famous Tata

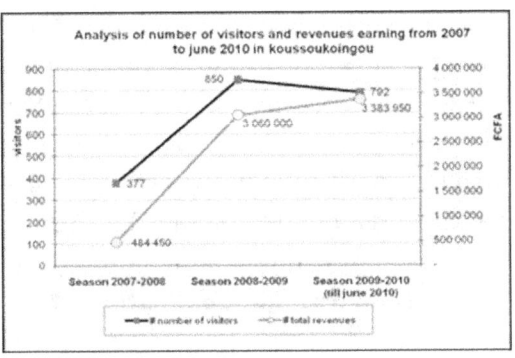

Somba that serve as a prime example of how cultural identity can be enhanced by responsible tourism. With the steady increase of tourism from 2007 on, lodging options for visitors became scarce. This motivated community members to build two new Tata Somba houses in 2008 where none had been built for 30 years. The owners of these new Tata Somba have already joined the CBO to offer home-stays and signs are numerous that this project will continue to stimulate the conservation of local building traditions through the added value that can be gained by tourism.

• *Minimise damage and environmental compatibility*

In order to avoid begging and to facilitate a healthy relation between hosts and visitors, it is strictly forbidden to give money and small gifts to the village children. Instead, the latter are strictly advised to donate their gifts to the CBO who records all monetary and non-monetary donations from visitors and subsequently ensures a balanced distribution, primary to deprived families and schools. "Walking and watching" characterizes most the guided tours offered by the CBO. Concerning the housing of the visitors in the Tata Somba, comfort is kept very basic and natural. Visitors sleep open air on the roof, using robust mats, mattresses as well as oil- and rechargeable lamps. Environmental compatibility of sanitation is sought by combustible dry toilets for the visitors. For other tourism-related waste, a village waste agent is considered to supervise the established measures. Beyond the minimization of negative environmental impacts, the project in Koussoukoingou also aims to foster pro-actively environmental reconstitution. As an ideal consequence, the usually negative ecological balance of tourism would not only be neutralized but even turned into positive in Koussoukoingou. Since June 2008, the association members have already planted about 1100 seedlings (local tree species) on the land around the future Tata Somba ecolodge.

• *Deal with gender Justice*

45% of the CBO members are women. They are involved in all of the activities. Two of them even guide tourists. In addition they reported to have gained more self-esteem and respect among family and community members. It is also worth noting that in the beginning, their husbands tried to put their wives off from engaging in tourism. But with the first revenues arising from their work, those women reported that now they become even encouraged by their husbands to do some side-work in tourism! The women who have already been in the village association from the beginning additionally reported to be considered by other women to be forerunners. As a consequence, those women are increasingly and seriously asked by other women about the way their engagement in the CBO and ecotourism works out and how to participate. This indicates that changes are under way, enhancing the self-confidence and respect of the women in the village, going along with an economic autonomy. A remarkable change in the self-confidence and empowerment of the village women is also illustrated by the successful garden project that has been initiated by the female members of the CBO. Even if assistance is still necessary, the prior self-mobilization of the women states a high degree of participation and empowerment a development unthinkable a couple of years ago.

CASE 2 TOURISM AND THE DESTINATION LABOUR MARKET IN HIMALAYAS OF NEPAL

By Monica Oliveros Delgado - SNV – Global Project Management Team and Sustainable Tourism Expert

THE SITUATION

Despite the great potential of the Manaslu region of Nepal, this destination has not been able to reach the same number of trekkers that Everest, Annapurna or Langtang yearly receives. One of the reasons for this is the limited availability of accommodation and restoration facilities for trekkers. If tourists are interested to trek in Manaslu, they have to join a fully organized camping trek, which is costly and allows limited contact with, and benefits for, host communities.

Recognizing the income and employment opportunities home-stays could generate for people in remote mountain destinations, SNV through the implementation of the EC funded High Impact Tourism and Training (HITT) programme, and in collaboration with the Himalayan Academy of Travel and Tourism (HATT) and its sister organization Explore Himalaya, implemented market driven, practical and High Impact Trainings to homestay owners in the Manaslu region. The objective of this intervention was to support the development of a home-stay trekking product in this region, make trekking in this area easier and cost friendly, and generate income and employment opportunities for entrepreneurs in this destination.

CASE BACKGROUND/CONTEXT

Through an inception analysis conducted at the start of the HITT programme, it was evidenced that camping treks are a costly activity for the inbound operator and allowed limited or none interactions with local populations. It was also evidenced that in some areas, the establishment of lodging facilities could decrease trekking operator costs up to an estimated 50% (e.g. Kanchenjunga, Dolpa) and that trekking companies, in order to expand their offer and decrease their operational costs, were interested to invest in the development and establishment of home-stays and tented camps managed by properly trained local people. The analysis also evidenced that commercially viable home-stay products could generate income and employment opportunities for people living in remote mountain districts.

THE MAIN OBJECTIVE OF THE CASE

The main objective of this intervention was to support the development of a commercially viable home-stay trekking product in the Manaslu region by equipping local entrepreneurs interested to host tourists in their houses with essentials skills to manage and operate homestays.

ACTIONS TAKEN

The HITT programme in Nepal worked in close collaboration with stakeholders in the tourism and hospitality sector. Through consultations with the private sector, HITT Nepal identified best approaches and models that were designed and refined in order to reach and target the needs of the beneficiaries. Using innovative teaching and training approaches, the HITT programme delivered high-impact results that were market driven and enhanced the employability of the beneficiaries.

For home-stays, HITT developed a training of trainers course (ToT) to equip trainers to deliver vocational training to small lodge and homestay operators in remote trekking areas. Trainers trained came from different backgrounds, including trekking guides from Explore Himalaya and hospitality professionals. Subsequently, the best trainers were sent for the first training of beneficiaries, which took place in Kakani in July 2012. The first beneficiaries trained hailed from the Manaslu region. 31 teahouse operators were trained during a 10 day period and they were provided with technical and practical knowledge on lodge management, housekeeping skills, cooking skills and lodge maintenance.

Upon the completion of the course, beneficiaries were awarded with work as interns in nearby hotels and guesthouses in order to put into practice the skills they had learned during the training.

The training was designed and developed based on sound educational theory and selected to lead to a higher retention of learning and actively engage participants in thei own learning, thereby enabling them to master skills and knowledge more easily. The course was organized around three modules: *Understanding Tourism, Lodge and Homestay Operations and Food Preparation.*

For the delivery, training courses were structured under the following logic:

Training resources were developed integrating findings from the learners analysis conducted during the inception phase of the HITT programme (e.g. low literacy and numeracy levels of end beneficiaries, limited understanding of tourism and tourist needs, and most home-stays are run by women, etc). Materials developed included a Trainer's Manual, a Trainer's Guide, 3 Flip Files, a CD detailing the content of the Trainer's Kit and Two Learner's hand-outs.

POST TRAINING ACTIVITIES

The collaboration established with Explore Himalaya was crucial for the implementation of post training following up activities and ensure the commercial viability of the home-stay products. In this partnership Explore Himalaya took the responsibility of carrying out regular supervisions on the improvements and actions participants of the trainings committed to implement in order to host tourists in their homes. Instead of outsourcing the monitoring to a service provider, Explore Himalaya embedded this monitoring task in the operationalization of tours in this destination. In this respect, during the ToT local guides were trained to assess service quality of the home stays and coach home-stay owners to implement better management practices in their enterprises. Likewise, the company also involved their clients by informing them about this initiative and encouraging them to provide constructive feedback to the home-stay owners.

As in most cases home-stays could only host few tourists, in order to develop the product and be able to cater the needs of trekking groups, this company supported local entrepreneurs by providing tents and other necessary equipment required to cater the basic needs of tourists. Entrepreneurs engaging in this venture were renting these tents in a nominal price from Explore Himalaya and free to provide the service to any other tour operator.

In terms of marketing and promotion of the product, Explore Himalaya promoted treks in Manaslu in several national and international events. For the operationalization of treks in this region, they use the services of the home-stays trained.

LEARNING

Out of the implementation of this intervention, the following bullet points summarize key learning and best practices related to the design and development of high impact skills development interventions in tourism destinations:

- Design training models in close collaboration with end beneficiaries as they are in a good position to indicate their needs and availability, appropriate content, material, time or logistical constraints
- Involve the private sector since the outset of the skills development intervention is essential to ensure that trainings are well adapted to their needs of qualified labor / services
- Recruiting competent material writers is the first and most crucial step as it determines how much time and energy will be spent on writing materials. In order to manage this effectively, there should ideally be a subject matter expert in the project team to manage the writing of materials and to check the quality, content and methodology included in the materials. In addition, sufficient time must be planned for the recruiting process of the writing teams to make provision for throwing the recruiting net as wide as possible to get good material writers.
- Conduct a revision of the training materials after the first piloting involving the master trainer and the trainers is crucial. Revisions

should look at improvements in terms of content but as well organisation (taking into consideration beneficiary access to training constraints) and logistics.

- Include mock-up exercises of material content and tools at the time of revising the training materials as a final test of the applicability and usability of the materials.

- Developing in-house trainers to deliver on-the-job-training is an interesting approach to minimize the risk of drop outs. In particular if the trainers are owners/ supervisors, as their motivation to train well is driven by the fact that their business service could improve and revenue could increase (happy customers = more consumption + return clients = more profits);

- However in-house trainers require specific follow-up and a good understanding of the context in which trainings are delivered (especially linkage with other in-house trainings);

- Private companies are willing to cover the costs of training their employees and providers in their supply chain if these interventions will lead to reduction of costs and higher satisfaction of clients.

Two

Principles of Sustainable Tourism Development

"The welfare of a nation can scarcely be inferred from a measurement of national income".

— SIMON KUZNETS, PRINCIPLE ARCHITECT OF THE GDP CONCEPT, IN 1934.

In 1962, he added

"Distinctions must be kept in mind between quantity and quality of growth, between its costs and return, and between the short and the long term. Goals for more growth should specify more growth of what and for what."

By Federico Vignati and Bruce Prideaux

OBJECTIVES OF THE CHAPTER:

- Define the concept of sustainable tourism development in both its ethical and pragmatic dimensions.
- Describe the technical principles on which sustainable tourism development is based.

- Analyse the relationship between sustainable tourism development and long-term competitiveness.
- Present and describe ways to promote sustainable tourism development.
- Spur critical thinking on the future of sustainable tourism development.

INTRODUCTION

How can tourism contribute to sustainable development? Does it have a meaningful role to play in fighting poverty and promoting the growth of strong, prosperous communities? Or protecting the biodiversity and cultural heritage of developing countries? To integrate sustainable tourism into a broader strategy for promoting inclusive, broad-based, equitable and ethical long-term growth and development, it is necessary to build a comprehensive understanding of sustainable development as a wider concept and practice, one capable of shaping policy on a global scale. In this way, we as leaders and managers will be in a better position to create innovative programs and initiatives capable of influencing stakeholders at all levels of the development process—from local communities to national governments, to private-sector firms and international agencies—to pursue a more conscientious and ethical path for the future of the global tourism industry.

Sustainable development is increasingly recognized as a global issue that requires coordinated action and support in both developed and developing countries. Moreover, there is an emerging consensus in the development community that "sustainability" is not just a passing fad, a facile buzzword, or a vague, idealistic objective: rather, sustainability is a meaningful, practical philosophy capable of delivering superior and enduringly positive outcomes for a wider range of development stakeholders. The already urgent need to adopt sustainable development practices will become even more important as the impacts of climate change and rapid population growth in developing countries continue to strain available resources, disrupt local ecologies, and adversely affect human welfare. In many ways, sustainable development can no longer be thought of as "optional"; it is an essential component of successful long-term policy in an ever-widening range of subject areas. Among these, the tourism industry is especially well-situated to benefit from changing attitudes towards sustainability, but only if development practitioners and policymakers fully understand the complex issues involved in sustainable tourism development.

In considering the nature and objectives of sustainable development, it is important to recognize three key facts:

(1) Despite the rapid march of economic globalization, the spread of new productive technologies and massive investment in international development and humanitarian aid, one third of the world's population continues to live in absolute poverty.[3] 2.6 billion people lack access to adequate sanitation, and 1.5 billion have no electricity.[4] While poverty is most densely concentrated in least-developed countries, it is not restricted to them: as many as half of the world's poor live in middle-income countries. Although the growth of the global economy and the diligent efforts of development practitioners continue to provide millions with the means to lift themselves out of poverty, for millions more these efforts have failed.

(2) Although sustained efficiency improvements and innovative advances have greatly expanded the world's production possibilities frontier, raising the average consumption levels of the entire global population to the current standards of advanced economies is unachievable: the world's sum total of productive factors

---

3 Poverty is defined here according to the UN standard as a per capita income of less than US$2 dollars per day.
4 UNDP (2011) "Sustainability and Equity: A Better Future for All."

is simply not equal to the task,[5] and the world's capacity to absorb the environmental damage of mass industrialization is not limitless.[6] These binding constraints on global production require a critical reassessment of traditional theories of economic growth as well as the long-term objectives of the international development project. Yet this difficult situation also presents valuable opportunities to explore broader concepts of human welfare that extend beyond private consumption and material abundance. Sustainable development can offer a more holistic approach that accounts for environmental quality, cultural preservation, social integrity, community pride and the continuity of tradition as crucial dimensions of human wellbeing—dimensions which do not depend on physical wealth and which often cannot be satisfied by physical wealth alone.

(3) According to UN estimates, by 2050 the global population will reach 9.1 billion. This huge expansion of humanity is being driven by developing countries as they continue to undergo the demographic transition.[7] Together with climate change and the inevitable depletion of fossil fuels, population growth in the developing world will entail major challenges for food production, public

---

5 An estimated 20% of the world's population currently consumes 80% of the world's resources. Moreover, consumption in advanced economies will likely continue to increase even as developing countries attempt to converge with them, and thus ensuring global equality in average consumption would require far greater total resources. See WWF (2011).

6 "The argument that the expansion of the economic system as we know it will make it possible for (poor) people to secure their rights is simply not realistic. If the world's inhabitants generated greenhouse gases at the same rate as some developed countries, we would need nine planets" UNDP (2008)

7 The "demographic transition" refers to the typically rapid population growth experienced by countries that are in the process of developing, as better nutrition and medical care cause death rates to fall dramatically while birth rates remain high. As countries continue to develop their birth rates gradually fall as well, and in many advanced industrial economies birth rates are at or below replacement rates. However, during the demographic transition the explosive growth of the population—and the downward shift of the median age—can put severe strain on a country's economic, social and institutional resources.

health, economic stability and physical security, at both the national and international levels.

In many ways, our vision for the future is largely an extrapolation on the conditions of the present, on the ideas, ideologies and production systems that have been developed to meet the world's current needs, desires and aspirations, and which may not be suitable—or even practicable—in years to come. In much of the world, national governments, private firms and even development agencies continue to operate on the premise that continuous and unlimited economic growth and the expansion of advanced-economy consumption patterns is always desirable and indefinitely feasible. The perceived success or failure of development policies continues to hinge on GDP growth, with perhaps a brief nod to simplistic equity indicators such as a declining poverty headcount rate or a reduction in the Gini coefficient, which are generally regarded as positive, but fundamentally subordinate measures of progress. There is no doubt that GDP tells one story about a country's growth and development. But does it tell the whole story? The following case study paints a very negative picture of tourism and is based on the government failing to implement development strategies that harness the potential of tourism. This not always the case but as the following case study highlights, without effective government, negative outcomes are possible.

BOX 1 THE ISLAND PARADISE

Imagine for a moment that you live in a small island nation in the Caribbean. Your country has limited arable land and few other natural resources, it exports a few basic agricultural commodities, and for generations most people in your community have fished and farmed on a semi-subsistence basis. By global standards you are considered quite poor, because the estimated value of your average production per person is low compared to the average for people who live in the world's industrialized countries. And indeed conditions are far from ideal: education rates are low, mortality rates are high, and economic opportunities tend to be limited to a handful of traditional occupations. Nevertheless, within your community few people consider themselves poor, as poverty and wealth are largely relative determinations: being poor by global standards is often very different from being poor by local ones.

One day a large international tourism firm buys a stretch of land on one of your island's many beaches, where it constructs a massive, all-inclusive resort hotel. This project causes your country's GDP to rise; the hotel is a major new piece of productive capital, and the process of building and then operating it add significantly to the total value generated by your small economy. The foreign direct investment required for the construction of the resort has a highly positive impact on your country's external balances, and initial tax payments or public-land purchases may provide a welcome boost to the fiscal accounts as well. The government lauds the project as ushering-in a new era in your nation's development. However, to what extent, if any, does life actually improve for you and your community?

The hotel imports nearly all of its inputs from abroad: from bed linens to silverware to parasailing equipment to scotch for the bar, almost everything the hotel offers its guests is produced elsewhere, often in countries that enjoy a strong comparative advantage in manufacturing these goods. Most of the highest-paid staff at the resort—managers and accountants, chefs and scuba instructors—are foreigners as well, since few people in your country's workforce possess these specific skills. And because the company is foreign-owned, all of its profits are ultimately repatriated abroad. Perhaps some of your neighbours take jobs as unskilled workers, cleaning hotel rooms, washing dishes and cutting grass on the grounds, and maybe a few local farmers or fishermen sell their produce to the hotel's restaurant; *ceteris paribus* these things are good, but overall you and your community are not much better off than you were before the hotel arrived. In fact, in many ways, your quality of life may be significantly worse.

If the hotel is very big and very busy, while the local community is very small and economically isolated, the hotel's food purchases may cause local food prices to rise. This is good for some people—the ones supplying the hotel—but it may be very bad for others, especially the poorest people in your community, for whom food represents a very large share of their household budget. Upward pressure on food prices can also have dire environmental consequences by encouraging overfishing, soil erosion, deforestation, and even the slaughter of local wildlife for food.

Meanwhile, there may be more complex economic effects going on at the national level. Although most people don't think of it this way, tourism is actually an export industry, but instead of selling goods and services to consumers in a foreign country, foreigners come to your country to buy them. Hotel rooms, restaurant meals, recreational activities, souvenirs and anything else sold to foreign tourists counts as an export, because foreign tourists exchange their currencies for your country's currency in order to buy those things. Now a great many tourists start exchanging their currencies for yours in order to buy your service exports, creating a trade surplus. This sounds like a good thing, and it may indeed be good, for some people, because increasing demand for your currency abroad causes its value to rise relative to that of other currencies. This is good for consumers of imports, who can now buy them more cheaply, but bad for domestic producers of similar goods, who have to compete with increasingly cheap imports, and it's especially bad for exporters, who have a harder time selling their effectively more expensive goods in foreign markets. Over time, your country's domestic import competitors and its few non-tourism export industries gradually decline, and tourism becomes increasingly central to your nation's economy.

At first, you might expect the hotel to generate important tax revenue, which could allow the government to fund better schools and clinics, or improve the local road system. Over time, this should help your economy become more diverse and sophisticated. However, the hotel company is a single, powerful entity with a very narrow interest, whereas your country's body politic is a complex collection of individuals and groups with a variety of diffuse, often competing objectives. Even in a functioning democracy the hotel company may be remarkably effective at promoting policies that suit its highly specific objectives at the expense of the public interest: perhaps it lobbies for lower taxes on tourism firms, or maybe it promotes the use of tax money (or external development funding) to support expanding the dock that its cruise ships use or the airport where tourists arrive, or both. Meanwhile, the schools, clinics and roads that would facilitate broad-based growth go unfunded, ultimately lowering your country's long-term development path. The hotel, its cruise ships, tour busses and many tourist consumers may also generate pollution and garbage, which your local ecology and waste-management infrastructure may be ill-equipped to handle. Rising tourism activity may put a strain on basic infrastructure, while the industry contribute may contribute little to its maintenance. As a result of these and a host of other potential adverse consequences, your country's underlying stock of wealth (its "adjusted net savings") may actually be depleted over time, actually making your country poorer even as the flow of GDP continues to rise.

Finally, it's well worth considering what you, as a citizen of your country and a member of your community, might think of all this. What do you think of the wealthy foreigners who come to your home to snap pictures of your "exotic" lifestyle and tell you how lucky you are to live in such a paradise? Some people you know have probably benefitted from the hotel, but others have lost; your local economy is changed forever, and with it your way of life. Are you richer than you were before the hotel came? Do you *feel* richer? The answer to those questions may not be the same.

This is not to say that traditional development indicators are irrelevant, or that conventional objectives and values are inappropriate. Prosperity is unquestionably better than poverty; health is better than sickness; literacy is better than illiteracy. But have we in the development community failed to consider broader measures of utility? Have we ignored crucial aspects of human happiness and wellbeing for no other reason than because they cannot be easily quantified or succinctly summarised? Does the existence of universal goals preclude the possibility of unique, non-generalizable, context-specific aspirations?

Achieving sustainable development requires that policymakers, practitioners and stakeholders devote serious consideration to these questions. Indeed, the experience of many highly developed economies highlights the inadequacy of growth-for-growth's-sake as an overriding objective. Many advanced industrial countries have reached a point where, once the provision of near-universal access to basic economic infrastructure and essential social services has been accomplished further economic growth has had only a minimal impact on people's satisfaction and happiness. Reviewing the research on subjective wellbeing in developed countries, Inglehart and Klingemann (2000)[8] argue that above a certain level of national income, the continued growth of per capita GDP has no measureable impact on

---

8   Inglehart R. and H.D. Klingemann (2000) <u>Genes, culture, democracy and happiness.</u> Cambridge, MIT Press.

average utility.[9] As Aldred (2006) puts it, "Once poverty is alleviated, further increases in income may not bring greater happiness." [10]

Frey and Stutzer (2002) bring an interesting perspective to this question. According to their Income and Life Satisfaction study, conducted in Japan, the overall happiness of the Japanese people is roughly unchanged from its 1963 level, despite the country's fivefold increase in income over the past 40 years. [11] If there is a point at which further economic growth ceases to produce further increases in satisfaction, there is an argument to be made for rethinking a number of the core values and underlying assumptions that have shaped development thinking. Regarding continuous increases in production and material abundance as the ultimate objective of social and economic policy is as much as subjective, normative judgement as any other, and one that may become decreasingly useful and increasingly infeasible as countries progress towards it.

SUSTAINABLE DEVELOPMENT AND NATIONAL WEALTH

Modern economic growth has enabled an explosive increase in personal consumption through advances in productive technology and the ever-increasing sophistication of systems for specialization and trade. However, traditional measures of growth often fail to account for its impact on national wealth—a country's underlying capital stock—and especially

---

9 See also Constanza and Farley (2010), "From a quality of life perspective, Brazil is already one of the richest countries, next to the USA and the EU. This is based on the high level of satisfaction of Brazilians, their lifestyle and ecological wealth." From another perspective the "gross national happiness" concept suggested by the King of Bhutan in 1972 offers an alternative way of viewing national development. This measure underlies the nation's approach to planning and in 2007 Bhutan ranked eighth out of 178 countries in measures of subjective wellbeing (White 2007). Interestingly, Bhutan was the only country with a very low GDP to be ranked among the top 20 happiest countries.

10 Aldred J. (2006) "Incommensurability and monetary valuation" *Land Economics* 82(2): 141-161.

11 Frey, B. and A. Stutzer (2002) Happiness and Economics. Princeton, Princeton University Press.

its environmental costs.[12] In this context, the increasing use of national wealth accounting, such as the calculation of adjusted net savings described in **Error! Reference source not found.**, below, represents a major contribution to the theory of sustainable development.

A country's GDP is a flow: it is the total value of the country's economic productivity during a given period, typically one year; in other words, GDP measures a country's annual income. National wealth, by contrast, is a stock: it represents the total value of all capital, produced and natural, possessed by a country. It encompasses physical, financial and human, capital, as well as the value of natural resources and environmental quality. To draw an analogy to personal finance, GDP is much like your annual salary, it's what you make; national wealth is like your net worth, it's what you own.

BOX 2 ADJUSTED NET SAVING

Among the most common methods for calculating national wealth is "adjusted net savings" or "genuine savings". A brief description of this method and its importance as a measure of sustainable development are provided by the World Bank (2013)[13]:

ADJUSTED NET SAVING – A PROXY FOR SUSTAINABILITY

Adjusted net saving, (also known as genuine saving), is a sustainability indicator building on the concepts of green national accounts. Adjusted net savings measure the true rate of savings in an economy after taking into account investments in human

---

12 Beckerman, W. and J. Pasek (2001) <u>Justice, Posterity and the Environment</u>. Oxford, OUP.

13 This text and the accompanying figure are taken directly from the World Bank website. See: http://web.worldbank.org/WBSITE/EXTERNAL/TOPICS/ENVIRONMENT/EXTEEI/0,, contentMDK:20502388~menuPK:1187778~pagePK:210058~piPK:21006 2~theSitePK:408050,00.html. For more on natural resource management in macroeconomic policy, see:

capital, depletion of natural resources and damage caused by pollution.

Negative adjusted net saving rates imply that <u>total wealth</u> is in decline; policies leading to persistently negative adjusted net savings are policies for unsustainability. In addition to serving as an indicator of sustainability, adjusted net savings has several other advantages as a policy indicator. It presents resource and environmental issues within a framework that finance and development planning ministries can understand. It reinforces the need to boost domestic savings, and hence the need for sound macroeconomic policies. It highlights the fiscal aspects of environment and resource management, since collecting resource royalties and charging pollution taxes are basic ways to both raise development finance and ensure efficient use of the environment. And it makes the growth-environment trade-off quite explicit, since those countries planning to grow today and protect the environment tomorrow will be notable by their depressed rates of adjusted net saving.

How to calculate adjusted net saving

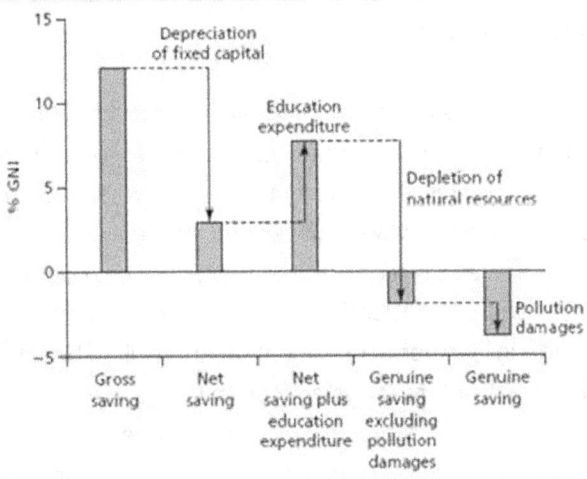

The method that the Bank uses for calculating adjusted net saving can be downloaded here.

- Calculating Adjusted Net Saving (PDF, 77 kb) [http://siteresources.worldbank.org/ENVIRONMENT/ Resources/Calculating_Adjusted_Net_Saving.pdf]

Adjusted net savings are derived from standard national accounting measures of gross national savings by making four types of adjustments. First, estimates of capital consumption of produced assets are deducted to obtain net national savings. Then current expenditures on education are added to net domestic savings as an appropriate value of investments in human capital (in standard national accounting these expenditures are treated as consumption). Next, estimates of the depletion of a variety of natural resources are deducted to reflect the decline in asset values associated* with their extraction and harvest. Finally, pollution damages are deducted. Many pollution damages are local in their effects, and therefore difficult to estimate without location-specific data. Here we estimate health damages due to urban air pollution. As for global pollution damages, the estimates include damages from carbon dioxide emissions.

Although a thorough discussion of national wealth accounting is beyond the scope of this analysis, a few key concepts should be noted. First, wealth and productivity are fundamentally different, but the two are inextricably linked. A country's GDP is in many ways a function of its underlying stock of national wealth, as the latter may be regarded as the sum of the country's productive assets. Second, current production can increase a country's wealth stock over time through investments in education and public health (human capital), economic infrastructure (physical capital), or environmental protection and conservation (natural capital). However, a failure to invest or to responsibly manage national weal can cause a country's underlying wealth stock to be depleted by production, leaving a country poorer over time.

Consider, for example, the small West African nation of Equatorial Guinea. At first glance, Equatorial Guinea would appear to be a roaring economic success. In one of the world's poorest regions, this country boasts an annual per capita income of over US$15,000,[14] higher than that of Russia, Chile and Hungary, and not far behind Saudi Arabia. As a result Equatorial Guinea is officially classed as a high-income country. Yet a closer look reveals that more than 75% of Equatorial Guineans live in poverty, and average life expectancy is just 51 years.[15] How is this possible?

With a population of less than 1 million and vast oil reserves Equatorial Guinea's productivity is overwhelmingly focused on the exploitation of its resources, and has little to do with the livelihoods of the overwhelming majority of its people. Income inequality is dramatic, and although the oil industry generates enormous public revenue, the government does not efficiently transform this revenue into new either new productive capital or basic social infrastructure, and as a result, less than 50% of the rural population has access to safe drinking water. Moreover, during the past 15 years the annual depletion of the country's natural resources has equalled between 40% and 135% of GDP, and while there is no comprehensive accounting of trends in the national wealth stock is currently available, given its public investment and social spending dynamics it is virtually certain that the country's adjusted savings rate is severely negative.

This is, of course, an extreme and in many ways atypical example, but it highlights the multidimensional inadequacy of GDP as a measure of economic development. The fact that GDP figures do not account for the depletion of natural wealth—whether from resource exports or environmental degradation, or a combination of both—is a matter of particular concern. Management of the natural capital stock is as essential for a

---

14 World Bank (2011). This figure is represents GNI per capita, Atlas method, which is a different metric than GDP (and arguably more appropriate in this case), but like GDP it is a measure of annual economic productivity per person.

15 All statistics in this and the following paragraph are derived from the World Bank's World Development Indicators: http://data.worldbank.org/country/equatorial-guinea

country with a thriving tourism industry as it is for a resource exported like Equatorial Guinea. Failure to appreciate the long-term impact of economic growth on environmental quality, from the local level to the global, represents a major threat to sustainable development.

SUSTAINABLE DEVELOPMENT AND THE ENVIRONMENT

In 1984 the World Commission on Environment and Development, also known as the Brundtland Commission, was established at the request of the Secretary-General of the United Nations. The Commission had three objectives:

"(a) to re-examine the critical issues of environment and development, and formulate innovative, concrete, and realistic action proposals to deal with them; (b) strengthen international cooperation on environment and development, and assess and propose new forms of development that can break out of existing patterns and influence policies and events in the direction of needed change; and (c) raise the level of understanding and commitment to action on the part of individuals, voluntary organizations, .business, institutes and governments."[16]

Three years later the commission published its findings in a document titled "Our Common Future" often referred to as simply the Brundtland Report. This study recognized the need to address developmental disparities between nations through a shared policy of "sustainable development", designed to make certain that further economic growth in both advanced and developing countries would not do irreparable damage to the planet or compromise its ability to sustain a growing world population.

Sustainable development was defined by the Brundtland report as, "balanc[ing] the imperative of economic growth with the promotion of social equity and the preservation of our natural heritage, thereby ensuring

16 Brundtland, Gro Harlem (1987) "Address at the Closing Ceremony of the Eighth and Final Meeting of the World Commission on Environment and Development" Tokyo: United Nations

that the needs of present generations are met without compromising the care taken of needs of future generations." This was among the first uses of "sustainable development" in this specific context, and it remains the most frequently cited definition of the term.

Using this definition as a reference point, we can observe a critical realignment in the way development is understood. Previously, "development" tended to be regarded exclusively in terms of its implications for economic growth.[17] "Sustainable development", by contrast, requires that the long-term impact of present decisions and consumption habits be taken into account, so as to promote "intergenerational equity."

This concept, which is closely related to sustainability, had been developed a decade earlier to define a principle of investment management,[18] but which was quickly expanded upon in a number of different contexts, and became widely influential not only in environmental management and economics, but in law, philosophy and public policy as well.[19] As a matter of sustainable development, intergenerational equity is the ethical obligation to manage the current stock of resources in such a way as to "maintain capital intact" and thereby ensure constant returns across indefinite future generations.[20] As UNDP (2011) noted, "The great development challenge of the 21st century is to safeguard the right of generations today and in the future to live healthy and fulfilling lives." The practical application of intergenerational equity to the development of the tourism industry often involves the conservation of ecology, biodiversity and

17 Daly, H.E. (1968) "On Economics as a Life Science". London: Journal of Political Economy

18 Toobin, James (1974) "What is Permanent Endowment Income?" *American Economic Review* 64(2): 427-32

19 Wiess-Brown, Margaret (1992) "Intergenerational Equity: A Legal Framework for Global Environmental Change" in Environmental Change and International Law: New Challenges and Dimensions. Tokyo: United Nations University Press

20 See: Solow, Robert M. (1974) "Intergenerational Equity and Exhaustible Resources" *Review of Economic Studies, Symposium* pp. 29-46. See also: Hartwick, John M. (1977) "Intergenerational Equity and the Investment of Rents from Exhaustible Resources" *American Economic Review* No. 67, December, pp. 972-74

overall environmental quality, as well as the preservation of cultural heritage, including not only historic sites and artefacts, but also traditional practices, knowledge, and ways of life.

The concept of sustainable development has been described by some as an attempt to simplify the complexity of natural wealth and cultural diversity so that "nature" and "culture" can be superficially integrated into the rhetoric of what is still a fundamentally destructive and exploitative process. However, this objection has less to do with sustainable development in principle than it does with the process of global economic development in practice. Consequently, proponents of this view are frequently associated with "anti-globalisation" or "anti-capitalist" movements.

While this and other philosophical debates will certainly continue, over time the concept of sustainable development has gradually moved from a theoretical construct to a concrete policy objective based on specific and measurable indicators. Nor has sustainability as a concept ever been entirely fixed; rather, it is the subject of an on-going process of elaboration, modification and adaptation to changing circumstances, both and in terms of its ethical underpinnings and the practical approaches that may be employed to achieve its objectives.

Similarly, the idea that defining public policies is a shared responsibility involving multiple stakeholders is also continuously evolving. Sustainable development strategies are formulated through consultative and collaborative processes, going beyond simply majority rule to build broad and enduring consensus. This is not simply a matter of feel-good democratic pluralism: widespread, multi-stakeholder support is a pragmatic necessity for sustainable development derived from hard-won experience. Among the most important lessons from the history of international development is that well-meaning interventions have failed far too often because they lacked the consent and active engagement of either their intended beneficiaries, or the broader community of actors affected by the intervention, or in some cases both.

It is especially important to note that there remains a great deal of general scepticism regarding the economic viability of sustainable development. The concept of sustainability should broaden our understanding of economic utility, augmenting an appreciation of material incentives with an understanding that human happiness and wellbeing extend beyond personal monetary gain. Far too often sustainable development practitioners have allowed a focus on nonmonetary values to eclipse their appreciation of vast power of economic incentives. This is deeply unfortunate, because economic viability is an essential component of sustainability—without it, no intervention, no matter how successful, will survive. Sustainable development policies must, by definition, be informed by a rigorous understanding of economic principles.

For a sustainable development intervention to be successful it must (i) meaningfully serve the self-defined interests of its intended beneficiaries (i.e. development), and (ii) ensure that these gains are maintained over time (i.e. sustainability). A failure to appreciate the diversity of aspirations within a group of stakeholders, or to create consultative and collaborative processes that can incorporate those diverse aspirations into a commonly supported agenda, can severely undermine either or both of these components. Without consultation during the design phase the intervention's stated goals may not actually serve the interests of its beneficiaries; without ensuring broad public support before implementation the intervention may simply fail to reach its goals; and without adequate mechanisms in place to guarantee that the interventions achievements will endure, even the most productive gains may be swiftly undone.

Sustainable development challenges individuals to assume an increasingly active role in political life, as citizens, as private-sector agents, as members of civil-society groups, and as stakeholders in a wide variety of interests and causes. This engagement in turn challenges society to improve its responsiveness and build more participatory civic institutions. This challenge is perhaps one of the most important direct contributions of sustainable development to the strengthening of democratic governance in the developing world.

WHAT IS THE PRACTICAL VALUE OF SUSTAINABLE DEVELOPMENT?

Sustainable development is more than a system of ethical principles for orienting development policy; it is a mechanism for improving the efficiency of development interventions, a practical system for ensuring that the vast sums spent and countless hours invested in the global development project live up to their enormous potential. There is a growing understanding among national policymakers, international agencies and local communities that sustainable development strategies are capable of delivering innovative, resource-efficient interventions that enhance individual and social welfare in ways that accommodate the diverse interests of multiple stakeholders. Sustainable development also has the capacity to give voice to marginalised groups by incorporating dissenting and minority views into the design of development strategies. An overarching objective of sustainable development is to formulate solutions that are not only effective economically, but that also efficiently internalize the social, cultural and ecological costs and benefits of the development process.

- **Economic sustainability** refers to the ability of a project or program to become economically self-sufficient, allowing it to continue operating indefinitely, or to a situation in which a temporary intervention yields a permanent welfare improvement. [21] Often, this means that a project, once completed, generates adequate financial returns to ensure its continued operation, or that a temporary economic intervention effects a lasting change in production methods, consumption patterns or commercial systems. For example, an agricultural NGO might provide farmers with new tools and equipment that allow them to increase their productivity. However, if the marginal productivity increase generated by the new capital is not sufficient to offset the cost of operating, maintaining and replacing it, then the famers will either sell their tools

---

21 In certain cases sustainable funding (e.g. through a permanent endowment) may also be an option.

and equipment or use them until they wear out and then revert to their previous production methods. In a larger sense, economic sustainability can describe the completed movement of an entire economy from one steady-state equilibrium to another,[22] as opposed to a partial movement caused by a temporary distortion that does not result in the achievement of a new equilibrium—as in the example of the farmers and their new tools. When assessing the economic viability of a proposed intervention, it is always essential to examine why the private sector may not consider a similar investment worthwhile, or why the prospective beneficiaries are not already adopting the new methods or systems that your intervention seeks to establish.

- **Social sustainability** refers to the need to balancing the personal costs and benefits of a development intervention with its costs and benefits to society. Development is economically viable if it generates private benefits that more-than-offset its private costs, but it can be much harder to incorporate the larger social consequences of development into the calculus of economic viability. For example, building a new paved road in remote community may have the potential to significantly increase incomes by boosting commerce, benefitting people as individuals, but it may also have deeply adverse social consequences: cars and trucks on the new road may generate significant pollution or present a serious safety hazard, especially if traffic is poorly regulated, while commercial truck drivers passing through the community may spur demand for bars, gambling and prostitution. In these and countless other ways economic development may leave people personally richer but socially poorer—and even the former is hardly guaranteed. Social sustainability requires

---

22 Any change in economic equilibriums entails trade-offs: gains and losses among the different parties involved. The distributional component to sustainability is the concept of Pareto efficiency: movements between steady-state equilibriums must generate more total gains than they do total losses, and those that are made better-off from the new equilibrium must be able to compensate those that are made worse-off.

that social consequences, both positive and negative, be internalized in the cost-benefit calculations of development policies and interventions.

- **Cultural sustainability** refers to the intangible, typically unquantifiable yet undeniably real value that people ascribe to their cultural heritage and identity. As noted above, 'culture' is not just a matter of historical sites and artefacts, or indigenous arts, crafts, music and dance, it is also a sense of traditional continuity and authenticity, and pride in a particular way of life. Economists have made great progress in attaching specific figures to social costs and benefits, and have worked to establish systems for incorporating these costs and benefits into public policy decisions. Yet the value of cultural integrity, and the costs of experiencing a 'cultural loss', have proven far more elusive. Complicating this problem is the question of intergenerational equity: to what extent will future generations suffer from 'cultural costs' incurred today? In some ways they will not suffer at all, or even notice, because culture is inherently fluid, and new cultural forms are constantly being created. In other ways, however, their lost will be more severe than any monetary value could describe, because it while new culture is constantly being created, the loss of culture is irreplaceable. For example: denser economic integration tends to eradicate local languages through cultural homogenisation and the economic 'network effects' of the dominant language. By some estimates, a language is 'dying' every 14 days, and within the next century a full half of the world's languages may disappear. What has a generation lost if it grows up speaking Russian instead of Tuvan, or Spanish instead of Seri, or English instead of Amurdak? From one perspective it has lost nothing; from another perspective its loss in incalculable. And how does the death of a language affect its last generation of native speakers? What is it like to be the only person on Earth who speaks your language, and have no one left to talk to? [23]

23 Rymer, Russ (2012) "Vanishing Languages" *National Geographic* http://ngm.nationalgeographic.com/2012/07/vanishing-languages/rymer-text

- **Ecological sustainability** is the imperative to protect the Earth's biodiversity and to maintain the balance of local ecosystems through environmental conservation and the responsible management of natural resources. Intergenerational equity is especially important to ecological sustainability, as its ethical predicate is the right of future generations to a natural environment that is at least as rich, diverse, healthy and productive for them it is for us today. One of the keys to ecologically sustainable development is the recognition that human communities are part of their local ecosystem—they are masters of it only in the sense that they can destroy it, not in the sense that they can bend it perfectly to their will—and the fate of one is ultimately bound to the fate of the other. Economists and social scientists have spent decades developing a sophisticated conceptual framework for understanding environmental degradation, and some of its key elements and practical applications are described in **Error! Reference source not found.**, below.

BOX 3 THE TRAGEDY OF THE COMMONS AND THE PROBLEM OF COLLECTIVE ACTION

The principles of economic, social, cultural and especially ecological sustainability are informed by research and analysis from multiple academic disciplines. Starting in the mid-20th Century, a number of exciting developments in mathematics, economics, political science, sociology and the environmental sciences, greatly advanced mankind's understanding of the challenges facing it in the future and the limited extent to which contemporary theories were able to describe, much less address those challenges.

In 1968 ecologist Garret Hardin published "The Tragedy of the Commons",[24] which proposed a groundbreaking approach to the analysis of economic and social problems. Previously, microeconomic interactions had been largely viewed through the lens of indi-

---

24 Hardin, G. (1968) "The Tragedy of the Commons." *Science* 162(3859): 1243–1248

vidual self-interest: people attempted to do what was best for themselves as individuals, and market mechanisms aligned their individual interests to produce a prosperous society.[25] Hardin, however, demonstrated that while in some circumstances an individual's pursuit of narrow self-interest promoted his or her broader interests as a member of group, in other circumstances a myopic focus on self-interest severely undermined and subverted those broader group interests by incentivising the unsustainable exploitation of common resources, leading to the eventual depletion of those resources and catastrophe for people who depended on them. Hardin's example involved herders attempting to share a common grazing area, but the principle applies to the use of any "common pool" resource. The tragedy of the commons hinges on property rights: if the ownership of a resource are not or cannot be clearly defined, then multiple individuals may attempt to satisfy their narrow self-interests by exploiting that resource as completely as possible, until they have destroyed their common resource and impoverished themselves.

The problem of ownership was not new.[26] In 1940 libertarian economist Ludwig von Mises noted that, "If land is not owned by anybody, although legal formalism may call it public property, it is used without any regard to the disadvantages resulting. Those who are in a position to appropriate to themselves the returns — lumber and game of the forests, fish of the water areas, and mineral deposits of the subsoil — do not bother about the later effects of their mode of exploitation. For them, erosion of the soil, depletion of the exhaustible resources

---

25 This view had its roots in Adam Smith's 1776 treatise <u>An Inquiry Into the Nature and Causes of the Wealth of Nations.</u> E.g.: "As every individual, therefore, endeavours as much as he can both to employ his capital in the support of domestic industry, and so to direct that industry that its produce may be of the greatest value; every individual necessarily labours to render the annual revenue of the society as great as he can. He generally, indeed, neither intends to promote the public interest, nor knows how much he is promoting it. [...] By pursuing his own interest he frequently promotes that of the society more effactually than when he really intends to promote it."
26 Indeed economists going back to Smith himself had been aware of this problem, in one form or another.

and other impairments of the future utilization are external costs not entering into their calculation of input and output. They cut down trees without any regard for fresh shoots or reforestation. In hunting and fishing, they do not shrink from methods preventing the repopulation of the hunting and fishing grounds."[27] More troubling was the question of how to address the lack of property rights, since privatization was not always possible (how would one privatize the ozone layer?) and frequently presented significant problems of its own.

Hardin's contribution was to demonstrate that common-pool resources were often maintained *without clearly defined property rights* through traditional social systems and environmental constraints on population growth. When development disrupted traditional societies and boosted population growth rates, the result could be a disastrous overconsumption of resources followed by extreme scarcity and privation. This was a very timely observation, as by Hardin's day the evidence of widespread ecological devastation throughout the developing world occurring as a direct consequence of the development process itself, had already become staggering. Deforestation, desertification, the collapse of biodiversity and the extermination of whole species, along with famines, dust storms, mudslides, acid rain and a host of other natural and man-made disasters—including the rapidly rising temperature of the Earth—are the direct result of an ongoing failure to address the misuse of common-pool resources.

How do we overcome this failure, as well as numerous related problems involving public goods, free-ridership, adverse selection and moral hazard, the overproduction of negative externalities and the underproduction of positive ones? Political science, law, and even mathematics have all yielded important insights, ranging from the

---

27 Ludwig von Mises Nationalökonomie: Theorie des Handelns und Wirtschaftens Geneva: Editions Union. English translation (1949) New Haven: Yale University Press.

game-theory concept of Pareto-optimal Nash equilibrium,[28] to the more recently formulated social identity model of collective action.[29] However, as Nobel prize-winning economist Elinor Ostrom noted in her 1997 Presidential Address to the American Political Science Association, overcoming the failure of collective action remains one of the most critical unanswered questions in economics and the social sciences, and one which is utterly fundamental to the future of human society.[30] In the end there may be no single, universal solution to the tragedy of the commons or the problem of collective action: each real-world situation is unique and to some extent it must be addressed on its own terms. The process of research and analysis is always ongoing, but for the present these questions will remain at the frontier of sustainable development theory.

The vital role in sustainable development played by the public sector is sometimes referred to as "political sustainability", though it is more accurately described as two distinct, but related concepts: **policy continuity** and **democratic institutions**.[31] The former refers to the importance of maintaining a firm political commitment to sustainable development that is reflected in continuous, consistent policies, which may extend beyond the mandate of any single political leader, party or administration. Erratic, unreliable or unenforced policy actions may in fact be worse than making no attempt at sustainable development, because ineffective policies generate uncertainty and discredit their underlying principles. Before ad-

---

28 See: Nash, John (1951) "Non-Cooperative Games" *The Annals of Mathematics* 54(2):286-295

29 See: van Zomeren, M., T. Postmes and R. Spears (2008) "Toward an integrative social identity model of collective action: A quantitative research synthesis of three socio-psychological perspectives" *Psychological Bulletin* 134 (4): 504–535

30 Ostrom, Elinor (1998) "A Behavioral Approach to the Rational Choice Theory of Collective Action" *American Political Science Review* 92(1): 1-22

31 It should be noted that "democratic institutions" does not necessarily refer to a country's system of national governance. It refers to the establishment and maintenance of effective mechanisms for citizens to collectively influence policy decisions, which can include popular elections and direct referenda, but the precise nature of these mechanisms may vary significantly by country and community.

vocating sustainability-focused reforms, whether at the local or national level, it is important to ensure a strong and stable constituency is in place and prepared to see them through. Building this constituency requires the type of active multi-stakeholder collaboration described above, but transforming a general consensus into a political force in turn requires responsive, participatory democratic institutions. Good governance and public-sector integrity, checks and balances on the exercise of authority, decentralised decision-making, and a commitment to equality before the law are all crucial elements of a lasting political commitment to sustainable development.

SUSTAINABLE DEVELOPMENT: OPPORTUNITIES FOR TOURISM DESTINATIONS

While sustainability has implications at the local, national and even global levels, in terms of economic sectors sustainable development is especially relevant to the tourism industry. There are several reasons for this, including: (i) the extremely important role that the tourism industry plays in the economies of many developing countries, (ii) the unusual sensitivity of tourism to local social, cultural and ecological conditions, (iii) the negative repercussions of unsustainable tourism practices or inappropriate sectoral policies and, conversely, (iv) the enormous—and still largely untapped—potential of tourism to generate positive outcomes across all dimensions of economic and human development.

The tourism industry currently generates an estimated 230 million jobs worldwide, or roughly 8 per cent of the global workforce; it has great capacity to raise incomes, reduce poverty, preserve historical and cultural patrimony, and conserve biodiversity.[32] Yet the industry is also a major polluter, especially considering the carbon damage involved in tourism-related air travel, and in its destination markets the industry is often a major local consumer of energy, land, water, biodiversity and other scarce

32 UN International Labour Organization (2008) "Guide for Social Dialogue in the Tourism Industry" *Sectoral Activities Programme Working Paper* No. 265, prepared by Dain Bolwell and Wolfgang Weinz

resources. Tourism can be extremely disruptive, even when it is well-regulated and governed by well-intentioned policies, while unrestricted, unethical tourism development can transform healthy developing communities into seedy, soulless, crime-ridden, culturally impoverished outlets catering to the worst impulses of wealthy foreigners.

From a tourism destination's perspective, sustainable tourism development may be described as a system for the strategic management of resources that will generate enduring returns in accordance with the objectives of broader national or local development policies. Sustainable tourism development encompasses practices and programmes that take a holistic approach to the industry and its community, including its ecosystems, social structures, cultural forms and self-defined aspirations not only in addition to, but as an essential component of the industry's long-term economic viability. According to a definition provided by the UN Environmental Programme's World Tourism Organization (2005) sustainable tourism "takes full account of its current and future economic, social and environmental impacts, addressing the needs of visitors, the industry, the environment and host communities." Expanding on this definition Ivars (2004) locates sustainable tourism within the broader framework of sustainable development, describing it as:

> [A] process of qualitative change, a product of political will, which, with the indispensable participation of the local population, adapts the institutional and legal boundaries as well as the planning and management instruments to development based on a balance between the preservation of the natural and cultural heritage the economic viability of tourism and the social inclusion and equity of the development.

Thus we understand that sustainable tourism is a process of qualitative change that not only reorients development policy and programming toward broader objectives that encompass the quality of life of local populations and the responsible use of resources, but which views the tourism industry, its host community and local ecology as elements of a complete, and interdependent system. Sustainability is the task of ensuring that that system is capable of balancing interests and aligning incentives in order to generate constant (even increasing) benefits for all of its stakeholders: tourists, local residents and industry workers, private sector agents both within and outside the tourism sector, the broader national community, and both the local and global environment. Sustainable tourism is both an ethical and, crucially, a *practical* framework, one which touches on all elements of sectoral development policy and programming.

Figure 2.1, below, illustrates this concept and highlights the importance of multi-sector collaboration and the engagement of civil society in sustainable tourism development.

SOCIAL EQUITY   **ECONOMIC EFFICIENCY**

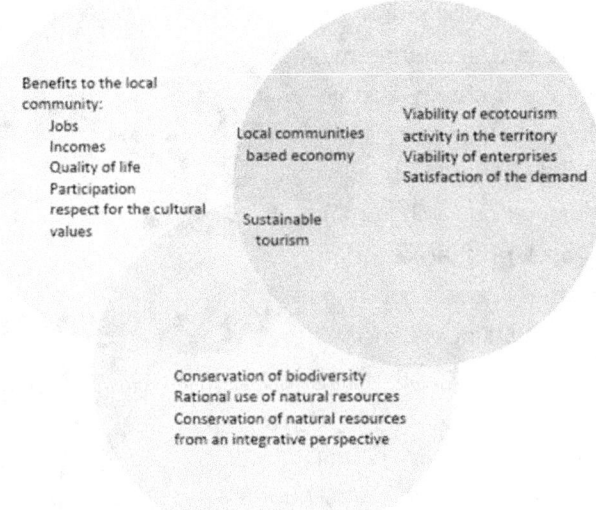

Benefits to the local
community:
    Jobs
    Incomes
    Quality of life
    Participation
    respect for the cultural
    values

Local communities
based economy

Sustainable
tourism

Viability of ecotourism
activity in the territory
Viability of enterprises
Satisfaction of the demand

Conservation of biodiversity
Rational use of natural resources
Conservation of natural resources
from an integrative perspective

ENVIRONMENTAL CONSERVATION

Figure 2.1: Intersectorial Collaboration

Sustainable tourism has introduced a new set of values and standards to the tourism industry. In many tourism destinations this has prompted a process of gradual change, with governments, private firms, local communities and international agencies all working redefine their visions for tourism development. This involves augmenting existing economic imperatives with an explicit commitment to ensuring social, cultural and/or environmental sustainability, as well as supporting the active participation of the local population in sectoral decision-making and promoting continuous reinvestment in ecological capital and the cooperative conservation of biodiversity. In a larger context, the tourism industry's greenhouse-gas output, its oceanic impacts and other global environmental effects must be more thoroughly understood, and various mitigation strategies for reducing carbon emissions and other forms of pollution must be rigorously evaluated, and the best available options must be tirelessly pursued.

While sustainability is often framed as an ethical obligation, the central political and economic motivation for investment in sustainable tourism development is the observable reality that sustainably managed destinations will remain competitive and profitable indefinitely, while the success of firms that rely on unsustainable models is inherently time-bound. Emerging destinations such as the United Arab Emirates, especially Dubai,

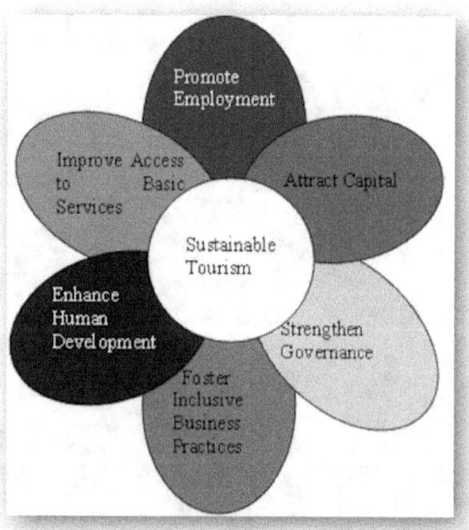

Qatar and Abu Dhabi, have made huge investments in promoting sustainable tourism and formulating strategies for leadership in a greener global economy. Although there is growing demand on the part of international tourists for ethically managed and environmentally responsible services, sustainable tourism is not, and should never be viewed as, merely a specific form of tourism or an exploitable niche market. Efforts to treat it as such will likely prove superficial and fail to achieve the core objectives of sustainability. These efforts may also be viewed as cynically opportunistic or otherwise illegitimate by sustainability-minded tourists, which would negate the value of this putative "sustainability" in the eyes of its target demographic.

If it is supported by a broad-based, genuine and enduring commitment, the integration of sustainable-development principles into tourism policy and sectoral management may act as a catalyst for other structural reforms and even give rise of new institutional mechanisms and forums for dialogue between policymakers and tourism stakeholders. Through a collaborative effort to promote sustainable tourism the private sector can be encouraged to switch to more responsible business practices, both by demonstrating the economic value of sustainability and by adopting a set of sectoral policies that favours investment in sustainable tourism.[33] The ability of governments to promote and support sustainable practices will require a commitment to good governance. While a more thorough description of the relationship between governance and sustainable tourism is presented in Chapter 3, it is important to outline its most salient elements.

In examining the impact of governance on the success of sustainable tourism development a number of key underlying themes become apparent. These include the fundamental importance of: (i) a credible and enduring political commitment to sustainability, (ii) the availability of adequate financial and institutional resources to complete the required legal, institutional and regulatory reforms, (iii) sufficient enforcement capacity to ensure that new laws and policies are meaningfully implemented, and (iv) accessible and responsive mechanisms for incorporating the input and feedback of affected communities and other stakeholders into the design of subsequent policy actions.[34]

---

33 However, it is important to recall that the principles of sustainability require that these policies themselves be sustainable: that is, they must encourage the growth of a sustainable tourism industry that is ultimately self-supporting and does not require continuous public-sector assistance to remain viable.

34 UN Environment Programme World Tourism Organization (2005) <u>Making tourism more sustainable: a guide for policymakers</u>

These prerequisites for the success of sustainable development should appear familiar, as they are all elements of **policy continuity** and **democratic institutions**, defined above.

SUSTAINABLE TOURISM AND PUBLIC POLICY: OBJECTIVES AND INDICATORS

Fostering the growth of sustainable tourism through public policy requires clear, well-defined, and measurable objectives consistent with the multidimensional nature of sustainable development. The design of policy objectives is critical, but in order to transform good intentions into demonstrable success, sustainable-development indicators must be integrated into the monitoring and evaluation of policies and interventions. Indicators are essential tools not only for gauging success, but also for incorporating feedback and establishing best practices, and in some cases they may be vital to the enforcement of laws and regulations and the implementation of policies. Indicators can be quantitative, qualitative or even a combination of the two, but in all cases reliable baseline data is critical, as it allows for the measurement and evaluation of trends over time. Objectives and indicators each play an essential role in operationalizing the sustainability paradigm. In terms of the governance and public-policy agenda for sustainable development, key objectives and related indicators include:

- **Local prosperity**, which reflects the extent to which communities impacted by the tourism industry are able to benefit from it economically. Policymakers often tend to focus on the national benefits of tourism—tax revenue, service export growth, positive changes in the external balances—at the expense of tourism's economic impact on local communities. That a community will become richer as a result of tourism development is in no way guaranteed and cannot be taken for granted. Local prosperity indicators include, but are not restricted to, increased income generation, more equitable income distribution, increased employment rates (especially in the formal sector), expanded employment opportunities for marginalized and disadvantaged groups, greater gender parity in labour-force participation, and broad-based poverty reduction. Popular satisfaction with employment quality and the changing nature of the local economy are also core elements of local prosperity and can be measured through regular household surveys. In addition, local prosperity also requires that a share of the revenues derived from the exploitation of environmental, social, or cultural resources is reinvested in the local community, and that this share must adequate to offset the loss of local capital arising from tourism development. This can be difficult to assess given the imperfectly quantifiable nature of certain forms of capital, and evaluating it requires:

- **Local empowerment**, because sustainable tourism is dependent on continuous stakeholder dialogue and collaborative, participatory decision-making. Local communities must be able to influence the tourism strategy, policy and management agenda. Local empowerment is predicated on strong, responsive political institutions capable of incorporating local perspectives into a dynamic development agenda; and establishing regular forums for consultation with a balanced and representative group of stakeholders. Because of the major role public institutions play in local empowerment, one of its essential prerequisites is:

- **Institutional integrity**. That policies, regulations, and legal protections are enforced with basic reliability, impartiality, transparency, and accountability is at the core of good governance, and fundamental to promoting sustainable development. In the context of sustainable tourism policy, institutional integrity involves a continuous commitment to ensuring that those affected by the tourism industry have access to official mechanisms for registering complaints, investigating claims, adjudicating disputes, and redressing grievances that arise from tourism development, not only at the individual level, but at the community and civil society levels as well. The universal enforcement of legal protections, the clear definition of property rights, and the efficient settlement of conflicts is critical to ensuring that local capital stocks are managed wisely and that the returns to development are equitably distributed, and essential to avoiding the destruction of common-pool resources through competitive exploitation as described above. At the national level, institutional integrity can be measured by various international evaluation systems, including the Transparency International Corruption Perceptions Index [35] and the Polity IV Project, but it can be much harder to measure at the local level. Surveys can be a useful tool, but it should always be borne in mind that perceptions are subjective and may be conditioned by implicit comparisons to other communities or neighbouring countries. Nevertheless, safeguarding individual and community rights and ensuring the protection of environmental resources is essential, as it allows for the preservation of:

- **Social, cultural and ecological integrity**. Sustainable tourism strategies pursue values that extend beyond easily quantifiable indicators of economic success, and which encompass a broader understanding of private utility and public welfare. Because they are both inherently subjective and contingent on evolving personal and community aspirations, the definition of specific social, cultural and ecological goals is a continuous process. Public policy must actively support this process by promoting local empowerment and ensuring institutional integrity, but policymakers must also recognize the sustainable management of social, cultural and ecological resources is a highly complex process and cannot easily be measured; in many ways, it represents the definitive challenge of sustainable tourism development.

---

35 To learn more, visit : http://www.transparency.org/research/cpi/overview

CONCLUSIONS

It is clear that the tourism industry in general, and sustainable tourism in particular, may play a significant role in achieving the development objectives of nations and communities alike, and that it is capable of simultaneously satisfying a great many of the diverse interests, hopes and desires of the countless stakeholders involved in international tourism. However, the benefits of tourism and of development in general do not accrue automatically and cannot be taken for granted. Good governance, well-designed public policies and strong, responsive institutions guided by inclusive dialogue and decentralized, collaborative decision-making are crucial to maintaining the multiple forms of capital—social, cultural and ecological—that extend beyond traditional economic assets. The central challenge of sustainability is to ensure that capital in all its forms remains intact and able to generate constant, or even increasing, returns for generations to come.

While the global debate regarding the value (or even the imperative) of sustainable development is on-going, but the fact that such a debate is taking place can be interpreted as positive evidence of a global society that is actively evaluating the necessity of undertaking fundamental, structural changes in the way it understands and interacts with the world in order to for developed nations to maintain the standard of living they currently enjoy, and for developing to define and pursue their own aspirations. Whatever the ultimate outcome, the influence of this debate on global tourism development is already clear and evidently gaining strength. It is our duty as residents of the world and members of a global society to reflect on these evolving dynamics and, as far as possible, to serve both our ethical obligations to one another and our own self-interests by ensuring that the wealth of tomorrow is never less than the wealth of today. In this context economic productivity cannot be regarded as an end in itself, but as only one dimension in a far more intricate, more comprehensive, and fundamentally more accurate understanding of human welfare.

EXERCISES

1. Explain each of the four dimensions of sustainable development.
2. Propose two ways to define social sustainability.
3. Explain the difference between GDP and national savings and list some of the factors that influence the latter.
4. What is environmental sustainability, and how does it affect the economic viability of tourism?
5. Briefly describe the "tragedy of the commons".
6. Investigate how environmental sustainability is managed in Mozambique's Bazaruto Archipelago.
7. In your opinion, why are stakeholder dialogue and consultative policy processes important to sustainable tourism development?
8. Name three major obstacles to sustainable tourism development.

CASE 3 - MAKING COMMUNITIES BENEFIT FROM WILDLIFE TOURISM IN WESTERN SERENGETI
Rinus van Klinken, SNV – Netherlands Development Organization.

BUTTERBEANS IN NATA
It is a Tuesday afternoon in Nata, one of the villages along the western corridor of Serengeti National Park. A group of farmers is sitting under a shed, listening to the secretary of the farmers' cooperative society (GHOMACOS), reading out the list of crops t0 be delivered this week. The farmers' cooperative has a contract with Grumeti Reserves, one of the major tourism and conservation investors in the area, to supply their 600 staff and tourists with agricultural produce. The requirements range from the mundane maize and rice, to more seasonal fruits and vegetables and up to the more exotic (e.g. butterbean, rosemary, thyme and other crops for which no Swahili translation has been invented yet).

Going down the list, the secretary notes who can supply by reading on the list: "tomatoes: 50 kg", five hands of farmers go up. He asks each of them how much they can supply this week; and if the quota is over-subscribed, they agree on supplying by rotation (with the excess sold in the local market). Although the list has some 40 different crops, with a total value of TZS 26 million (USD 26,000) per week, during this fairly typical week only one third of the requirements can be met by the 60 or so farmers, who are members of GHOMACOS. With further support and improvements, the supply system (which was established only 3 months ago), can generate some USD 1 million per year for the farmers, and represents one of the most concrete results yet from the tourism sector interventions in the Lake Zone.

BACKGROUND

Tourism is one of the fastest growing sectors in Tanzania's economy, contributing 17 % of Tanzania's GDP and 25% of total export earnings. Tourism generates more foreign exchange than any other sector of the economy, US$1.269 billion in 2008. Currently, tourism directly employs an estimated 300,000 Tanzanians and this number is sure to increase. SNV Tanzania regards tourism as a driver for local development. The aim of our support in tourism development is to increase opportunities for the poor to benefit. For higher impact of tourism on the poor, linkages between tourism and poor people in the local economy are strengthened (increasing the slice of the tourist cake for the poor). This goes hand in hand with strengthening the performance of the overall tourism sector (increasing the overall size of the cake), both at national and destination-level. SNV Tanzania is applying this approach in three destinations, i.e. the Pangani-Saadani coastal area, Zanzibar and western Serengeti.

The western Serengeti DMA is covered from the Lake Zone portfolio. It is a well established destination, a UNESCO World Heritage Site and recognized and appreciated worldwide. In 2006/07, some 135,000 tourists visited Serengeti National Park (almost 20 % of all international arrivals in Tanzania!). Most of those visited Serengeti as part of the Northern Circuit game viewing safari (also covering Ngorongoro Crater, Tarangire and Manyara National Parks), with a total average package price of $ 1,600. It can be estimated that tourists spend at least $ 70 million per year in Serengeti.

In a first diagnostic study in 2008, it was established that there was plenty of scope to make wildlife-based tourism in Serengeti more pro-poor. Using the 7 pro poor tourism mechanisms developed by the UN World Tourism Organisation to assess the pro-poor content of the existing tourism industry, it was noted that the linkages with local communities and small businesses were extremely low. For example, only 20 % of the employees working in the tourism industry (estimated at 7,000 direct jobs) came from the surrounding communities, while most produce originated either from Arusha or from outside the country, but was hardly sourced from neighbouring communities.

KEY ISSUES

Through a carefully crafted process the key challenges in holding back pro-poor impact of the current mainstream tourism in western Serengeti were teased out. The process consisted of a multi-disciplinary community survey ('swarming'), followed with individual consultations with key stakeholders, and culminating in a high-level multi-stakeholder platform, convened by the Regional Commissioner for Mara Region by end of last year (2009). Through this process consensus was created that more efforts need to be made for creating community benefits from wildlife and tourism.

While wildlife is fairly in abundance in the Serengeti eco-system, it is under severe pressure from increasing population, changed land-use practices and illegal hunting (with an unclear boundary between commercial poaching and traditional hunting practices). Both wildlife conservation and wildlife-based tourism generates large revenue flows, not only from business activities but also in form of payments of fees, taxes and remittances to local and lower-level government. Some villages have an annual income of TZS 300 million (USD 0.2 million) from camp fees, land rent and other income, yet with very little visible effects on village amenities or livelihoods. Underlying this is an accountability agenda, with tourism companies and wildlife agencies making payments to government institutions and leaders, yet with constituents not being made aware of this.

Based on the above analysis and understanding between the key stakeholders,
the following activities are being supported by the Lake Zone portfolio.

1. Tourism Enterprise Mapping

Creating systematic insight into the relations between tourism enterprises, local communities and government, as a basis for accountability interventions

Partner: EKN (PATA Innovation Fund); Client: Serengeti District Council, Bunda District Council and Mara Regional Secretariat; LCB: IBDI, Musoma

This activity is based on village-level mapping. For each village, bordering western Serengeti, a detailed survey is made of all tourism enterprises and how they relate to the communities and payments made. This information is then tri-angulated with both District Council and village government records. Finally, a village dialogue meeting is convened with all parties concerned, in order to share the available information and agree on action points on how improved use can be made of tourism-based revenues for village development processes.

Results: The mapping has undergone some delays for operational reasons. Only a pilot in 2 (out of the 25) villages has been concluded, while a survey on all enterprises within the Park is now under way.

The village dialogue meeting in one of the pilot villages exposed the lack of a contract between the local investor and the village as well as the lack of guidance from the Bunda District Council in this respect. As a result of the dialogue, the Council has now prepared a standard contract, to guide this and other villages in their relationships with investors.

Plans: Based on current planning, the Mapping exercise will be completed in early 2010, and will be concluded with two district dialogues, laying the basis for further accountability interventions, focusing on improving collaboration between tourism investors, local and lower level governments and citizens.

Example of village contract

2. Cultural and community-based tourism

Developing cultural tourism enterprises with links to mainstream wildlife-based tourism

Partners: Tanzania Tourist Board (TTB) – Cultural Tourism Project; LCB: IBDI; Consultant: Miradi Associates; Clients: On-going cultural tourism initiatives

The main route to Serengeti National Park is from Arusha, with tourists coming and going back through the same route. There is a small, but growing, trickle of tourists coming from Kenya through the Sirare border post, and entering Serengeti through the western corridor. Either way, the contact between tourists and local communities is minimal, as once the tourists have entered the Park they do (generally) not come out. Yet, interviews with tourists and tour companies have proven that there is a market demand for cultural and community-based tourism attractions, to diversify the holiday experience.

A number of individuals and groups have taken the initiative to establish local attractions, facilities and events. Jointly with TTB/CTP, a consultancy was commissioned to make an inventory of these initiatives, make an assessment of their status and give advice on their further development. Based on the outcome of this consultancy, a joint programme with TTB/CTP will be developed, focused on first developing the capacity of the initiatives (guide them into becoming enterprises) and secondly linking these to the market.

Results: Partly as a result of hitherto rather incidental interventions, a number of cultural tourism initiatives have been established, both within

Serengeti District (now grouped as Serengeti CT association) as along the Musoma – Bunda corridor. Examples are: Serengeti Cultural Centre, Ikoma Cultural Centre and the Butiama/Nyamuswa cultural programme.

3. Strengthening Supply Chains

Building and strengthening supply chains between local communities and producers and tourism enterprises in and around the Park

Partners: Honey Guide Foundation; Grumeti Fund; LCB: IBDI, TSAEE, Match Makers Associates; Clients: Grumeti Farmers Cooperative, Mara Milk and Musoma Dairy

The opportunities for linking communities to tourism enterprises can be captured in two statements:

- Tourism enterprises obtain their agricultural and dairy supplies from Arusha, with a substantial part of it being imported.
- The area bordering western Serengeti is agriculturally highly productive, with both developed and potential irrigation, and Mara Region is the second highest region in terms of number of cattle in Tanzania.

There are equally two key constraints for linking the two:

- Tourism enterprises prefer to obtain their supplies from a single source, and there is internal resistance for modifying their purchase procedure to accommodate local produce from communities;

- Communities are used to operate within an opportunistic and ad hoc market, with market behaviour characterised by risk aversion and short-term horizon.

Breaking through these established and entrenched positions is not easy. A two-pronged approach is being followed: providing support to small steps (specific initiatives for establishing chains) and seeking audience with chief executives for strategic support.

Two specific initiatives being supported are the linking of the farmers cooperative to Grumeti Reserves (see introduction story) and linking milk processors to tourism industry in the Park (see text box). Efforts to link these processors to VCCF (equity finance) have met reluctance from the entrepreneurs.

Plans: support will be provided to the Grumeti farmers in improving production, and based on these results the establishment of a farmers wholesale market will be further explored. The Mara dairy processors will be linked to the Serengeti hotel industry. These activities are supported by the Grumeti Reserves.

Linkages beetween the tourism sector and the local dairy producers in Serengeti, is based in the following market highlihgts:

- Local tourism sector spends as much as US$ 1.5 million/year in dairy products.
- Currently most of dairy products bought are imported from EU, Kenya and South Africa.
- There in raising interest in supporting local quality standards to buy local.

4. Mwanza as additional gateway to Serengeti

Creating Mwanza City as a destination and additional gateway for entering Serengeti National Park

Partners: Cluster Competitiveness Programme (TPSF), Mwanza Regional Secretariat, Tanzania Tourist Board; LCB: Kiroyera Tours, Mwanza Guide on Line; Client: Mwanza City Council (MCC); Mwanza Tourism Association.

Very few tourists are entering Serengeti National Park through the western corridor (most come through Arusha), and almost none travel through Mwanza. Yet, Mwanza is only 2 hours by road from the Park. Part of the reasons for Mwanza not featuring on the travel map is the lack of connections, tourism facilities and developed attractions.

For the last one and a half years, SNV has supported efforts to establish Mwanza as a destination, which could then link up with the well established Serengeti market. While initially a task force was established under the City Council umbrella, private sector stakeholders have gradually taken over the task force, which is now in the process of being transformed into the Mwanza Tourism Association. Key activities have been the opening of a Mwanza tourism information office, lobbying TTB for opening a zonal office in Mwanza and TAA (Tanzania Airport Authority) to improve airport facilities, joint marketing efforts (through Karibu Fair) and development of tourism routes.

Results: A vibrant, private sector led Mwanza Tourism Association is operational, and is in the process of opening and operating a Mwanza tourism information office. TTB will be opening a zonal office before the year end. Community-based cultural tourism modules are being developed, and will be operational by the end of the year.

Plans: Link the Mwanza Tourism Association to investment opportunities (through CCP-TPSF), create link between Mwanza and Serengeti (through tour operators) and develop cultural tours.

- Tourism accounts for 25 % of foreign exchange earnings
- The sector contributes about 17.2 % to the GDP
- It directly employs an estimated 250,000 - 300,000 people

Federico Vignati • Don Hawkins • Bruce Priedeaux

CASE 4 - WORLD BIRDING RALLY: RAISING AWARENESS OF THE VALUE OF BIODIVERSITY IN PERU
By José Koechlin and Gabriel Meseth - Inkaterra

CONTEXT

Inkaterra has pioneered ecotourism in Peru since 1975 and is currently renowned as a world leader in sustainable tourism. In order to underscore Peru's cultural and natural values, the hotel company employs a holistic approach that generates added value in rural areas: it encourages scientific research for biodiversity conservation, education and the economic growth of local communities. Its areas of influence are in the Amazon rainforest of Madre de Dios; the Andean cloud forest of Machu Picchu; and the Cabo Blanco tropical sea and desert in Northern Peru.

Through the NGO Inkaterra Asociación, many scientific research projects have been developed since 1978, including flora and fauna inventories designed to set a benchmark to compare Inkaterra's impact on biodiversity. For instance, a total of 747 bird species have been inventoried within Inkaterra hotel properties in Madre de Dios and Machu Picchu, almost as many as in all of Costa Rica.

Aiming to promote Peru as a top destination for birding, Inkaterra conceived the World Birding Rally. This international non-stop competition attracted renowned ornithologists such as Thomas Schulenberg (Cornell Lab of Ornithology) and Daniel Lane (LSU Museum of Natural Science), co-authors of the comprehensive guidebook *Birds of Peru*. Teams from the United States, Great Britain, Spain, South Africa, Brazil and Colombia – main markets for this particular segment – were invited to participate in both events of the World Birding Rally: the Inkaterra Route, a 6 day 800km journey across Madre de Dios, Cusco, the Sacred Valley and Machu Picchu; and the Nor Amazon Route, spanning 1503km in 9 days through 12 life zones in the regions of Lambayeque, Cajamarca, Amazonas and San Martin.

Foto: Ernesto Benavides

Foto: Carmen Soto

A COLLABORATIVE INTERVENTION LOGIC

The World Birding Rally was designed to validate bird inventories within Inkaterra properties stressing immediacy and low costs. Since the first rally in December 2012, its main objectives were to raise awareness of confirmed values of biological diversity in Peru and to support its conservation though an eco-friendly activity: bird watching. It aims to prompt the establishment of more local reserves to preserve natural habitats for endemic bird species, thus improving the quality of life of rural communities while preserving their environment. Career opportunities related to local ecotourism reduce emigration, helping to safeguard local cultures.

There are 2.42 million birdwatchers interested in visiting Peru during the coming three years (2015-2018); according to a study sponsored by PromPerú, each will spend an average of 19 nights (average travel expenses: USD$2741-$3300). Thus the World Birding Rally is a key element in the national strategy to promote Peru as a bird watching hotspot. It is worth mentioning that Peru has the world's third largest number of bird species (1816 species, including 120 endemic to Peru). Thus, Peru is in a prime position to generate opportunities for biodiversity conservation, job creation and the economic growth of local communities directly catalyzed by the development of bird watching tourism.

Since that first rally in 2012, the World Birding Rally has been organized and overseen by Inkaterra with a matching financial investment by the Ministry of Foreign Commerce and Tourism (MINCETUR) and PromPerú. Itineraries in Madre de Dios and Machu Picchu take place within the Inkaterra areas of influence, with excursions to Lake Sandoval and Lake Valencia; Inkaterra Canopy Walkway – a system of hanging bridges at 100ft above the ground, built to study flora and fauna at the rainforest canopy in Tambopata; and the cloud forest surrounding Inkaterra Machu Picchu Pueblo Hotel.

The event was replicated in June 2013 for the Nor Amazon route. The itinerary was planned by Inkaterra Asociación and CORBIDI (Centro de Ornitología y Biodiversidad), after a series of inspections across the Lambayeque-San Martín route. Regional governments encouraged the participation of local communities and showcased potential for ecotourism activities during the event. Additionally, the National Service of Natural Protected Areas (SERNANP) and the Ministry of the Environment (MINAM) gave access to ecological reserves; while the Ministry of the

Interior (MININTER) – in charge of the National Police of Peru – was involved via the National Road Plan, allowing participants to travel safely.

There have been four World Birding Rallies to date, two of which took place on the Inkaterra Route (December 2012 and 2013) and two along the Nor Amazon Route (June 2013 and May 2014).

PROJECT MEANS AND GOALS

Following a scheme similar to Big Days and Big Years, the World Birding Rally's goal is to register the largest number of bird species in a determined time and itinerary. Each team is made up of three to four members and is assisted by a local or Inkaterra guide who contributes specific knowledge of each checkpoint's characteristics. Species are registered in a checklist which at the end of each day is handed to two judges. Final results for all editions can be observed in the following table:

Dates	Participants	WBR Event	Total Species
Nov. 29–Dec. 5, 2012	24	Inkaterra	692
Jun. 9–20, 2013	24	Nor-Amazónica	864
Dec. 4–10, 2013	15	Inkaterra	457
May 13–21, 2014	16	Nor-Amazónica	777

The number of species registered in these week-long competitions surpassed all expectations and confirmed Peru as both a mega-diverse country and a top destination for observable bird species. For instance, the Nor-Amazon route allowed competitors to observe in only nine days up to 864 species – equivalent to 10% of the total number of bird species in the world.

The World Birding Rally also has a positive impact on the conservation of natural areas, as local communities were able to learn more about ecotourism trends and opportunities.

In Machu Picchu and Madre de Dios, Inkaterra Asociación and CORBIDI organize training sessions on bird watching techniques and species identification, which helps raise awareness on the value of bio-diversity among several communities. Local guides from Inkaterra con-stantly organize birding excursions during their spare time, keeping records of their findings through field reports – published in the Inkaterra Newsletter, a monthly public listing for orchids, mammals and medicinal plants. Additionally, Inkaterra organizes educational games and experi-ments for children in local communities, offering key messages on con-servation and environmental care for future generations.

For the Lambayeque-San Martin route, town halls and regional gov-ernments began to encourage ecotourism, rural tourism and biodiversity conservation as suitable methods towards development. Since the World Birding Rally, the communities of Conga and Limón (Cajamarca) consider experiential travel an effective alternative to mining and other extractive industries, and they are growing fruits, bushes and trees in their fields to at-tract birds overflying the area. In Luichupucro (Cajamarca) the 'Campanilla' flower has been seeded in forests and riverbeds, its nectar the main feed-ing source for an endemic species thought to be extinct and currently can only be found in this zone: the Grey-Bellied Comet (*Taphrolesbia grisei-ventris*). In Leymebamba (Amazonas) – habitat of the Marvelous Spatuletail (*Loddigesia mirabilis*) – Inkaterra trained and furnished local inns on hospi-tality international standards in order to welcome a group of 102 travellers, an unprecedented event in Chachapoyas province. In Moyobamba (San Martín), villagers offered a warm welcome to birders with food tastings, emphasizing native goods such as cacao and coffee.

The reaction of the international media to the World Birding Rally has been extremely enthusiastic, as well as in social media (specially the Cornell Lab of Ornithology official Facebook page). An equivalent of $2,000,000 in free publicity has been generated. The events' massive outreach allowed natural areas in Peru to have increased international awareness, favoring bird watching and rural tourism.

LESSONS LEARNED

Bird inventories commissioned by Inkaterra since 1979 aimed to create a replicable model based on scientific knowledge, conservation and sustainability. The World Birding Rally helped to validate more than 30 years of collected data and confirmed Inkaterra's proposition that nature has a social function. It proves the need to establish natural reserves across Peru in order to conserve endemic species. Through ecotourism and sustainable development, local communities can preserve their own environments, while migration is reduced and native cultures are safeguarded. Improving quality of life for humans and biodiversity can be achieved by this approach.

From a new tourism product development perspective, the World Birding Rally allowed organizers – including Inkaterra, PromPerú, SERNANP and other affiliates – to learn more about the profile of birdwatchers and their expectations of their visits to Peru.

It is worth enhancing the creation of awareness of biodiversity conservation in local communities after the event. This will allow rural communities to be more committed to research endeavors, the conservation of natural areas and, overall, to ecotourism as a new source of income.

RECOMMENDATIONS

The World Birding Rally offers a chance to expand bird watching throughout diverse routes in Peru, promoting social inclusion, tourism diversification and the decentralization of economic development, providing income and working opportunities in remote areas with very little economic alternatives.

A public-private alliance accelerates research programs to help learning and the conservation of protected natural areas. If research and species validation is publicized worldwide, the result will be Peru being acknowledged as the world's top destination on bird watching.

A thorough photographic record should be produced during the next rally, to help promote bird watching tourism through publications and advertising on a global scale. This would consolidate bird watching in Peru as a successful business model. In that sense, further studies would determine the impact of bird watching on biodiversity and community development.

Inkaterra and CORBIDI are currently working on an initiative to ensure proper conservation strategies for bird species to be shared with neighboring countries (Safe Migratory Routes). Peru is situated in a privileged spot for bird observation, being a sort of crossroads for migratory birds, as well as a hotspot for endemics due to its geography, 84 life zones and favorable weather conditions.

Three

Sustainable Tourism and Governance

Be the change you want to see in the world.

— MAHATMA GANDHI

OBJECTIVES OF THE CHAPTER:

- Describe the influence of governance, public policy and the local political economy of tourism destinations on the sustainability of the tourism industry.
- Highlight the key role that local citizens, private-sector representatives and civil-society organizations all play in sustainable tourism development.
- Identify a number of important political challenges to sustainable tourism.

INTRODUCTION

The term 'governance' refers not only to the quality of a country's public institutions, the integrity of its legal and regulatory structures, or the effectiveness of its policies, but also to the responsiveness of governments to the diverse, ever-evolving interests, views and aspirations of their constituents. The concept of good governance therefore encompasses the multiple institutions, mechanism and processes through which citizens, private-sector representatives and civil-society organizations articulate their needs and goals, resolve conflicts, and exercise their rights and obligations at both the local and national level.[36] Good governance involves active partnerships between public institutions and stakeholder groups in order to facilitate the formulation of transparent, accountable and equitable public policies and the delivery of high-quality public goods and services. Good governance has a profound influence on the success of all sustainable development efforts, and it is absolutely essential to sustainable tourism.

Due to the often intense local impact of tourism development, good governance in a tourism destination is especially reliant on highly empowered local governments. Local institutions must be invested with sufficient authority, independence and resources to build the sophisticated capacities necessary to sustainably manage a growing tourism industry, while ensuring transparency in its operations and accountability to its citizens. There is no single blueprint for high-capacity local governance: the laws defining public authority and institutional relationships across multiple levels of government (local, regional, provincial, national) are different in every country. Moreover, some jurisdictions may include peculiar local power arrangements, such as special ethnic or tribal protections, unique provisions for religious institutions or communities, or even some of regional semi-autonomy; conversely, some localities might face a loss of local control through remote administration, or through various forms of institutional marginalization, whether based on ethnicity, regional origin, religious affiliation, or some other distinction.

Consequently, good governance, like so much else in sustainable development, is locally specific; it must be constantly conceptualised and re-conceptualised to suit the particular contours of each case. Successes are unique, and cannot necessarily be replicated in other circumstances, while failures need not reflect a weakness of underlying theory, but may instead represent its reckless application to an inappropriate context. Nevertheless,

---

36 See UNDP 2004

a sound understanding of the general principles of governance and the international experience is vital to the development of locally specific strategies that incorporate good governance and institutional strengthening into a comprehensive sustainable-development agenda.

GOVERNANCE, THEORY AND ANALYSIS

In 1989 the World Bank defined governance as "the manner in which power is exercised in the management of country's economic and social resources for development," a definition which remains in frequent use.[37] The concept of governance, however, is continuously being enriched through dialogue, debate and new research. In 1997 UNESCO described governance as the "process whereby citizens' needs and interests are articulated for the positive social and economic development of the entire society and in the light of a perceived common good. Governance means more than government: it refers to a political process that encompasses the whole society and contributes to the making of citizens, active contributors to the social contact that binds them together."[38]

Today, the World Bank provides a more comprehensive definition of governance in its introduction to the Worldwide Governance Indicators (WGI) database, a subset of the more widely known World Development Indictors:

Governance consists of the traditions and institutions by which authority in a country is exercised. This includes the process by which governments are selected, monitored and replaced; the capacity of the government to effectively formulate and implement sound

---

37 This definition was introduced in the 1989 report "Sub-Saharan Africa: From Crisis to Sustainable Growth" and remains in common use. See, e.g., World Bank (1992) "Governance and Development" and Kaufman, D. and A. Kraay (2008) "Governance Indicators: Where We Are, Where Should We Be Going?" World Bank Policy Research Working Paper No.4370.

38 UNESCO (1997). Tourism in European Heritage Cities. UNESCO World Heritage Center.

policies; and the respect of citizens and the state for the institutions that govern economic and social interactions among them.[39]

The WGI dataset, which is available to the public online,[40] enables both cross-country comparisons of various governance indicators and the evaluation of trends over time; though, as noted above, broad findings on governance do not necessarily lend themselves to concrete policy conclusions in specific cases.[41] The WGI is compiled from 30 different data sources, including surveys and assessments undertaken by bilateral and multilateral agencies, non-governmental organisations and private information service providers. These data are aggregated according to six dimensions of governance: (i) voice and accountability, (ii) political stability and absence of violence, (iii) government effectiveness, (iv) regulatory quality, (v) rule of law, and (vi) control of corruption. The WGI is similar to other international development indexes and shares both the strengths and weaknesses of comparable systems.

However, its six dimensions provide a useful framework for breaking down the broad, somewhat nebulous concept of governance into clearer, more definite components. [42]

---

39 See: World Bank (2013) World Governance Indicators http://info.worldbank.org/governance/wgi/index.asp

40 *Ibid.*

41 *Ibid.* "The six composite WGI measures are useful as a tool for broad cross-country comparisons and for evaluating broad trends over time. However, they are often too blunt a tool to be useful in formulating specific governance reforms in particular country contexts. Such reforms, and evaluation of their progress, need to be informed by much more detailed and country-specific diagnostic data that can identify the relevant constraints on governance in particular country circumstances."

42 This is far from the only definition of governance in common use. OECD (2004), for example, lists seven components of good governance: (i) democratic accountability; (ii) transparency in the public sector; (iii) public participation at all levels of government ; (iv) the functional division of administrative and political roles; (v) respect for citizens' rights and enforcement of legal protections; (vi) a service-oriented civil service; and (vii) public financial accountability.

- **Voice and Accountability.** The first dimension of the WGI is arguably the most important, as it represents the fundamental ability of citizens to influence the course of public affairs. Voice and accountability is closely related to the principle of **democratic institutions**, one of the prerequisites for sustainability described in the previous chapter; it refers not only to the essential mechanics of democracy, such as free and fair elections, but also less intuitively obvious measures of political responsiveness and responsibility, such as press freedom, transparency in policy processes, and the political influence of powerful groups.

- **Political Stability and Absence of Violence.** This dimension measures the extent to which political processes are compromised by the use or threat of violence, the violation of constitutional norms or the unlawful usurpation of power. In addition to its obvious implications for public safety and economic security, political stability and absence of violence reflects the overall reliability and predictability of government, and its susceptibility to violence. It is essential to note that this refers not only to violence committed against the government, but also to violence committed by it, or on its behalf.

- **Government Effectiveness.** The concept of government effectiveness focuses on the quality and efficiency of government operations. Does the government develop policies that further its stated objectives? Does the government adhere it its commitments over time? Are its policies implemented by a proficient, incorrupt public administration? Are public services accessible and dependable? And, in general, are interactions between citizens and the government characterized by expeditiousness and professionalism, or by costliness and incompetence? All of these are measures of government effectiveness, which encompasses the principle of **policy continuity**, another necessary condition for sustainable development defined in the previous chapter.

- **Regulatory Quality.** Closely related to government effectiveness is regulatory quality, the ability of the government to establish a private-sector policy and institutional framework favourable to economic growth. Regulatory quality includes measures of the overall efficiency of business regulation, such as the administrative and time costs required for opening, operating and closing a firm, as well as the extent to which preferential or discriminatory policies, such as tax incentives, subsidies and trade restrictions, may distort the development of specific industries or sectors. Measures of regulatory quality tend to be more controversial than government effectiveness, as many economic policies involve trade-offs between pure market efficiency and other policy objectives that are matters of domestic political economy, not objective indicators of good governance. For more on trade-offs between economic efficiency and other policy objectives, see Box 4, below.

- **Rule of Law.** This dimension reflects public confidence in the integrity of legal processes and institutions; it measures the willingness of both citizens and agents of the government to abide by the law and to act within official systems and in accordance with legal norms. On the criminal side, rule of law indicators include, *inter alia*, overall crime rates, the prevalence of bribery and extortion, and general trust in police forces and in the independence and impartiality of the judiciary, while the civil side includes the protection of property rights, contract enforcement, and the size of the informal sector relative to the economy as a whole.

- **Control of Corruption.** The final dimension of governance captured in the WGI is control of corruption. Similar to rule of law, but specific to the improper exercise of government authority, this concept describes the degree to which citizens believe that government officials abuse the public trust for private gain. Though it includes direct bribery, "corruption", broadly understood, is not simply a matter of cash-filled envelopes changing hands in back rooms, but also encompasses numerous forms of influence trading, patronage and graft. "Influence trading" typically refers to *quid pro quo* agreements (whether explicit or informal) between public agencies and powerful interest groups. "Patronage" is the establishment of systems of political protection and reciprocity within the public administration, or between officials and favoured constituencies. "Graft" can refer to any number of illegal or quasi-legal methods for profiting from public office, the most common of which is the use of insider political information to gain advantage in economic transactions.

These elements of governance are overlapping and mutually reinforcing. Control of corruption, for example, is partially encompassed within rule of law, which, along with political stability and absence of violence, is as vital to economic growth as regulatory quality. Consequently, a persistent weakness in any one aspect of governance can severely undermine gains in other areas; or, conversely, a focus on the most deficient elements of governance may be greatly magnified by the relative strength of its other elements.

Having these in mind, some of the fundamental aspects related to governance and sustainable tourism destinations can be resumed in the following:

- Governance, Sustainability and International Tourism;
- Interest Groups and Rent-Seeking;
- Tourism and Local Politics; and
- Participation and the Quality of Public Policies.

BOX 4 TRADE-OFFS, BIG AND SMALL

A new student of macroeconomics, considering the role of government as protector of individual rights and freedoms, might be tempted to assume that the ultimate objective of macroeconomic policy should be to promote economic liberty and the returns to industry by ensuring an efficient allocation of economic resources. She might conclude that the government's focus should be on safeguarding property rights, enforcing contracts, maintaining the rule of law and levying taxes only for the purpose of providing public goods, and never to redistribute wealth. The resulting policy mix would likely produce the most rapid rate of economic growth; however, it would do nothing to address inequality, which would inevitably be passed on to subsequent generations, and a rapidly expanding and increasingly unbridgeable gulf between rich and poor could result in entrenched deprivation, and hopelessness, encouraging criminality and even provoking violent attempts to reallocate wealth by force.

Or, that same student might draw a radically different conclusion: that given the government's unique position as guarantor of the public interest its primary role is not to facilitate the market but to correct its injustices, and that the goal of macroeconomic policy should be to promote the general welfare by ensuring an equitable allocation of resources. She might determine that the government should use redistributive policies, such as progressive taxation, transfers and social programs, to offset the inequality generated by the market. This would certainly result in a more even distribution of wealth, and relative equality would yield important social benefits, but individuals' rights to the product of their labor would be compromised, while the distortive effect of redistribution on economic incentives would likely have a devastating impact on growth, leaving the country poorer as a whole.[43]

As a matter of economics, which course is best? There is no real answer to this, because the question is not in fact a matter of economics. Once normative judgments are introduced—what "should" the government do, what is "best" for society—the discussion leaves the territory of economics proper and enters the realm of political economy. Efficiency and equity are each valid

---

43 For a more thorough discussion of these and related issues see: Scully, G. (2002) "Economic Freedom, Government Policy and the Trade-Off Between Equity and Economic Growth" *Public Choice* 113(1-2): 77-96

policy objectives and the tension between them, often referred to as "the big trade-off," is the driving force behind political-economy debates in democracies throughout the world. The science of economics can inform conclusions about how this trade-off works, about the consequences of moves in either direction, but the ultimate determination of how the trade-off should be made can only be decided by the people who will be affected by it, whether directly or through their representatives in government.[44]

From the perspective of sustainability, the ultimate balance between efficiency and equity is not nearly as important as respect for the sovereign right of the people affected by it to determine that balance for themselves. This applies at the national level, but it is equally critical in local communities, where efficiency-equity tradeoffs take many forms and balancing private incentives with the public interest is always an unfinished process. What rules should govern land use? How should pollution be controlled? What natural resources should be conserved, and how? Sustainable development hinges on broad-based participation in economic decision-making, and the democratic resolution of these countless "small trade-offs" is central to the relationship between governance and sustainability.

GOVERNANCE, SUSTAINABILITY AND INTERNATIONAL TOURISM

The relationship between local and national governance is critical to locally focused development efforts, and especially to sustainable tourism. In particular, the respective roles and mandates between local, regional and national authorities must be clearly defined. As noted in OECD (2004), "local governance has often been supported in political contexts where the status of the decentralization process, in terms of legislation, policies and implementation,

---

44 See, e.g.: Dietz, S. (2010) "The Equity-Efficiency Trade-off in Environmental Policy: Evidence from Stated Preferences," *Land Economics* 86(3): 423-443

is unclear."[45] The failure to determine the precise, legally sanctioned purview of local governments represents an immediate threat to the sustainability of local development efforts, as those efforts may rely on a government that lacks the legal power to support and protect them. Moreover, attempting to empower a local government beyond its sanctioned authority itself violates the principles of good governance, particularly government effectiveness and the rule of law. Although it may be very tempting to ignore inconvenient legal arrangements in the service of an obvious good, as Machiavelli points out in the epigraph to this chapter, maintaining respect for official rules and procedures is the foundation of good governance: disregarding lawful norms for noble reasons makes it easier to disregard them for malicious ones.

Good governance is not essential for the success of all economic endeavours; indeed, a great deal of industry takes place in countries and regions where governance is weak or even virtually non-existent.[46] However, it is indispensable to international tourism because good governance factors into the consumption preferences of tourists. Although there is a lack of reliable quantitative data on the relationship between governance and tourism demand, evidence from individual cases makes it very clear that tourists consider certain elements of governance to be highly desirable, and will express their preferences for those elements of governance through their decisions as consumers.

For example, in 2011 the small West African archipelago of Cape Verde experienced a boom in its tourism sector. Although tourism had long been an important element of the Cape Verdean economy, and

45 OECD (2004), "Supporting Decentralization and Local Governance: Lessons Learned from Donor Support
to Decentralization and Local Governance" Paris: OECD
46 This is particularly true of extractive industries, which frequently operate—and even thrive—under profoundly corrupt regimes and in nearly-lawless regions. In many cases extractive industries themselves are a major contributor to the deterioration of governance. See, e.g.: Runge, J. and J. Shikwati (2011) Geological Resources and Good Governance in Sub-Saharan Africa: Holistic Approaches to Transparency and Sustainable Development in the Extractive Sector CRC Press.

the government had done much to foster its growth, the sharp spike in tourism demand it experienced was not due to any domestic initiative or private investment in the industry; rather, it was among the most unanticipated consequence of the Arab Spring.

Although far removed from North Africa, Cape Verde's major competitors for tourists from the European source markets are Egypt, Tunisia, Algeria and Morocco. When several of these countries suffered temporary but severe governance shocks—mass demonstrations, political violence, the collapse of whole regimes—and others faced considerable political uncertainty, European tourists abandoned these destinations and opted for the calm, sunny shores of Cape Verde instead.[47] It is perhaps worth noting that Cape Verde is one of only two West African countries never to have experienced a coup d'état, and that its WGI scores are comparable to those of Italy and Brazil.[48] While the boost provided by the diversion of European tourist from North Africa is already beginning to subside, it is expected that the positive reputational effects generated during this period will have a lasting impact on Cape Verdean tourism.

However, tourists do not value all dimensions of governance equally. Cape Verde's governance scores had been far higher than those of its North African competitors for many years before large-scale unrest shifted the demand calculus of European tourists. Anecdotal evidence strongly suggests that political stability and absence of violence has the greatest influence on tourism demand, as destination countries that experience paroxysms of instability and conflict often see their tourism industries virtually shut down overnight. This was the case in Thailand in 2010, when a confrontation between the country's major political factions dealt a serious blow

47 See: World Bank (2013) Cape Verde: Overview http://www.worldbank.org/en/country/capeverde/overview (updated as of April 2013)
48 World Bank (2013) World Governance Indicators http://info.worldbank.org/governance/wgi/sc_country.asp

to one of the world's most vibrant tourism industries.[49] While order was swiftly restored and Thailand's tourism industry rapidly recovered, the reputational effects of conflict and bloodshed can prove remarkably enduring. Rwanda boasts some of the greatest national parks in Africa, including the spectacular *Parc National des Volcans*, home to rare and beautiful lowland gorillas, yet Rwanda's tourism industry has never recovered from the genocide of the 1990s, even though the country has been at peace since 1994.

While political stability and absence of violence have a major impact on tourism, other dimensions of governance appear far less important. The United Arab Emirates is home to global tourism hubs at Dubai and Qatar, which continue to thrive despite the UEA's repressive political climate and consequently abysmal WGI score for voice and accountability. Fiji remains one of the most storied tourist destinations in the Pacific notwithstanding its very low scores on both voice and accountability and the rule of law. The Dominican Republic is a rising star in Caribbean tourism even though it also scores very low on rule of law and on control of corruption, while Maldives maintains a tourism-based economy in spite of a corruption score that is below the average for Sub-Saharan Africa. Malaysia's corruption score is nearly as low, while Seychelles and Vanuatu both have very low scores for regulatory efficiency. Even political instability and violence are not necessarily crippling to the tourism industry provided that they can be contained to areas where they do not directly impact tourism activity, as appears to be the case in Indonesia and the Philippines.[50]

These findings should perhaps not come as much of a surprise. In most cases it is hard to imagine that someone planning a vacation would think to herself, "How free are people in this country to express their will in the political arena? Not very? Then I guess I'd better go someplace else." This is not meant to make tourists appear callous or uncaring—indeed

49 See: Horn, R. (2010) "Thailand Tourism Devastated by Political Unrest" *Time Magazine* http://www.time.com/time/world/article/0,8599,1982555,00.html
50 World Bank (2013) World Governance Indicators http://info.worldbank.org/governance/wgi/sc_country.asp

many of them care very much about these issues—but as a group they are simply consumers, indifferent to concerns that do not directly impact the quality or price of the service they demand. However, over the long term good governance can become very relevant to the quality and price of tourism services, and that will most definitely affect consumer demand.

INTEREST GROUPS AND RENT-SEEKING

At its core, governance is about the peaceful reconciliation of conflicting interests. There are many ways to accomplish this, and not all are democratic: a highly effective authoritarian regime can successfully rule by fiat, though history offers few examples of such governments proving sustainable over the long term, and many instances of catastrophic collapse.[51] Democratic systems have shown themselves to be more durable, but are subject to their own particular weaknesses. Among these is the tendency of powerful interests to influence the policy process, often creating outcomes that favour their narrow objectives and the expense of the general welfare. This is particularly true when valuable resources are at stake: political or economic elites may attempt to monopolize the returns to these resources, a phenomenon known as **rent-seeking**. At the extreme, the complete domination of economic policymaking by interest groups is known as **state capture**. Curtailing the excessive influence of elites is a continuous process; it requires strong democratic institutions and a high degree of policy transparency, but even the most comprehensive administrative systems to counter rent-seeking will not be successful indefinitely, as those who stand to gain from rent-seeking will work persistently to subvert these systems, and their efforts will become increasingly sophisticated over time.

Rent-seeking is especially important to the tourism industry, as tourism is predicated on the exploitation of resources—natural, social, cultural and economic—and the control of those resources can offer

---

51 In his theory of the "J-curve" sociologist James Chowning Davies argued that a period of sustained economic development may give the appearance of stability to a dictatorial regime, but in fact makes it more likely to be overthrown. See "Toward a Theory of Revolution" *American Sociological Review* 27(1962):5-19

considerable returns. The specific nature of tourism resources and their economic value will be discussed in greater detail in the following chapter, but for now consider a pristine stretch of beachfront property, and how it is like a diamond mine.

Although one might not think of it this way, property is a natural resource, and a finite one at that. There is only so much desirable property in the world, and ownership of it is similar to ownership of any other productive asset. Its returns are the utility gained from access to it, and these returns can be privately consumed (e.g. by building a house on the property) or they can be sold in the marketplace (e.g. by building a hotel). Just like the diamond mine, the beach may be either publicly or privately owned, but in either case its value is part of the national wealth[52] of the country as a whole; and just like the diamond mine, how the beach is managed has a major impact on the returns it generates.

Yet unlike the diamond mine, the beach is a sustainable resource: if managed well it is capable of generating returns indefinitely. Also unlike the diamond mine, the beach's value is highly dependent on the use of the land around it and on numerous other factors that cannot be directly controlled by the property owner. If, for example, the owner of the adjacent property decided to build a commercial fishing wharf and cannery, or if the local government decided to build a garbage dump nearby, the value of the beach as a potential residential property or hotel site would be greatly diminished. Conversely, the value of the beach could be greatly enhanced by other public or private decisions, if, say, the adjacent property owner decided to build a marina for pleasure boats or a high-end restaurant, or the government established a national park nearby. In either case, governance is the crucial factor, as the government both makes key decisions directly (garbage dump or national park?) and affects private decisions through its regulations and policies (cannery or high-end restaurant?). This power makes control of government decisions

---

52 For more on national wealth, see Chapter 1.

economically valuable, and interest groups will inevitably attempt to use that power for private gain.

There is nothing inherently wrong with individuals and groups attempting to influence public policy to their benefit; in many ways, this is a fundamental feature of democratic governance. It can become problematic, however, when an individual or group becomes sufficiently powerful that they are able to profit at the expense of the public interest. There is no rule of thumb for determining when this may be happening or how best to deal with it: rent-seeking must be identified in each specific instance and handled according to a country's applicable laws and procedures. However, in many cases the exploitation of public policy for private gain, which comes at the expense of society as a whole while contributing nothing of value to it, is flatly obvious.

BOX 5 POLICIES OUTLIVE THEIR USEFULNESS

Consider, for example, the case of American mohair producers. Mohair is a type of sheep's wool: it is lightweight, durable and good for outdoor clothing. During the Second World War the US used mohair for its military uniforms, and as the war dragged on it began to face a serious shortage, as producers were unable to keep pace with demand. In the 1950s the government established a subsidy[53] for mohair producers in order to boost the size of the industry and help to ensure an adequate supply in the event of a future conflict.

This was a reasonable policy from a strategic standpoint, but it had unintended consequences. It created a small, tight-knit constituency (the mohair producers) that derived a benefit (the subsidy) from a large, diverse group (American taxpayers). Because the marginal benefit of the subsidy to the mohair producers was very large, while the margin cost of the subsidy to taxpayers was very

---

53 This was not a single policy, but rather a set of subsidies and price supports introduced in the 1954 National Wool Act and the 1954 Farm Bill.

small, the mohair producers had a strong incentive to maintain the policy, while the taxpayers had only a weak incentive to end it.

By 1960 synthetic fibres had replaced mohair in military uniforms, and the US military removed mohair from its list of strategic materials; nevertheless, mohair producers were able to keep their subsidies through aggressive lobbying. Although briefly phased out in the 1990s amid embarrassment at the self-evident wastefulness of these policies, mohair subsidies were quietly resumed a few years later, and American mohair producers continue to receive various forms of public assistance to this day. This story is frequently cited as an example of how a small, but highly motivated interest group can bend the policy process to its will, reaping benefits at a clear cost to society as a whole. [54]

Although in principle they compete with one another in an open market, in practice tourism firms often share the same political interests because the policies that benefit one firm will likely benefit others as well. Tourism firms, and those in related economic sectors, may have a strong common incentive to support policies that benefit the tourism industry, even if their value to the broader economy or society at large is much more dubious. This phenomenon is in no way unique to tourism. All firms and individuals share a complex set of partially overlapping incentives; and all interest groups pursue agendas that serve their narrow objectives, typically with little attention to broad social costs and benefits. But because of its locally concentrated character the tourism industry's influence on local politics can be decisive.

TOURISM AND LOCAL POLITICS

Many tourism firms operate in small communities, where they represent a major force in the local economy. Indeed, a considerable number of small countries count tourism as one of their most important, or even

54 See, e.g. Zakaria, F. (2003) The Future of Freedom: Illiberal Democracy at Home and Abroad New York: W.W. Norton and Company

their principal, economic sector. In contexts where the local, regional or even national economy is dependent on tourism, tourist firms may wield extraordinary influence over the policy process.

Consider a hypothetical small island state in which tourism is a large and growing activity, while other sectors remain underdeveloped and relatively weak: say that through careful fiscal management the government has produced a budget surplus, and it now must decide how to spend its additional resources. Among society as a whole there are numerous competing interests all vying for those funds: some people think the money should go to the country's schools, other to its clinics and hospitals, and others still think the roads are badly in need of repair. Industry groups also have ideas: the fishing industry wants a bigger navy to police the country's territorial waters, while retailers want to deepen the seaport to allow for larger commercial vessels and cut transport costs, and the tourism industry wants to expand the airport to enable more international arrivals. How this choice is ultimately made is the essence of governance. Under the parameters we have established, the tourism industry in our example is most likely to see its agenda come to fruition, because tourism firms are agents of an economically important and prosperous sector, and they all share the same, highly focused objective that comes with an immediate financial reward: getting more tourists to the island.

The individuals and civil-society groups pushing for more social spending or investment in basic infrastructure have diverse objectives, even within the same general interest—Should increased education funding go to elementary schools or colleges? How about vocational training, special-needs education, or programs targeting disadvantaged groups? Should more funding go to urban schools, or to rural ones?—and this lack of common purpose greatly hampers their efforts. Moreover, few people who support this agenda stand to directly benefit from it financially. Some education-sector workers might get paid more, but the value of this policy mostly comes from improved education quality, and the extent to which a person (or their child) will personally gain from increased education funding is highly uncertain.

While other industries and trade groups may have incentives that are similar to those of the tourism industry, tourism firms are likely to have a several significant advantages. For example, many tourism firms enjoy complementarities arising from economies of agglomeration.[55] Put more simply, many tourism firms do not really compete with each other, and in fact they often benefit from one another's presence in the same area. A single tourist may stay in one or more hotels, eat at several different restaurants, hire a guide from a tour company, ride in several taxis, and buy souvenirs from a shop. Attracting more tourists is beneficial for multiple firms, and indeed the existence of multiple firms may itself attract more tourists, since tourists often demand a greater diversity of services than one establishment is able to provide. This reinforces group incentives among tourism firms, which can make it far easier for them to work together for their mutual benefit. The island's retailers, by contrast, have much weaker incentives to work together. Although better commercial infrastructure will lower costs for all of them, they are in direct competition with each other. At least in the short-run, the success of one retailer is likely to come at the expense of another; this creates mistrust and diminishes their ability to collaboratively pursue a joint policy agenda.

In many cases this is far from the only advantage enjoyed by tourism firms. As noted in the previous chapter, tourism is an export industry; this means it is a source of foreign exchange, which is critical to currency values and to a country's external accounts. Tourism is also frequently a strong contributor to a country's overall inflow of foreign direct investment, which also has important implications for fiscal and monetary policies, as well as the government's larger development strategy. For these and other reasons, policymakers may regard tourism as an especially critical priority and give its interests precedence over those of other sectors. A country that views the fishing industry as its past and tourism as its

55 This phenomenon is not necessarily negative, and can greatly accelerate the development of the sector. These and related issues are discussed in much greater detail in Chapter 8.

future is unlikely to devote additional resources to the former, no matter how sensible a policy this may actually be.

In this example there is no reason to believe that any particular policy course is superior to another. Increasing the shipping capacity of the port might be more worthwhile than boosting social spending, or it might not; and a refurbished road network might generate superior outcomes than better policing of fishing rights would, or the opposite might be true. Indeed, given there is no reason to believe that a bigger airport would not in fact be the best policy decision available; given the importance of tourism to the economy and the jobs and revenue that it generates, perhaps an expanded airport is the most cost-effective use the government's resources. The purpose of this example is to illustrate that good governance is not a matter of *which* policies to make, but rather *how* those policies should be made. It is also essential that in any specific public policy question with profound implications for a local community, that that community be given the opportunity to understand and determine not merely how that policy should be implemented, but whether it should be implemented at all. As noted by Hemmati (2002):

> The fundamental right of communities to self-determination needs to be respected. In cases where a potential agreement affects the future lives of a stakeholder group, they need to have the right to say 'No'. For example, if all stakeholders except the affected local community agree to a tourism development plan, the plan should not be carried out.[56]

Sustainability requires that policy processes in tourism destinations give voice to all stakeholders, promote a balance of power, support the building of a shared vision and create the conditions for on-going dialogue, negotiation and collaboration. Transparent democratic decision-making

---

56 Hemmati, M (2002)Multi-Stakeholder Processes For Governance and Sustainability: Beyond Deadlock and Conflict New York: Earthscan

is critical to the success of inclusive and sustainable tourism development. Good governance is not only a matter of democratic voting systems and equality under the law: equally essential is the constant vigilance required to offset the power of small, concentrated interests to ensure that the will of the majority is not subverted. Again, there is no single, universal blueprint for accomplishing this, but doing so in any unique context requires understanding the complex relationships between interest groups, policymakers and the public and defining a locally appropriate strategy to reconcile conflicting objectives and ensure that policy decisions accurately reflect the will of those impacted by them.

PARTICIPATION AND THE QUALITY OF PUBLIC POLICIES

Productive dialogue between the government, the private sector, and civil society generates more accurate and comprehensive information on which to base public policies, facilitating a more efficient and equitable allocation of scarce public resources.[57] The government needs the cooperation of local actors to identify problems, propose alternatives, monitor evolving situations, and provide first-hand evaluations of the impact of current and past policies. When the lines of communication between various stakeholders are strong and well-organized, governments are more likely to develop innovative approaches that satisfy a broad range of needs and aspirations, rather than focusing on the interests of a few influential constituencies.

Ensuring democratic participation in defining a sustainable tourism policy requires an organized system of representative bodies and inclusive forums capable of incorporating large amounts of feedback into the policy process and reconciling the interests of numerous individuals and groups. Building these systems is easier advocated than achieved, and the international experience suggests that experimentation with decentralized authority, collaborative policymaking, and multi-stakeholder partnership arrangements have produced mixed results in different

---

57 OECD (2004) "Supporting Decentralization and Local Governance: Lessons Learned on Donor Support to Decentralization and Local Governance" Paris: OECD

tourism destinations.[58] However, the international experience also reveals a number of best-practice principles for participatory decision-making in tourism policy.

From the standpoint of good governance, it is absolutely critical that the tourism development be organized and supported by a dedicated organization representing multiple stakeholders and recognized by the relevant government authorities.[59] Establishing a **multi-stakeholder team** can be a very complex and difficult undertaking, and it is important to remember that establishing such an organization is not an end in itself; it is an instrumental step towards the goal of inclusive, sustainability-oriented policymaking. Nor is it ever an entirely finished process, as the stakeholder team should expand and evolve over time to reflect a greater and more accurate diversity of opinion.[60] This team should be comprised of credible representatives from the tourism industry, other private-sector firms and organisations, civil-society groups, especially those representing marginalized or disadvantaged populations, and public sector agencies involved not only in the tourism sector, but in environmental management, cultural affairs, development planning and other relevant areas.

The success of multi-stakeholder teams is predicated on a general understanding among its members that ensuring sustainable tourism development is beyond the capacity of any one individual, and that the team's purpose is to create superior outcomes for all of its members by overcoming the **collective action problem** identified in Chapter 1. The objective of the multi-stakeholder team is to build an enabling policy environment capable of addressing systemic constraints to inclusive, locally

---

58 Goeymen, K. (2000), "Tourism and Governance in Turkey" *Annals of Tourism Research* 27(4):1025-1048

59 For more on governance structures see: Hall, C. M. (2011) "Framing Governance Theory: A Typology of Governance and its Implications for Tourism Policy" *Analysis Journal of Sustainable Tourism*

60 Getz, D. And S. Timur (2005) "Stakeholder Involvement in Sustainable Tourism: Balancing the Voices" in Theobald, W.F.F. (ed.) <u>Global Tourism: Fourth Edition</u> Burlington, MA: Elsevier

self-determined economic development and promoting an appropriate balance between short-term economic growth and the long-term competitiveness of a tourism destination. As SNV (2010) puts it in a broader discussion of capacity development:

> Over time we have learned that society develops and solves its problems through collective capabilities. No matter how experienced and skilled individuals or single groups are, if this type of capability cannot be coordinated for the common good, progress in improbable.[61]

An effective multi-stakeholder team plays a number of key roles in the policy process. These include:

(1) Advisory Support. The multi-stakeholder team should provide government agencies, private firms and citizen groups with impartial analysis of sustainable tourism development informed by an in-depth understanding of the international experience, in particular at the destination level. Where it lacks specific competencies the team should seek out specialized assistance from international agencies and academic institutions, and it should actively solicit perspectives and opinions and draw on experience from within the community, working continuously to expand its advisory capacity through a process of:

(2) Knowledge Development. A multi-stakeholder team is not an academic organisation, but it is in unique position to collect, compile and share valuable information about the destination market. This information can be used by policymakers, private-sector representatives and the general public to influence development processes and make sound economic decisions. Although sustainable tourism development is highly context-specific, and it may

---

61 SNV (2010). "Capacity Development in Practice" London: Earthscan. It should perhaps be noted that "Connecting People's Capacities" is the slogan of SNV – Netherlands Development Organization.

be difficult to apply lessons from one case to another, information gathered by a multi-stakeholder team about experiences in one community may be germane to policy decisions in other, nearby communities that share similar characteristics. In many cases this degree of local focus is almost impossible for traditional academic organisations public-sector institutions and international development agencies to achieve. Sophisticated local knowledge is also necessary to reassess standard development policies and practice and to promote change through evidenced-based:

(3) **Advocacy.** Sustainable tourism development will inevitably require the reform of institutional arrangements, structures, policies and practices; while ensuring the integrity of governance in the tourism sector requires continuous efforts to balance the immediate economic interests of powerful firms with the more complex and diverse interests of the general public. In many cases, a multi-stakeholder team may be ideally situated to build a broad coalition for sustainability capable of influencing the policy debate. The team should encourage the joint formulation of innovative policies, strategies and institutional reforms designed to promote sustainable tourism development, and when such measures enjoy widespread endorsement, the team should support them through active:

(4) **Leadership.** Sustainable tourism depends on good governance, which in turn relies on transparent negotiations between civil society, the private sector, and the government. A multi-stakeholder team can lead this collaborative process, and pursue policy measures that reflect the consensus of its members and of the broader interests of the tourism destination. Multi-stakeholder teams must lead by building shared visions, influencing policy processes through advice, knowledge and advocacy.

A multi-stakeholder group is often initially an informal body with a changing composition and an evolving leadership structure. But over time it should develop into a formally recognised organisation with a clear role in the policy process. In some destinations these stakeholder groups that could have the form of a Tourism Development Observatory, a Tourism Council or as the UNWTO has strongly advocate in the past years as a Destination Management Organization - DMO.

CONCLUSIONS

On practice there is no single recipe on how to better address governance in tourism destinations. What remains essential is that good governance is at the core of sustainable tourism development, enabling dialogue, supporting a search for balance of power, and feeding, through active multi-stakeholders feedback, a continued learning process that should lead in to shaping inclusive and sustainable development.

Local stake-holders need to find creative and practical ways to guarantee that their voice is properly understood and through political instruments integrated in to destination management decisions. Although the big-trade-off efficiency over equity is a permanent question and challenge for government institutions, the responsibility to find the right balance should not remain at the government shoulders, assuming that the government representatives do understand society diverse thinking and interests.

It is through active collaboration, strong multi-stakeholders communication channels and driven by a balance of economic, social and definitely biodiversity concerns, that the path for development needs to be setup. As this is exactly why governance as a concept and a practice has risen strongly over the last decades, to push society in to much more active civilian participation, moving away from a the first and second industrial social behaviour of obedience to top down decision making, presuming that through efficiency we would all, find a place under the sun.

Governance practice, more than ever is being boost by information technology, social medias and a progressive global awareness on issues such as climate change and the loose of biodiversity. More than a decade ago, young generations are much more interested in new and more horizontal forms of participating in public interest issues. Have as an extreme example the Arab Spring. As we move forward and internalize in to society behaviour new information technologies which are promoting open source knowledge sharing, new ways of learning and civil participation, governance tends to strength as a fundamental practice and tool for political decision taking. While hearing the voice and understanding the concerns of a group of Ashanikas in the Peruvian amazon, was extremely difficult a few decades ago, today through internet, this same people can be online, and being part of a global conference to discuss directly their concerns and interests. This is how governance is moving in to a rising and dynamic practice, that should be through time one of the most powerful tools societies have to shift from the current mainstream economic thinking in to a less utilitarist and more horizontal capitalism.

EXERCISES

1. Identify and evaluate how multi-stakeholders platforms have contributed to effective tourism destinations management in 2 emerging destinations;
2. Identify and evaluate 2 different financing models for DMO's.

Group discussion:

- what are the major challenges in promoting multi-stakeholders participation in tourism governance?
- who should lead destinations governance platforms?
- identify and discuss 5 key role that successfull destination governance platforms should play.

CASE – 5 ENHANCING TOURISM IN THE RICHTERSVELD WORLD HERITAGE SITE, SOUTH AFRICA

By Andrew Rylance and Anna Spenceley

1. Problem/Opportunity Identified

In June 2007 the Richtersveld World Heritage Site (WHS) was de-clared, covering 160,000 hectares of the Northern Cape in South Africa. A remote wilderness, with few passable roads and sparsely populated by sheep and goat herders, it was nominated as a natural site for its high plant diversity, and as a cultural landscape shaped by the semi-nomadic Nama pastoralists: one of the last transhumance cultures in Southern Africa. Prior to the southern migration of Bantu peoples the indigenous Nama were more extensively spread across the sub-continent; now they live in the northern part of South Africa and Namibia, but only practice pastoral transhumance in and around the area (UNESCO, 2007).

UNESCO state that the Richtersveld Cultural and Botanical Landscape demonstrates Outstanding Universal Value (UNESCO, 2007). The extensive communal grazed lands are a testimony to land management processes, which have ensured the protection of the suc-culent Karoo vegetation. They demonstrate a harmonious interaction between people and nature. The rich diverse botanical landscape of the Richtersveld, shaped by the pastoral grazing of the Nama, repre-sents and demonstrates a way of life that persisted for many millennia over a considerable part of southern Africa and was a significant stage in the history of this area.

The Richtersveld Community Conservancy, which manages the WHS, identified that there were a number of opportunities for tourism, but there was a problem that few benefits were realised for the local community.

They also recognised tourism opportunities should not be in conflict with other activities in the conservation area (i.e. stockfarming).

2. Approach

The Richtersveld Company for Sustainable Development (RCSD) commissioned a feasibility study. The objective of the study was to link the vision of the local communities for the Richtersveld with current and future demands of the market, in order to promote financially-sustainable tourism and nature-based business.

Information on the current situation of the Richtersveld WHS was drawn from a number of sources, including previous reports, a participatory planning workshop, and interviews with key stakeholders. Field visits to the WHS and a tour of the existing tourism facilities and attractions were also conducted. A series of participatory planning workshops were held with local multi-stakeholder groups. A draft report on the workshop results was circulated for comment to the participants, and was also sent to other stakeholders that had been identified during the workshops. Additional comments were also obtained from the chair of the Communal Property Association (CPA) in separate meetings.

Landscape and flowers in the
Richtersveld National Park

Stockfarming and nature

2. Outcome

Based on the results of the market demand study to identify viable conservation-based businesses, the following opportunities were prioritised by local stakeholders for further investigation:

Priority 1: Cultural attractions and Guided hiking trails
Priority 2: Guest houses and learning about conservation
Priority 3: Desert botanical gardens, Boat/Canoe trips, and Medicinal plant tours
Priority 4: Camping, Birding tours, and Botanical tours.

PRIORITY 1: CULTURAL ATTRACTIONS AND GUIDED HIKING TRAILS

1.1 Cultural attractions

Local guides could provide tours of cultural attractions, such as stock farming (traditional / nomadic), dancing groups, Nama choirs, Nama villages (e.g. with traditional houses), traditional clothes, villages, traditional foods (e.g. styne pap/ asbrood/ stampmielies), traditional drinks (e.g. honey beer, qombotih, ginger beer), story telling "Groot slang" and petroglyphs as well as the opportunity to partake in traditional activities, such as donkeys cart rides. Local guides could provide a broad range of natural and cultural knowledge of the Richtersveld area. Furthermore, providing opportunities for tourists to purchase arts and crafts as well as food and refreshments from local enterprises would be advantageous.

1.2 Guided Hiking Trails

Guides could take visitors on tours through the WHS, which either aim to achieve something (i.e. climb Black Face Mountain) or provide a route through the varied habitats of the site (i.e. mountains to Orange River). Self guided tours, with interpretive sign boards and well marked trails, would also be created. Guides would be trained to acquire a broad knowledge of botany, medicinal purposes of plants, geology, birding and cultural heritage.

PRIORITY 2: GUEST HOUSES AND LEARNING ABOUT CONSERVATION

2.1 Guest Houses
There are two 10-bed guest houses (Rooiberg and Kom Rus-'n-Bietjie), and chalets in Sanddrift and Kuboes. There are also and two 8-bed (4 chalet) facilities in Sanddrift and Kuboes (Stofbakkies and Nou! Plek). An 8-bed guest house (Koerdap) that was initially owned and operated by community members in Lekkersing, is now leased by a private sector operator (Richtersveld tours). Rather than establishing new guest houses in the area, it is recommended that improving the management, operation, hospitality, facilities and marketing of the existing guest houses be improved.

PRIORITY 3: DESERT BOTANICAL GARDENS, BOAT/CANOE TRIPS, AND MEDICINAL PLANT TOURS

3.1 Desert botanical gardens
A demonstration area with local guides providing tours and specialist information on local flora in the WHS with an emphasis on the species endemic to the Richtersveld area, and the 33 plants endemic to the WHS itself. The demonstration area could provide interpretation information for tourists on local conservation issues, conservation issues for desert areas, endemic and interesting in the area, medicinal plant use, and new research findings.

3.2 Boat / canoe trips on the Orange River
River trips are operated by approximately 12 private companies located to the east of the WHS. These run multi-day rafting and canoe trips along the Orange river, which in part travel along the eastern boundary of

the WHS. Community members could either become guides or provide meals, entertainment and rest camps for rafting guests.

3.3 Medicinal plant tours

Local guides could provide specialist information on local flora in the WHS with an emphasis on endemic species to the Richtersveld area. Additional information provided by trained guides could include local conservation issues, local geology, history, endemic birds in the area, medicinal plant use, existing cultural practices using plants.

PRIORITY 4: CAMPING, BIRDING TOURS, AND BOTANICAL TOURS.

4.1 Camping

There are currently five camping sites, each with space for 5 tents and a compost toilet (Tierhoek, Rosynbos, Fluorspar Valley, Sunvalley, Kannikaip), although occupancies at present are extremely low (2.1% in 2008). It is recommended that improving the management, operation, hospitality, facilities and marketing of the existing facilities should be prioritised.

In addition, a series of solutions to various barriers identified were proposed covering 6 major bottle neck for sustainable touriems development:

- Policy and planning framework
- Infrastructure
- Destination management and working skills
- Resources Management and Sustainability
- Marketing and promotion:
- Tourism facilities and attractions:

4. Conclusion

This case study demonstrates that through a process of systematic participatory planning with multi-stakeholder groups, viable tourism opportunities can be evaluated and prioritised. Elements of any feasibility study for a tourism destination should address the policy and planning framework, infrastructure, human resources, utilities, marketing and promotion, tourism facilities and attractions, financing and business management.

Four

Economic Impacts of
Tourism Development

In the vastness of space and the immensity of time, it is
my joy to share a planet and an epoch with you.

— CARL SAGAN.

OBJECTIVES OF THE CHAPTER:

- Describe the unique economic characteristics of tourism and how
the composition of the tourism sector impacts the destination
economy
- Discuss the potential consequences of tourism development in
terms of income, employment, public revenues, and macroeconomic management
- Introduce the conceptual framework and technical basis for formulating effective economic policies to maximize the benefits
of tourism in line with the self-defined objectives of destination
stakeholders

INTRODUCTION

Over the past several decades in countries around the world the tourism
industry has evolved from a minor, secondary element of development

policy to become one of the principal drives of economic growth. The rising prominence of tourism in both international economics and development theory is reflected in the ever-increasing body of analytical work focusing on tourism's potential contribution to social and economic development, as well as its limitations and liabilities.[62]Because of the industry's unique characteristics tourism can produce a wide range of radically different impacts on a¨ destination economy, and the ultimate effects of tourism development depend in large part on the local economic policies that condition its growth.

The rise of global tourism has established all the necessary elements to enable destination economies to diversify production and boost consumption, generate new income opportunities among the poor and marginalized, and promote robust and sustained job creation for the workforce as a whole. More fascinating—and controversial—is tourism's potential to quantify the value of social, cultural and environmental resources, transforming them into economically productive assets, and the "commoditization" of social, cultural and environmental resources will be discussed throughout the chapter.

Some destination countries have harnessed the power of tourism, making it an engine of growth in the broader economy and accomplishing a range of positive social and economic outcomes. Many others, however, have enjoyed only marginal and narrowly focused benefits from tourism, and these limited returns have often come at a significant cost. The difference between success and failure in sustainable tourism is in the management of tourism destinations. This goes beyond the foundational issues of good governance discussed in Chapter 3 and encompasses the specific policy mix that destination governments adopt to shape the growth of the tourism industry.

Recent decades have witnessed important advances in research into the economics of tourism. These have helped lay the foundation for new development policies in a number of key areas, including air-travel

---

62 For a broad overview of the literature on international tourism and economic development see: Theobald, W.F.F., ed. (2005) Global Tourism: Fourth Edition Burlington, MA: Elsevier. See also: Mathieson and Wall (1982); SNV and UNWTO (2010).

Federico Vignati • Don Hawkins • Bruce Priedeaux

regulation, visa policy, decentralized tourism administration, and demand-driven product and service development. In many countries national administrative agencies have been created or reorganized in order to focus on sector-specific policies, while administrative decentralization and capacity-building efforts at the provincial and local levels have helped to promote more efficient, democratic, and sustainable tourism policies. This chapter provides a brief analysis of the tourism industry's potential economic impacts on destination countries, and describes how tourism policies can be calibrated to yield the greatest benefits for all stakeholders, in particular at the local level and with a special focus on the poor and members of vulnerable groups. As noted in previous chapters, the impacts of tourism go far beyond economics, but economic effects are extremely important and must be thoroughly understood before going on to examine the social, cultural and environmental implications of tourism development.

THE ECONOMIC IMPACTS OF TOURISM

As noted in Chapter 1, international tourism is an export industry. Tourists come from abroad and exchange their currencies for the currency of the destination country. They spend that money on goods and services, which effectively return home with them—just as if the producers of those goods and services had packed them on a ship and sent them off to a foreign market.

How tourism exports impact the destination economy is highly dependent on how the tourism sector is organised, what types of firms and individuals operate within it, and what policies the government has adopted to shape it. Because tourism brings foreign exchange into the domestic market, tourism revenue has a large potential multiplier effect[63] on the destination economy. This multiplier effect is directly related to the ways in which tourists satisfy their demand for accommodation, food and beverages, transportation, entertainment and other forms of commerce

---

63 Ashley, C. (2006), "How Can Governments Boost the Local Economic Impacts of Tourism?" SNV and ODI: The Hague/London

and industry, and it is this effect that massively increases the tourism industry's potential to leverage broader economic development.[64]

BOX 6 - ON HOLIDAY

Image for a moment that you are taking a vacation abroad. You are a foreign tourist, and you are doing a number of very common "touristy" things. You stay in a hotel, eat at restaurants, take a tour of some local sights, do some outdoor activities, eat at some more restaurants, buy a few souvenirs, and then return home. You enjoyed yourself immensely, and all the people you interacted with were pleased to do business with you. But what impact did your trip have on the local economy?

This will depend a great deal on where you went, and on the type of trip you went on. Let's say you come from a relatively developed country and that you vacationed in a relatively less developed one—a "sun, sea and sand"[65] destination, perhaps in the Pacific, or the Caribbean, or the Indian Ocean. How did you get there? Did you buy a seat on a commercial airline, or did you book a charter flight with a tour operator or arrive on cruise ship, perhaps as part of a package deal? And where did you stay? A smaller, locally owned hotel, or a large resort, maybe run by the same company that sold you the airline ticket? And where did you eat and drink while you were there? At restaurants, cafes and bars in the local area or at the restaurants, cafes and bars in your hotel and in others very much like it? Where did you book your tour of the local sights? With whom did you do your activities? And where did you buy those souvenirs?

The answers to these questions will place your trip somewhere along a spectrum, with small-scale, independent, locally oriented tourism at one end, and large-scale, all-inclusive-resort-package

---

64 Pearce, D. (1989). Tourism Development Harlow, Essex: Longman.
65 In tourism industry terminology this is often referred to as a "3-S" destination.

tourism at the other. While the world rarely fits neatly into academic categories, the available evidence shows that, *ceteris paribus*, small-scale, independent, locally oriented tourism tends to have a dramatically deeper, more equitable and more poverty-focused impact on the destination economy.[66] Exactly why this is the case, and what can be done to extend the benefits of tourism throughout the local economy, will be the subject of much of this chapter.

The "multiplier effect", noted above, is at the heart of the matter. Tourism revenue enters the destination market as tourists spend money on locally produced goods and services, both within and beyond the tourism industry proper. As the local firms and individuals that produce those goods and services earn income, they spend much of it on other locally produced goods and services, and the producers of those services spend much of it in the domestic economy again, and so on, stimulating growth well beyond the tourism sector. However, in practice much potential revenue is lost to the destination market because local firms are not able to compete with large international tourism firms in supplying the services tourists demand.

International hotel chains and tour-package operators are frequently based in tourism source markets in developed countries, rather than in destination markets in developing ones, and the profits of these companies are "repatriated" abroad—transferred, in many cases, back to the same country that the tourists came from. These firms

66 See, e.g.: UN Environment Programme (2013) "Resource Efficiency and Sustainable Consumption and Production: Negative Economic Impacts of Tourism Development" http://www.unep.org/resourceefficiency/Business/SectoralActivities/Tourism/FactsandFiguresaboutTourism/ImpactsofTourism/EconomicImpactsofTourism/NegativeEconomicImpactsofTourism/tabid/78784/Default.aspx See also: Swarbroke, J. (1999) Sustainable Tourism Management New York: CABI Publishing; and Harrison, L., C. Jayawardena and A. Clayton (2003) "Sustainable Tourism Development in the Caribbean: Practical Challenges." *International Journal of Contemporary Hospitality Management* 15(5):294-299.

enjoy direct access to their customer base, as well as to the sophisticated capital markets and other microeconomic assets of their home country, and they typically have considerable institutional experience in the international tourism industry. By contrast local tourism operators, especially in emerging destinations, may have few or none of these advantages. Large international firms also typically have ready access to skilled professionals in their home countries, who they may hire to fill the more advanced and better-paying jobs in the destination market, relying on the local labor force only for unskilled or semi-skilled work. They may also "insource" many of their administrative functions to home offices or outsource them to countries other than the destination market.

Large international tourism firms enjoy considerable economies of scale in the production of tourism services. These are not a bad thing in and of themselves; indeed they tend to make these firms more efficient, which helps keep prices low. However, these economies of scale also tend to give large international firms a decisive advantage against smaller local competitors with far less access to capital or other resources. Moreover, the large scale at which many international resort chains and package-tour companies operate tends to make imported inputs more competitive against local goods by allowing for bulk purchasing at consistent levels of quantity and quality. [67] This encourages them to source inputs from abroad, unlike smaller firms who are more likely to buy from the local market, further limiting the impact of each tourist's spending on the destination economy.

Relatedly, all-inclusive resort chains and package-tour operators typically derive a strong competitive advantage from **vertical integration**: that is, they often own or are contractually tied to other firms in the

---

67 See UNEP (*supra*); and Telfer, D. and G. Wall (1996) "Linkages between Tourism and Food Production" *Annals of Tourism Research* 23(3):635-653

tourism sector.[68] A single company may sell you a plane ticket, a hotel room, all the food and beverages you can eat and drink, a range of activities at the destination, local transportation and many additional services, and that same company may offer similar packages at any number of other destinations you might care to visit during your trip. You could travel to numerous locations in multiple countries over the course of several weeks and pay thousands of dollars to do so, yet without ever spending a single cent on anything not directly supplied to you by that one tourism company.

This is certainly convenient, and among the many sound economic reasons why large international tourism firms continue to be successful,[69] yet the market structures created by these firms can severely constrain the tourism industry's ability to positively influence the destination economy. Foreign currency flows into the economy, but much it flows right out again in the form of imported inputs, salaries for expatriate workers, repatriated profits and other revenue **leakages**. As a result, the UN Environment Programme (2013) estimates that, "of each US$100 spent on a vacation tour by a tourist from a developed country, only around US$5 actually stays

---

68 "Vertical integration" refers to one firm's control over other activities in its own supply chain, such as a steel company that also owns its own iron mines, or an oil company that owns drilling rigs, refineries and gas stations. A vertically integrated firm cuts costs and increases profits by adding value at multiple steps in its supply chain, which can give it an extreme advantage over other firms, in some cases leading to the monopolization of whole markets. Although vertical integration is typically regulated in advanced economies, it remains common among international firms and especially those operating in less developed countries, where local legal systems either do not prohibit excessive (i.e. anticompetitive) vertical integration, or where such prohibitions are not enforced. For a more detailed summary of vertical integration see: The Economist (2009) "Idea: Vertical Integration" http://www.economist.com/node/13396061

69 For more examples of the advantages to this model from the prospective of tourism consumers, see: US News and World Report (2012) "The Financial Benefits of All-Inclusive Resorts"
http://money.usnews.com/money/personal-finance/articles/2012/02/07/the-financial-benefits-of-all-inclusive-resorts

in a developing-country destination economy,"[70] and provides a diagram showing how tourism revenue "leaks" out of the destination market.

Figure 1: Tourism Spending Structure and Leakages from the Destination Economy

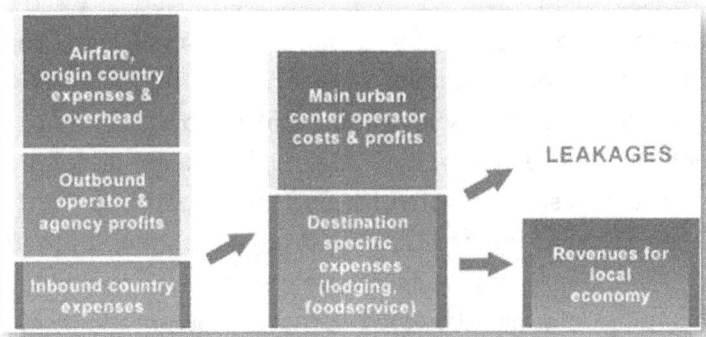

Source: UNEP

Despite this grim picture, some tourist revenue may go to locally sourced inputs, salaries for local workers, and taxes—the large-scale, all-inclusive resort and package-tour system does typically make a positive contribution to the local economy—but that share is often very limited. As summarized by Goodwin (2008):

> Promoting the consumption of domestically produced goods and services has become more and more difficult given the growing popularity of all-inclusive resort-style tourism and cruise tourism. Tourists who purchase these packages rarely venture into local communities. Spending is generally restricted to the cruise ship, tour operator, or resort operator, all of which tend to be owned by multinational corporations.... All-inclusive vacation packages siphon most spending

---

70 UN Environment Programme (2013) "Resource Efficiency and Sustainable Consumption and Production: Negative Economic Impacts of Tourism Development" http://www.unep.org/resourceefficiency/Business/SectoralActivities/Tourism/FactsandFiguresaboutTourism/ImpactsofTourism/EconomicImpactsofTourism/NegativeEconomicImpactsofTourism/tabid/78784/Default.aspx

out of the country and minimize the potential multiplier effect that tourist spending might otherwise have on the local economy.[71]

Tourism's capacity to promote inclusive, broad-based economic development consequently depends on the extent to which the destination market is capable of creating linkages between the tourism industry and other domestic economic sectors, transforming tourist spending in the source market into income in the destination market.[72] Conceptually, a destination's ability to capture a greater share of tourism spending can be understood as a function of the economy's general sophistication (tourists in France tend to consume a smaller share of imports than tourists in the Dominican Republic) and the model of tourism most commonly employed (tourists in France don't generally stay in all-inclusive resort enclaves). Both of these, in turn, are largely determined by the destination country's tourism policies.

On the fiscal side, tourism can have a similarly mixed impact. The tourism industry may represent a significant source of government revenue, which can be used to spur economic growth and promote a range of positive social outcomes.[73] However, tourism can also entail considerable public expenditures ranging from expensive sector-specific infrastructure, such as passenger docks capable of servicing cruise ships, to media campaigns designed to promote the destination in source markets. Tourism may also indirectly prompt the need for increased public spending on law enforcement and other public services, especially when

---

71 Goodwin, J. (2008) "Sustainable Tourism Development in the Caribbean Island Nation-States" *Michigan Journal of Public Affairs* The University of Michigan: Ann Arbor
72 Ashley, C. and G. Haysom (2008) "The Development Impacts of Tourism Supply Chains: Increasing Impact on Poverty and Decreasing Our Ignorance," in: Spenceley, A. (ed.) Responsible Tourism: Critical Issues for Conservation and Development Earthscan: London
73 See: SNV & UNWTO (2010) Manual on Tourism and Poverty Alleviation: Practical Steps for Destinations Madrid; and Balaguer, L., and M. Cantavella-Jorda, (2002) "Tourism as a Long-Run Economic Growth Factor: The Spanish Case" *Applied Economics*, 34: 877–884.

poorly regulated tourism development encourages an increase in excessive drinking, drug use, prostitution, or other forms of criminality.

Finally, tourism can have important inflationary and exchange-rate effects with serious economic and welfare consequences for the destination economy. Demand for tourism exports (like all other exports) prompts foreign consumers to exchange their home currency for the destination's currency, and as export volumes rise, increased demand for the destination market's currency boosts its value relative to other currencies. This typically causes two primary effects: (i) it encourages imports, since foreign products are now relatively cheaper to buy in the destination country's currency, which can harm domestic producers of goods that compete with those imports and especially non-tourism exporters, whose goods become less price-competitive in foreign markets; and (ii) it causes inflation, as income from tourism exports stimulates demand for non-tradable[74] goods and services in the domestic market, especially real estate and often food, energy and retail services as well.

Inflationary and exchange-rate effects are among the most complex economic dynamics of the tourism industry, and they have critical implications for policymakers attempting to expand the share of tourism spending that remains in the destination market. Because these effects are caused by foreign exchange inflows, expanding the share of foreign revenue captured by domestic firms is tantamount to increasing the country's total export value. This will enhance the destination's external-account position, particularly its trade and current-account balances, and it will boost consumption and spur growth in the destination economy; however, capturing more foreign revenue will also exert inflationary and exchange-rate pressures, which can have deeply negative impacts on competitiveness, both in the tourism and non-tourism sectors, as well as potentially serious effects

---

74 "Non-tradables" are goods and services that cannot be traded across borders, often because they cannot physically be moved (e.g. real estate), because they are too costly to transport (e.g. electricity), or because they are services that must be locally consumed (e.g. a haircut or a car wash).

on the poor, especially if inflation increases food prices. Monetary policy measures, such as the sterilization of foreign-currency inflows, can help to mitigate these effects; and a destination government should carefully consider its monetary policy stance before attempting to introduce large amounts of foreign exchange into the domestic economy.

Figure 2: Diagramming the Tourism Industry

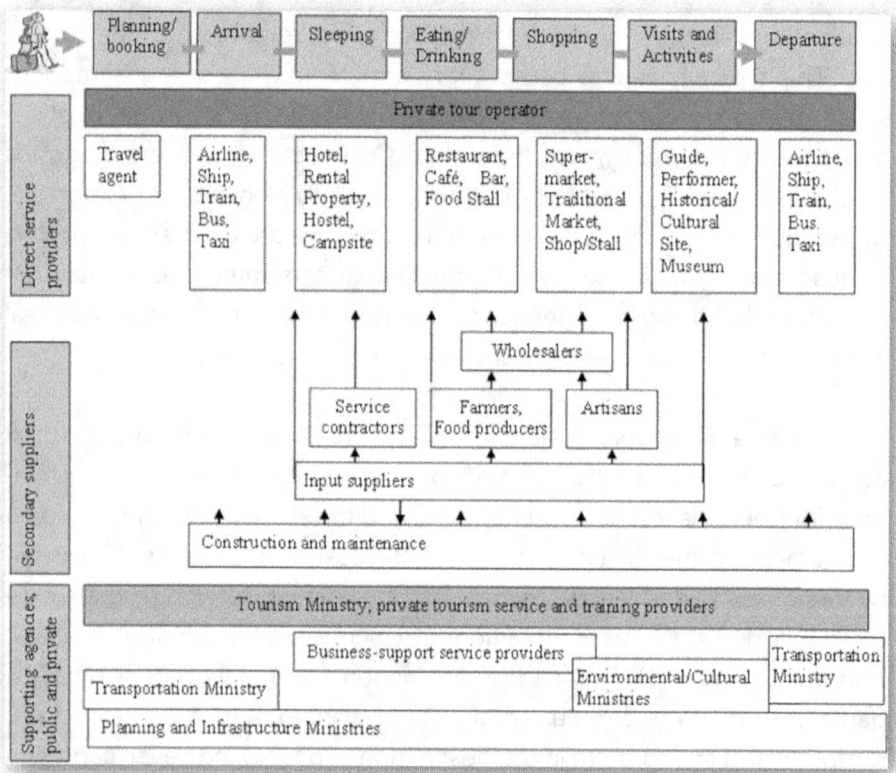

Source: SNV & UNWTO (2014)

THE TOURISM INDUSTRY AND DOMESTIC PRODUCTION

Tourist spending impacts a destination economy in a number of ways, some of which are quite subtle. Although important, the impact of tourism is not restricted to direct inflows, that is, purchases of tourism-specific goods and services. This direct spending is distributed through inter-sectoral linkages to local, regional, national, and international value chains. In this way, the development of the tourism sector may affect producers far outside that sector itself, generating important (and perhaps unnoticed) benefits throughout the economy.

Tourism spending affects the economy through three transmission channels. These are: (i) direct tourism inflows, the revenue of firms directly linked to the tourism industry; (ii) indirect tourism inflows, the revenue of firms in sectors that supply the tourism industry; and (iii) induced tourism inflows, revenues accruing to other sectors of the economy that, even without directly supplying the tourism industry, benefit from its positive impact on the economy as a whole.

Direct inflows tend to be most strongly associated with the transportation and accommodations industries, and the extent to which domestic producers benefit from direct inflows is heavily dependent upon the ownership of transportation and accommodation capital. If tourists overwhelmingly arrive on foreign-owned airlines or cruise ships, very little revenue accrues to the domestic economy from these industries, and what revenue is captured by the destination is likely in the form of taxes and fees paid by foreign firms. Food service is also an important component of direct inflows, and here the use of the all-inclusive resort model is a major determinant of revenue "leakage". If most tourists stay in hotels where they have paid in advance for food and beverages, they are unlikely to seek out local restaurants, cafes and bars, further limiting the ability of domestic firms to benefit from direct inflows.

Food production, however, may still be a major part of **indirect inflows**. Even all-inclusive resorts must source their food from somewhere, and in some cases they may purchase food and beverages from local producers. However, all-inclusive resorts are far more likely than local eateries to rely on imports to meet their food and beverage needs. Other hotel, restaurant, and activity-related inputs may or may not contribute to indirect inflows, based largely on the ability of the local economy to meet the demand of tourism firms. And, in most cases, a substantial share of this demand will have to be met by imports, as structural factors will preclude the development of all possible local industries.[75] Again, however, large, foreign-owned hotels tend to be less conducive to indirect inflows, as they are more likely to cater to tourists' taste for home-country goods that may be difficult to replicate locally. This is a decided market advantage for large, international hotels and resorts, which are often able to dominate markets for tourists who want to enjoy the 'comforts of home' wherever they are, but it constrains the ability of destination firms to supply the tourism sector.

Wages, salaries and other forms of income in the destination's labour and capital markets are a major component of **induced inflows**. While different segments of the industry have varying labour-to-capital ratios, the tourism sector as a whole tends to be relatively labour intensive, employing workers of many different skills levels and providing an entrance point into the formal labour force for youth, women and the poor. The tourism sector can also be a major contributor to informal employment and to various forms of self-employment and entrepreneurship, offering opportunities for workers with little education or training and for marginalized or vulnerable groups to an extent that other industries are not always capable of matching. However, these effects are not automatic and cannot be taken for granted. The destination must develop a workforce with the skills and experience demanded by tourism firms, and it must adopt policies that encourage the participation of domestic entrepreneurs in the tourism sector.

TOURISM AND THE DESTINATION LABOUR MARKET

Tourism is a substantial contributor to global employment, and in many smaller, tourism-focused counties, the sector accounts for a large share of

---

75 For example, although scuba diving is an important component of the Bermudan tourism sector, it is highly unlikely that it will ever be economically viable for Bermuda to produce its own scuba equipment.

the national labour force.[76] As with the flow of revenue into the destination economy, the employment effects of tourism follow several distinct transmission channels. **Direct employment** refers to people employed in the tourism industry proper. This includes airline, hotel and restaurant staff, as well as guides, artisans, local transport providers, recreational activities specialists and anyone else whose livelihood is directly connected to the tourism industry.

Indirect employment includes workers in sectors that supply the tourism industry, including tourism-related food and beverages suppliers, input wholesalers, banks, insurance and accounting firms, certain government agencies, and producers and importers of consumer and capital goods used in tourism. Indirect employment has an even greater impact than direct employment: it is estimated that, on average, two new jobs in the tourism industry indirectly generate three additional jobs in related economic sectors.

Induced employment refers to jobs generated in other sectors of the economy as a result of the growth of the tourism industry, though they are not necessarily linked to the tourism supply chain. Induced employment is often focused on meeting the demands of tourism industry workers, and includes jobs in non-tradable service sectors such as consumer retail, food and beverage production, food service, and entertainment. The extent to which the tourism industry generates induced employment is directly related to the total employment, wages and working conditions of the tourism industry. It is also subject to the same liabilities as direct and indirect employment in tourism, including **contingency** and **seasonality**.

---

76 In 2010, tourism is estimated to have accounted for over 235 million jobs worldwide, equivalent to about 8% of global employment, or 1 in every 12.3 jobs on Earth. In small, tourism-focused countries such as Barbados, Fiji, Mauritius, and Seychelles tourism represents a major or even a plurality share of national employment.

Contingency refers to the sensitivity of employment to changes in market conditions. Tourism industries face considerable variation in demand, which in any given destination can fluctuate dramatically from one year to the next. Employers are aware of this, and attempt to structure their workforces so that they can quickly increase or decrease their staff in response to changes in tourism demand, for example, by laying-off a portion of their least-skilled workers and having the remaining workers perform multiple roles. This enables tourism firms to survive when demand is low, but it leaves many tourism workers—especially the least-skilled and lowest-paid—with very little job security, as they are highly vulnerable to negative market shocks and may have considerable difficulty estimating their future income prospects and making financial decisions accordingly.

The related problem of **seasonality** refers to the annual cycle of tourism demand experienced by nearly all locations. Tourism demand does not remain constant: it varies both between years and within years, as each destination experiences its "high seasons" and "low seasons". Unlike employment contingency, employment seasonality can be at least partially planned-for in advance, but it leaves many workers unable to earn enough income during the year to break out of the seasonal employment cycle, and consequently contributes to the persistence of low wages and bleak employment prospects among many lower-skilled tourism workers.

Tourism also has important and complex implications for gender and youth. Women represent between 60 and 70 per cent of the tourism labour force, and half of all tourism workers are under the age of 25.[77] These dynamics are is some ways highly positive, as tourism provides a prime opportunity for women and youth to acquire wage employment—often in contexts where unremunerated domestic labour or semi-subsistence employment in farming or fishing may be the principal alternatives. However, most of the jobs available to women are in unskilled

---

77 ILO (2008) "Guide for Social Dialogue in the Tourism Industry" ILO Working Paper No. 265 Geneva: International Labour Office

or semi-skilled positions, with few opportunities for advancement beyond the entry level, and women are often employed in the informal sector where they face poor wages and working conditions.[78]

Improving wages, working conditions and terms of employment in the destination market involves substantial trade-offs between the interests of workers, employers and the economy at large. The job insecurity and negative income effects generated by contingency and seasonality can in principle be mitigated by stricter labour laws—e.g. regulations specifying minimum periods of service or preventing termination without cause—though in practice these restrictions on employers tend to create serious problems of their own. Employers that cannot easily terminate employees may be reluctant to hire new ones, contributing to unemployment and informality, while firms in industries that are inherently seasonal, such as tourism, may become uncompetitive if they are unable to adjust size of their workforces to reflect demand conditions. In the broader economy the latter effect is referred to as **labour market rigidity**; it negatively impacts both current employers, who are prevented from swiftly downsizing their workforces, and emerging employers, who find that a large share of their potential employees are already committed elsewhere.

This is not to suggest that either stronger labour laws or specific protections for workers in the tourism sector are inappropriate; these reforms entail both advantages and liabilities, and their value must be determined on a case-by-case basis through informed discussion in democratic forums. The International Labour Organization provides a useful definition of "decent work", which may serve as an orientation point to guide labour policy discussion. Decent work is productive, it delivers a fair income, workplace security and social protection for families, it offers improved prospects for personal development and social integration, freedom for people to express their concerns, organise and participate in the

---

78 *Ibid.*

decisions that affect their lives, and it provides equality of opportunity and treatment for both women and men.[79]

In addition, there are a number of specific concerns that deserve consideration in any discussion of sustainable tourism labour markets. These include the government's strategic objectives for the tourism sector and for the nature of employment within the sector, as well as the diverse goals and aspirations of the private sector and those of local civil society. Is the government's focus on using tourism as an engine of job growth, or do policymakers view it primarily as a public revenue source and/ or a means of stimulating job growth in other sectors? How does the business community perceive the skills and competencies of the local workforce? Are they hiring expatriate workers to fill gaps in the local labour market? How do people in the local community view tourism jobs? Is employment in the tourism industry considered desirable, or is the sector regarded as an employer of last resort?

Answering these questions will require addressing broader and more fundamental issues as to how the tourist industry is structured, what share of the tourist market is being targeted, and how do all of these stakeholders view the integration of tourists in the broader economy? Should they be encouraged to mingle freely with the local population, using smaller, locally owned hotels, restaurants and other facilities, or should they be sequestered in large, all-inclusive resorts? The former model is likely to have a much stronger impact on employment, and income, as studies show that small, dispersed, locally owned facilities generate more local employment than large-scale foreign-owned resorts. As noted by UNEP:

The Organization of American States (OAS) carried out a survey of Jamaica's tourist industry that looked at the role of the all-inclusives compared to other types of accommodation. It found that "All-inclusive hotels generate the largest amount of revenue but

---

79 ILO (2011)

their impact on the economy is smaller per dollar of revenue than other accommodation subsectors." It also concluded that all-inclusives imported more, and employed fewer people per dollar of revenue than other hotels. This information confirms the concern of those who have argued that all-inclusives have a smaller trickle-down effect on local economies.[80]

However, there are also serious social and cultural issues associated with opening local communities to large numbers of foreign tourists,[81] as will be discussed in greater detail in later chapters, and these must be weighed against the potential employment benefits of dispersed, socially integrated tourism. As always, the principles of sustainability require that these decisions be made transparently, democratically, and locally and that they substantively reflect the will of the people affected by them.

TOURISM AND MACROECONOMIC MANAGEMENT

In addition to its microeconomic effects on income, employment, and firms in the destination market, tourism has important implications for public revenues, the external accounts, inflation, exchange rates, as well as related fiscal, monetary and overall macroeconomic policies.

The tourism industry can generate significant revenue for both local and national governments through the various direct taxes and fees imposed on tourists and tourism firms, as well as from taxes on indirect and induced tourism revenues. **Direct taxes** include tourist visa fees and exit taxes, sales taxes or value-added taxes paid by tourists and by tourism firm, and all other taxes paid by tourism firms and employees, such as corporate income tax, property tax and payroll tax. **Indirect taxes** include

---

80 UN Environment Programme (2013) "Resource Efficiency and Sustainable Consumption and Production: Negative Economic Impacts of Tourism Development" http://www.unep.org/resourceefficiency/Business/SectoralActivities/Tourism/FactsandFiguresaboutTourism/ImpactsofTourism/EconomicImpactsof   Tourism/NegativeEconomicImpactsofTourism/tabid/78784/Default.aspx
81 Swarbroke, J. (1999) Sustainable Tourism Management New York: CABI Publishing

aircraft landing fees and other tourist transportation-related taxes, as well as tariff revenues from tourism-sector imports. **Induced taxes** include any additional sales tax, payroll tax, corporate income tax, property tax, and all other increases in tax receipts arising from the induced revenue effects of tourism.

Public agencies in many developing countries have limited tax-collection capacity, and derive a substantial share of their revenue from trade-related taxes (especially import tariffs) rather than more administratively challenging income and sales taxes. This often makes tourism very attractive from a public-revenue standpoint, since it presents numerous opportunities for relatively easy-to-collect revenue. Visa fees and exit taxes, property taxes on tourism-related real estate, and tariffs on tourism-related imports have low administrative costs and may represent nontrivial revenue sources in developing countries with thriving tourism sectors.

However, there are also significant public costs associated with the tourism sector. Some of these are fairly straightforward: the tourism industry in most countries relies on sector-specific public infrastructure, such as airports and passenger-ship docks, and shares other public infrastructure and services, such as roads, electricity, and sanitation, which must be built, operated and maintained by the government. There are also other fiscal costs that may not be as obvious, yet must also be considered in the public accounting of tourism development. The tourism industry is often a major consumer of infrastructure and public utilities, especially in remote areas, and may place considerable strain on roads, electricity, water, and sanitation services. Investments in expanded infrastructure and the depreciation of public capital as a result of the tourism industry's operations are also important components of public expenditures in the sector.

In addition, international tourism is a highly competitive industry, and countries with large or growing tourism sectors may spend considerable sums advertising the merits of their destination. Because destination countries generally hire advertising firms based in their target source markets, tourism promotion is often a significant source of revenue leakage. The destination government is purchasing advertising as a service import in order to sell tourism as a service export. As a matter of fiscal policy, these costs must be weighed against the direct, indirect and induced tax revenue effects of tourism. As a matter of macroeconomic management, the import and export dynamics of tourism can have an important and complex influence on a destination country's **balance of payments**.

The balance of payments is a national accounting method. It expresses a country's economic relationship with the rest of the world by comparing foreign-exchange inflows and outflows. These foreign-exchange dynamics are largely driven by the value of imports and exports, the sum of which is called the "trade balance." The trade balance combined with net financial transfers and returns on foreign investment (minus payments to foreign investors) forms the "current-account balance," one of the two components of the balance of payments. The other component is the "capital account", which measures changes in foreign ownership of domestic assets and domestic ownership of foreign assets. These occur through foreign direct investment and portfolio investment, as well as the operations of the central bank.

The effects of the tourism sector on the balance of payments can be divided into three categories: (i) primary impact, which occur when spending by foreign tourists brings foreign exchange into the country (this counts as export revenue), or, conversely, when a resident spends money as a tourist abroad (this counts as an import); (ii) secondary impacts, which occur through the direct, indirect or induced effects of the tourism sector described above, such as outflows of foreign exchange used to finance imports for the tourism sector or related sectors; and (iii) tertiary impacts, which occur through the purchase of imports or exports that are economically complimentary to the goods and services produced by the sector. International trade in luggage, cameras, sunscreen, bathing suits and other complimentary goods are part of the tertiary impacts of tourism on the balance of payments.

As this breakdown suggests, the effects of tourism on the balance of payments are complex, but tend to be very positive for the destination country. Tourism service exports bring in foreign exchange, as does foreign direct and portfolio investment in hotels, real estate, tourism facilities and other private capital, and these tend to outweigh the outflow of foreign exchange cause by tourism-related imports. The ultimate impact of rising foreign exchange reserves is similarly complex: on the one hand, substantial foreign exchange reserves can bolster a country's macroeconomic stability and may allow it to defend a fixed exchange-rate policy. However, the process of building these reserves puts upward pressure on the **exchange rate**, which can have a range of negative impacts on the destination country.

The exchange rate is the price of one currency expressed in units of another one, that is, the amount of domestic currency required to obtain foreign currency, or vice versa. As foreign exchange flows into an economy, it increases the foreign-currency purchasing power of domestic consumers. This makes foreign goods effectively cheaper in domestic markets, which can damage the competitiveness of other domestic industries. Ultimately, rising currency values can even damage the industry that prompted them, in this case making the destination market more expensive for foreign tourists.

A related monetary effect of tourism development is **inflation**. Tourist spending and tourism-related investment affects the amount of money in circulation and increases the speed with which money changes hands in the economy. These dynamics, plus increased demand for scarce resources, especially real estate, energy and food service, may contribute to rising prices. This phenomenon is sometimes known as "tourism inflation". Managing currency appreciation and curbing inflation involve highly sophisticated monetary policy operations, which can be administratively demanding for public agencies in developing countries.

In addition to monetary policy, transportation- and infrastructure-policy measures can help to alleviate inflation at both the local and national level, and in many cases these measures will also have broadly positive impacts on the economy as a whole. Tourism can raise prices for food and consumer goods by boosting local demand in a context where supply is constrained in various ways, such as through limited local production capacity and high transportation costs. Real estate is always subject to inherent supply limitations, and regulating land use involves complex trade-offs that are discussed in detail in later chapters, but prices for food, consumer goods and electricity can be moderated by responsible supply-side policies.

Reducing transportation and transaction costs for local and international trade can help to mitigate the inflationary effects of a tourism-related increase in demand. This may include paving or resurfacing roads, refurbishing rail lines, expanding or improving ports or other forms of transport infrastructure; in addition, measures to reduce the administrative costs of transporting goods, such as streamlining permit processes and customs-clearance procedures may help to reduce the cost of imports nationwide. Similarly, tourism firms tend to demand a large amount of energy, often in areas where power-generation is weak or structurally expensive, and water services are often subject to similar constraints. Rising utility prices or erratic supply can damage economy-wide competitiveness, while investments in new power and water capacity or technological upgrades can provide a boost to economic growth and diversification.

However, new investments in transportation and utility infrastructure are typically very expensive, and governments must ensure that tourism firms pay **cost-reflective tariffs**—that is, that the amount they pay for public services is commensurate with the cost of providing those services. While it may be tempting to offer transportation, energy, water systems and other public infrastructure at below-cost rates in order to promote the growth of the tourism sector, these policies may threaten the fiscal sustainability of local and even national governments, or result in the accumulation of contingent liabilities by state-owned enterprises. Fiscal sustainability is as important to the development of a sustainable tourism as the other forms of sustainability discussed elsewhere in this book, as it is critical to ensuring that tourism serves the public interest and makes a positive contribution to the general welfare of the destination.

CONCLUSION

The tourism sector interacts with the broader local and national economy in a variety of complex ways, and the economic policy framework that guides its growth will have a major influence not only on its sustainability, but also the extent to which it contributes to priority development objectives. Assessing the economic impacts of tourism requires analysing the multiple dimensions of interaction between the tourism industry, the broader private sector, and the local and national government.

First, it is important to evaluate the market structure of the tourism sector and its degree of integration with the destination economy. Which inputs used by the tourism industry are sourced locally, and which are imported? Does the industry have access to skilled workers that meet its labour demands, or does it hire foreign workers to fill key positions? How open is the tourism sector to domestic entrepreneurship? Understanding these linkages is the first step to enhancing the impact of the tourism industry on employment, income and livelihoods in the destination. Generally speaking, a tourism sector populated by numerous small firms, each providing a distinct service to independent travellers will have a greater local economic impact than a tourism sector dominated by a few large, all-inclusive resorts catering to package tourists.

Second, it is crucial to recognize and appreciate the ways in which the tourism industry is shaping the growth and development of the broader economy. How do tourism exports impact the exchange rate, and how does the sector influence the balance of payments? To what extent does the sector contribute to inflation or to local price distortions? What is its impact on the labour market? A large tourism sector will generate important macroeconomic changes, with implications at both the national and local levels. Understanding these effects will enable the government to design policies that support the development of tourism as a driver of growth of the broader economy.

Third, evaluating the relationship between the tourism industry and the local government will illustrate the extent to which tourism contributes to the fiscal health of the destination. How much revenue does the government derive from the sector, directly in the form of taxes and fees paid by tourists and tourism firms, indirectly though taxes on tourism-related goods and services, and via increased tax revenues generated by tourism-induced growth in the broader economy. How much does the government spend on public infrastructure and services used by the tourism sector? Do payments for the use of infrastructure and utilities accurately reflect the fiscal costs of providing them? Policymakers, development professionals and local civil society must remain abreast of these dynamics and maintain a healthy discourse on the political economy of the tourism industry.

EXERCISES

1. Describe how revenue flows into a local economy via the tourism sector. What are the differences between direct, indirect and induced inflows?
2. Explain the concept of "leakages". How do leakages affect the sustainability of the tourism industry?

3. How does the tourism industry affect the value of a destination country's currency? How does it impact the exchange rate, and how does it impact inflation?
4. Define "conditionality" and "seasonality" in tourism employment? How do these factors influence incomes and livelihoods in the tourism industry?
5. How does a local government derive revenue from tourism? What public expenses might be incurred by the tourism industry?
6. What does "fiscal sustainability" mean in the context of the tourism industry?

CASE 6 RANCHO MARGOT, A PERMANENT SEARCH FOR SUSTAINABILITY IN COSTA RICA.
By Eduard Müller – Rector Dean at University for International Cooperation. emuller@uci.ac.cr

Costa Rica is a well-known tourist destination, especially nature based, though mass tourism mainly linked to beaches in the province of Guanacaste has grown steadily over the last decades pushed strongly by the government. Under the slogan "no artificial ingredients", 2014 closed with over 2.5 million tourists with approximately US$2.6 billion in revenues, an 8.3% increase over 2013. Average stay was between 12 and 13 nights with an average spending between US$ 1300 and 1400 per tourist. The country is considered as one of the birthplaces for ecotourism, which developed in the 1960's and 70's. Peaceful conditions and good infrastructure offered excellent conditions for research which made information about its biodiversity available for tour guides very early on. In the 90's the country developed its own Sustainable Tourism Certification (CST), a pioneer initiative worldwide.

The Arenal area is located in the northern plains of Costa Rica and became a tourist destination about 20 years after the explosion of the Arenal Volcano in 1968. Locals owned the land around the volcano and they made their living in agriculture and cattle ranching but the steady increase in tourists in the early 90's and the decline in cattle production generated an almost spontaneous destination. Constant eruptions with lava flows where a magnet for growing number of visitors, many of which came in rental cars with few organized tours being offered during the first years. Farmers soon recognized that they had a world attraction in their back yards and at first simple lodging sprung up and more ambitious tourism oriented development soon followed. Initially most of the hotels and attractions were locally owned. As the industry grew, foreign investors and more sophisticated operators appeared on the scene forcing the local operators to improve or go out of business. Prices traditionally high in the area faced increase pressure from well-healed competitors. The high end market was quickly dominated by the few foreign owned operators, the mid-range was filled by the better organized local operators and all the rest forage in an increasingly competitive market for the lower end travelers.

In 2010 the volcanic activity stopped. During the first couple of years thereafter volcanic activity was still offered as the main attraction and images of volcanic eruptions where still widely used for promoting the area. With the realization that volcanic activity was not to restart any time soon, operators were forced to diversify activities and nature treks, skywalks, canopy tours, agrotourism, thermal spas and many others soon became common attractions.

In 2004, Juan Sostheim, a Chilean-American businessman coming from the mass food industry visited the area and decided to change his life, purchasing a farm with the intentions to create a self-sufficient intentional community anchored in tourism, production and education. Rancho Margot is a work in progress that in its first decade of development has already gained a reputation for setting the bar in sustainable tourism in Costa Rica and around the world.

Approximately 160 hectares of cow pastures are slowly being converted to a sustainable, working community. By March 2015, a substantial amount of infrastructure dots the landscape of the valley Rancho Margot is situated in. A fully functioning resort maintains a staff of 40 mostly local residents employed full time. In 2014, seventeen bungalows, a forty-student bunkhouse, restaurant, bar and tours generated $890,000 in revenues.

What was once desolate pastureland without trees and lacking biodiversity is now an indistinguishable part of the rain forest. Birds that had not been seen in years are now a regular feature of the landscape.

A rapid assessment exercise conducted in 2012 estimated a biodiversity gain valued at US$450,000. Green roofs are full of plants, orchids and small animals including lizards, snakes and squirrels. Two mini hydroelectric plants provide 100% of the ranch's electricity and 3 bio-digestors provide approximately 70% of all the gas needs. In 2012 the Ranch was certified as carbon neutral by Carbon Clear with a negative footprint of 1275 metric tons of carbon.

The food that is consumed on the ranch is also produced to a great extent on ranch premises. 100% of the dairy needs (milk, cheese and yogurt); 100% of the eggs and meats (pork, chicken and some beef) is produced on the ranch. All leafy vegetables, tubers (yucca, camote, malanga), squash and many others are also produced without the use of chemicals. All fertilizer, compost and mountain microorganisms used on the premises are also produced in Rancho Margot. Although Rancho Margot served over 60,000 meals to tourists, staff and volunteers in 2014, outside purchases including some outside food bought for animals was less than $0.90 per meal. The main source of purchases were rice, beans, oil and fruits which we were not able to produce nor eliminate from the diet so far. All the soap used is produced on the farm from used cooking oil from the kitchen. The furniture is also built on site.

Rancho Margot is located in a rainforest 4 km from the village of El Castillo on the shores of Lake Arenal in Costa Rica. In 2004 there were less than 200 people living in the village, in March 2015 there are almost 500 residents living in El Castillo. School was k-6 and with no hope of going to secondary school most children abandoned what little education opportunity they had.

It quickly became a priority to get these young people off the streets and back to school. The success of Rancho Margot would increasingly be dependent on the education level of the local work force. In February 2004 for the beginning of classes Rancho Margot hired a local van operator to take and bring the students who wanted to continue their education to the nearest school 35 km away in La Fortuna and back five days a week. Within six months Rancho Margot was operating a free bus schedule for the locals to go to La Fortuna with two 50 passenger school buses acquired through ebay.com for that purpose.

In 2006 the ranch was instrumental in finally getting secondary schooling to El Castillo and in 2005-2008 Rancho Margot spearheaded a successful community effort and received a $22,000 grant from the national institute for community development DINADECO for the El Castillo School. The funds were used for a two-year bilingual environmental science program, teachers and computers.

In the span of 11 years a sleepy village with a total of 5 landlines (3 public phones and 2 hotel phones) has seen an incredible transformation. Foreign direct investment to this area kept people employed, brought some local income and some of the locals began to invest themselves to take advantage of the boom. El Castillo has high-speed Internet and cell coverage and well as new landlines in almost every home.

Not all the growth has been orderly or legal for that matter. Hunting, logging and building in protected zones is a growing problem that needs government action and in the absence, private entities like Rancho Margot and the Children's Eternal Forest among many have to join forces to fill de void. This inevitably leads to conflicts between owners, park officials, community members and perpetrators. Lack of will power by local officials to enforce property and environmental laws only exasperated the problems giving lawbreakers acquired rights that are difficult, time consuming and costly to revert.

By 2010, El Castillo and the whole area surrounding the Arenal Volcano National Park was deeply embedded in the financial crisis. The world economy and the end of the period of activity for the Arenal Volcano coincided to form a perfect storm from which only half of the hotels in the area have been able to recuperate. Rancho Margot was vulnerable and survival was by no means assured. The year 2012 was perhaps the most difficult when an unscrupulous US citizen and neighbor from El Castillo started an anonymous defamation campaign against Rancho Margot which culminated in the top guide book of 2010 having a completely negative recommendation. The new edition 2012 brought back the top choice destination and by the end of 2012 Rancho Margot had begun growing revenues again.

Typically independent, the local tourism industry had never really developed cooperative mechanisms to market the region as a whole. Fighting and old rivalries impeded collective action by all the actors, many just looked for someone to blame. Eventually panic gave way to reason and some valuable initiatives are leading to a repositioning of the industry and region as a whole.

In 2007 an area of 916 thousand hectares corresponding to close to 20% of the country was nominated by UNESCO as the Water and Peace Biosphere Reserve. Rancho Margot quickly went on board to promote the consolidation of this biosphere reserve and cofounded and has presided since the Water and Peace Foundation, established to fill the gap of lacking institutionality to support the biosphere reserve. One of the important initiatives currently being promoted is the Lake Arenal Development Group which seeks the establishment of a bicycle track around the lake and the promotion of watersports. It can be argued that is the first truly multidisciplinary and inter-sector group working at the territory level.

Rancho Margot started taking on volunteers in 2004. These men and women aged 21 and older, college graduates for the most part come from all over the world and contributed 36 hours per week for one month in exchange for room and board. Since the program's inception over 800 volunteers have contributed to the development of Rancho Margot.

Approximately 20 Costa Rican university students come during the year for internship as part of their ongoing curriculum. Unless these volunteers have a specific skill, they usually help in all areas where they are needed.

Today, over 50 universities, several high schools groups, dozens of yoga and specialized groups as well as hundreds of families and individual travelers visit Rancho Margot annually. Over 4,000 tourists stayed an average of 4 plus nights at Rancho Margot during 2014 and accounted for approximately 75% of total revenue. The average combined occupancy throughout the year was approximately 31%. In addition to overnight guest we have more than 6,000 outside visitors that come primarily to take the ranch tour, horseback ride and eat at Rancho Margot. 2015 has seen a steady increase in visitation, assuring the consolidation of the initiative.

CASE 7 - MANAGING BAROTSELAND AS A TOURIST DESTINATION

By Beauty Moono-Chengala, SNV Senior Advisor

INTRODUCTION

The Lozi people of Zambia still call the large expanse of land they inhabit in the western part of the country Barotseland and guard the name and everything it stands for jealously. Theirs is a kingdom, one of Africa's last and it is ruled with traditional pomp and colorful splendor by the Litunga, Lubosi Imwiko II, the Lozi king.

The Barotse region is one area rich in culture and history and lies in an area that covers a unique and important ecological area on the western banks of the Zambezi River, bordering Namibia in the south (the Caprivi Strip) and Angola in the West. This area covers two National Parks, Sioma Ngwezi and Liuwa, The provincial capital, Mongu, hosts the famous Kuomboka Ceremony which attracts thousands of visitors, local and international over a period of two days.

Barotseland is 600 kilometers by road from Lusaka, the Zambian capital. By air, 1 hour 40 minutes flight —should you want to make the journey. Traveling by road is probably more interesting and public bus shuttles are available. The route passes through the Kafue National Park, the second largest Park in Africa and Zambia's oldest, for a distance of about 90km. Impala, puku, elephants are a common sighting and occasionally cheetah, hippo and other species of wildlife and birds can be seen on this route. From Livingstone, Zambia's tourism capital and home of the Victoria Falls, the destination can be reached by road using the Sesheke road, through Senanga covering a distance of about 330km. Four wheel drive vehicles are recommended on these sandy and rugged roads.

In 2010, SNV Zambia put in place a comprehensive Pro-Poor Tourism (PPT) Program in order to start implementing the SNV Zambia 2009 PPT

Strategy. The Barotse region is one of five (5) selected destinations (Kafue National Park, Mpika, Kasanka, and Barotse) that SNV Zambia chose to work and provide support in destination management. Among these destinations only Livingstone can be considered an established destination. Livingstone is also Zambia's tourism capital and home of the Victoria Falls. In spite of the Barotse's evident tourism potential, the destination is probably the least developed of the five destinations areas, and can be considered an emerging destination at best. The development of the Barotse destination will, for a large extent, depend on the ability to be linked to Livingstone and the Kafue National Park. The Kavango-Zambezi Transfrontier Conservation Area (TFCA) programme incorporates the Barotse area and its envisaged impact on tourism development is great, in particular through the opening up of the area to tourists making use of the to be completed Walvisbaai-Copperbelt highway.

The Nalikwanda, the Royal Barge being paddled to the Limulunga harbour. Photo courtesy: Lusaka Times

Main tourism activities in this region are boating, angling and game drives; Visits to the privately owned royal museum, the Nayuma Museum in Limulunga which offers an opportunity to learn about the Lozi Kingdom and buy beautiful handicrafts: woven, wood carvings, leather and pottery products. Heritage sites include spectacular man-made canals and mounds, traditional houses and palaces, royal burial sites, shrines and other sacred sites and objects of special significance mostly used as part of rituals and ceremonies.

The table below shows the visitor numbers received in the main tourist attractions in the Barotse region.

Table 1:
Visitor numbers and average length in main tourist attractions

Main Tourist Attractions	No of Visitors	Average length of stay
Liuwa National Park	500	2 days
Sioma Water Falls	200	1 day
Kuomboka Ceremony	5000	2 days
Senanga Fishing Competition	200	2 days
Business	100	2days
Conference/workshops	500	3 days
Sioma Ngwezi National Park	200	2 days
Total	6700	2days

The tourism industry comprises mainly of small guesthouses, small restaurants serving mainly local food and five campsites including three community managed campsites in Liuwa National Park. The area does not benefit much from tourism and participation by local people in tourism and other related sectors is extremely limited. Among the reasons for this poor performance is that the local hospitality industry does not have the capacity to provide the quality service that discerning tourists and visitors demand, lack of collaboration and networking among players and its unexploited potential as a tourism destination due to poor road infrastructure. Sadly, local peoples do Not benefit from the hordes who visit the area to fish and to watch the migration of wildebeest (in Liuwa).

This is because the visitors prefer to stay in their own tents and live on food and drink they would have brought with them, thereby depriving the lodges and guest houses in the area of much-needed revenue. During the Kuomboka ceremony, accommodation rates shoot up to prohibitive levels!

There are opportunities. The Kuomboka ceremony attracts thousands of visitors that stay for an average period of two (2) days. The number of days could be increased if events and packages were developed and marketed. The Ceremony itself is over a period of two weeks; cultural and historic sites are dotted throughout the region. The region fact that the region covers two national parks and a water fall, Sioma in the West provides opportunities for nature and cultural tourism. Further, Government plans to rehabilitate major roads in the region have reached an advanced stage.

SNV INTERVENTION

The destination management approach taken in the Barotse destination and the other four destinations,) is mainly in marketing and quality service delivery. SNV's intervention in the area, is in partnership with Open Africa (OA), a World Bank/GEF-funded South African Non Governmental Organization which provides marketing support (website and maps), and facilitates bio-diversity monitoring activities. The main thrust of the intervention is to build a practical framework for collaboration between local peoples as well as private and public players to exploit the area's tourism resources and spread the economic benefits all around.

The SNV support so far given to the tourism SMEs, the communities and other players has been seen as a catalyst and an eye opener to the tourism entrepreneurs and the community who have begun to explore the tourism opportunities in the region.

MULTI STAKEHOLDER PLATFORM

The idea to form an association started in November last year after a meeting jointly organised by SNV and Open Africa to introduce the Open Africa North South Tourism Corridor initiative and SNV capacity development services. At the time, the only tourism group that existed was the Hotel and Catering Association of Zambia but it was inactive and was limited to only accommodation and restaurants. The participants felt that they needed a platform that would provide them with an opportunity to deal with tourism matters, collaborate and encourage networking. SNV was approached to support and facilitate the organising of a Multi Stakeholder Platform (MSP).

This led to the first ever tourism MSP meeting that was held in May 2010, jointly supported jointly by OA and SNV.   Objectives were as follows:

- To develop a partnership framework to address key constraints and opportunities in the tourism sector in the Barotse destination area
- To build consensus on a common vision for the future of tourism in the Barotse destination area
- To identify core PPT activities to catalyze significant growth for the poor in the Barotse destination area
- To identify and support lead initiatives in a coordinated development approach to build on ongoing activities already being implemented

The underlying premise for the MSP was that any undertakings and activities that were developed and implemented would be coordinated and key to this would be to build on existing initiatives and leverage resources and the various competencies of the stakeholders invited to fulfill common objectives.

The stakeholders were from public, private sector, NGOs and the community representatives. 56 participants attended the MSP. These were from the Ministry of Tourism, Environment and Natural Resources, National Heritage Conservation Commission, Zambia Tourism Board, WWF, Kavango Zambezi Trans Frontier Conservation initiative (KAZA TFC), African Parks, the Barotse Royal Establishment, tourism and tourism related service providers.

Stakeholders agreed to work out a destination development plan, collect data on capacity of actors, attractions and types of activities and that the proposed Barotse Tourism Association (BTA) that stakeholders were proposing be registered, be the lead agency in managing the destination. The players also agreed that it was important for BTA to develop a strategic business plan and a communications strategy. SNV facilitated the registration of the Association and it was registered in July 2010. Its main objectives are to be the voice of the tourism industry, to develop and promote tourism in the Western Province. Membership to this Association is open to tourism, tourism related businesses and service providers. At present, SNV works with the interim Committee of the Association. Elections are scheduled to take place before the end of December 2010. Other services that have been provided to BTA is facilitating access to information on regulations and best practices in tourism and linkages to other similar associations in the country.

As a result of the MSP held in May this year, the mood and interest in the industry is changing. Industry players are beginning to show interest and willingness to explore new ideas and activities and to work together. In June, members of the tourism industry organized and sponsored a smooth familiarization tour for members of Hotel & Tourism Association of Zambia

MARKETING OPPORTUNITIES

The Association would also like to put in place a well documented database of cultural and historic sites and other attractions in order to be able to develop new tourism products and the process of collecting information has begun. SNV is finalizing an agreement to support this process. This is intended to lead to training of cultural sites care takers and women as village chefs and youths as village/cultural guides, an initiative expected to create new jobs for women and the youth.

SNV has facilitated linkages between the BTA to tour operators to market the destination. BTA has now been linked to a tour operator, Floating Skies, which is already bringing clients to the area. Package Tours by Floating Skies alone this year are expected to bring in about US $4,000 to the area. The operator has now started working through the Association to facilitate tours and is involving the Committee in designing the packages. The BTA is currently working on the 2nd tour which is being used as a fundraising activity. One major challenge is the lack of know-how in designing packages and handling international tourists. Other training needs that have been identified are basic hygiene and house keeping for women who teach and cook with visitors participating in this village cooking tours. The local training institution, Mongu Trades Institution has also risen to the occasion and has introduced short training programmes in front office, housekeeping, and food production to contribute to improved service provision in the region. The institution has identified BTA as a partner and plans to design programs relevant to the BTA and its members.

OA is also in the process of finalising its website and maps for the destination. This is a good marketing opportunity to attract self-drive tourists

Lessons Learned
The journey for SNV has just begun. As SNV continues to providing strengthening the capacity of the local tourism association and the various players, it is anticipated that collaboration and networking among the local people, private and public players will continue to improve and lead to more community linkages and involvement of the local people.

Furthermore, the destination management support is expected to contribute to the growth of the Barotse destination through marketing initiatives. Improved service delivery, management and marketing of these spectacular cultural and fishing events should, in the next few years, lead to increase the number of visitors and the length of stay and ultimately revenue earned by the SMEs and the local people. This would boost the handicraft industry in the region and increase direct pro-poor benefits to the communities - This is the Lozi peoples dream.

"I think time has come for us embrace tourism." Kekelwa Mundia, *Interim Chairman, BTA*

Five

Strategic Planning for Sustainable Tourism Development

The enemy of a good plan is the dream of a perfect plan.

— CARL VON CLAUSEWITZ, ON WAR

OBJECTIVES OF THE CHAPTER:

- Define the key concepts that guide the strategic planning process for tourism destinations.
- Identify the key differences between a tourism development plan, a tourism marketing plan, and a strategic plan.
- Discuss the complex political, social and economic factors that determine the success of destination planning.
- Introduce the analytical models used in destinations planning and describe their relevance to sustainable tourism.

INTRODUCTION

Tourism is more than just an industry; it is a complex social, economic, political, and cultural phenomenon, and a relatively recent one at that. The international tourism industry has grown exponentially since the mid-20th Century, matching or even leading the curve of economic and cultural globalization. Tourism has changed the face of the world, creating a new understanding of economic value and how it applies to non-traditional assets such as natural beauty, historical significance and cultural uniqueness.

This understanding continues to evolve, and the appreciation of tourism development planners for the nature of the industry and its influence on social and economic condition has not always proven adequate to ensure that a destination's resources are used responsibly, in some cases with tragic results. While conventional demand-driven approaches to development planning might succeed in increasing tourist arrivals, average spending, and length of stay, they may still fail to deliver lasting benefits to the local population, especially to the poor and marginalised, to women, minorities, youth, to the discriminated against and disadvantaged.[82] Tourism is resource-based industry, drawing on social and cultural as well as natural resources; in too many cases these resources have been expended in pursuit of short-term opportunities and immediate benefits, while overestimating the capacity and resilience of ecological and social capital or simply ignoring the long-term costs inflicted by tourism development.

Destination managers, policymakers, stakeholders from the private sector and civil society, and anyone else who is responsible for—or has a voice in—the planning and management of destination markets must cultivate a comprehensive grasp of how the tourism economy functions and of its complex relationship with the physical and social spaces in which tourism takes place. This appreciation for the complexity of tourism development, together with an understanding of the strategic approaches to sustainable development planning currently gaining ground in the international tourism industry, is the foundation for equitable, broad-based tourism development that conserves and augments the destination's

---

82 See Burns, P. (2004) "Tourism Planning: A Third Way?" *Annals of Tourism Research* 31(1): 24-43

capital, continuously building competitiveness and enabling the destination to generate consistent economic returns over time.

There is a growing range of local-level development planning approaches and policy instruments designed to ensure long-term sustainability, several of which are especially relevant to the tourism industry. For example, 'pro-poor' development strategies focus on maximizing the income-generating potential of economic growth among the lowest income groups. Pro-poor development is generally considered successful if overall increases in per capita income serve to reduce inequality; in other words, development is pro-poor only if its returns are progressively distributed. Meanwhile, so-called 'green growth' strategies put the environment at the centre of economic policy, regarding development as successful only if the environmental impacts of growth are minimal and reparable and the natural capital stock remains intact.

There are considerable advantages to these strategies, which are not limited to their equity, social-development and quality-of-life objectives. A growth model that generates broad-based returns is likely to enjoy enduring popularity and, consequently, **policy continuity**, while a model that benefits only a narrow constituency may be altered or reversed or even provoke political or social disruptions. Similarly, a development model that prioritizes the conservation of natural capital is more likely to produce consistent returns over the long run than a policy that focuses only on maximizing current profits.

However, these strategies are not without their cost. Promoting pro-poor growth and protecting environmental quality often involve limiting the tourism industry's capacity to generate immediate increases in income and employment, slowing the pace of growth for the sake of its quality. This trade-off can be enormously consequential: in the short-run concentrating on any policy objective other than maximizing private profits will almost certainly decrease the competitiveness of a tourism destination, and excessively restrictive development policies can undermine their own goals by stymying growth altogether. In more well-established destinations policymakers may have sufficient latitude to increase the participation of the poor or safeguard environmental assets without severely damaging investment incentives, but emerging destinations in low-income countries this may not be the case.

Determining how to make these types of trade-offs—between equity and efficiency, between investors and workers, between immediate returns and long-term competitiveness—is perhaps the most crucial issue facing destination managers. Formulating a strategy for sustainable tourism development involves balancing complex sets of competing interests, and in this context it is essential to establish and strengthen **democratic institutions**, political and administrative mechanisms capable of leveraging the participation of a wide range of stakeholders, including the marginal and disenfranchised. This is much easier said than done; it requires a considerable degree of administrative sophistication and, most critically, robust and sustained political will.

Tourism development strategies have typically fallen under one of two broad ideological categories, the "development first" model, which stresses social objectives and regards tourism as a means to accomplish the public interest, and the "growth first" model, which focuses on private economic incentives and views tourism as a means to generate wealth. Each of these approaches involves opportunities and risks, and neither is necessarily appropriate in any given case. Managing the tension between these two ideological poles, which is one aspect of **the big trade-off** described in Chapter 2, requires as pragmatic and a participatory approach. This can be achieved by adhering to the good practice principles for destination governance detailed in Chapter 3.

Table 1: Two Ideological Approaches to Tourism Development[83]

The "Development First" Model	The "Growth First" Model
Focuses on social development	Focuses on economic growth
Regards tourism as an element of a broader social system	Regards tourism as an industry operated by rational utility-maximizing individuals
Views tourism as a form of local culture	Views tourism as a form of universal consumerism
Considers primary consequence of failed policies to be the unsustainable exploitation of human, social, cultural and environmental capital	Considers primary consequence of failed policies to be low growth and persistent poverty
Concentrates attention on peripheral participants in the tourism industry	Concentrates attention on core participants in the tourism industry
Normative values: growth should be equitable and sustainable	Normative values: Growth should be robust and efficient
Main policy objectives: the establishment of a unique destination in which the returns from tourism are progressively distributed, cultural and environmental integrity is protected, and the industry itself is an instrument of human development.	Main policy objectives: A highly competitive, rapidly growing tourism destination that maximizes its market share by offering whatever cultural or environmental tourism products best satisfy international market demand.

---

83 , p. 3, see *supra*.

Key downside risks: Policies designed to achieve social, cultural, environmental and/or equity objectives prove excessively restrictive and distort economic incentives, weakening the destination's competitiveness and discouraging investment; tourism development proceeds very slowly or fails altogether.	Key downside risks: A myopic focus on private interests and short-term growth undermine the public interests and erode long-term competitiveness; tourism development depletes the destination's human, cultural and/or environmental capital stock; the industry grows quickly but eventually collapses, leaving the destination worse off than it was previously.

Source: Author, adapted from Burns (2014)

Again, it is important to stress that strategic planning for tourism development does not follow a single methodology, pursue a single set of objectives, or adhere to a universal set of norms and values. A strategic development plan that was highly successful in one context generally cannot be applied to another destination because it is the planning process itself that generates the local knowledge, self-defined objectives and broad-based political will necessary to implement a successful development strategy. Strategic planning mobilizes policymakers and stakeholders to study the social, cultural, environmental and economic ramifications of tourism development, identify various options, balance their competing interests, select feasible strategies, and commit to achieving a common set of objectives. From a sustainable-development perspective the planning process may in fact be every bit as important as the plan itself.[84]

In this chapter we will review key concepts and principles behind successful sustainable tourism destination planning and define a basic

---

84 As American President Dwight D. Eisenhower once said, "Plans are worthless, but planning is everything." See: *Public Papers of the Presidents of the United States, Dwight D. Eisenhower* (1957) Washington DC: National Archives and Records Service, Government Printing Office

methodological framework for formulating development, marketing and strategic plans to guide the growth of a sustainable tourism industry.[85] This process begins with the pre-planning stage.

THE PRE-PLANNING STAGE

The international experience has shown that effective tourism development programmes are based on two fundamental implementation prerequisites, both of which must be addressed before planning begins. These are (i) the "mainstreaming" of tourism policy into the broader policy process and (ii) the establishment of adequate governance structures for the tourism industry. If either or both of these elements are not in place it is highly unlikely that any plan, no matter how well-designed, will be implemented successfully.

1. **Tourism policy mainstreaming**: "Mainstreaming" means incorporating tourism policy and programming into the routine functions of a government. Simply put, a destination's government must be both willing and able to execute a tourism development plan, and where either the will or the ability does not exist, it must be created. Many destination plans have failed because they were conceived without regard for political realities or lacked a sufficient understanding of the way governments operate. Formulating an elegantly crafted, thoroughly researched, and comprehensively detailed tourism destination plan and then simply presenting it to a government that has little institutional understanding of tourism or no interest in implementing this particular strategy will almost certainly prove to be a waste of time. This is particularly the case

---

85 The following section draws heavily on the authors' fieldwork in Latin America, the South Pacific, and Sub-Saharan Africa, during which they participated in a number of tourism-development planning initiatives led by local governments and by both local and international development organizations. In some cases tourism development yielded clearly positive social and economic impacts, while in others there was a frustrating lack of useful results, with tourism development leaving behind significant resentment and cultural damage while delivering little improvement in economic or social indicators.

in emerging destinations and for community-based initiatives, as both the government's administrative capacity and the community's organizational resources are likely to be limited. Planning failures caused by inadequate policy mainstreaming are in many cases either caused or compounded by the fact that tourism development planners are often more focused on the methodological aspects of the plan itself than on the task of building local capacity to understand, engage with and ultimately sustain the planning process.

2. **Effective destination governance:** Successful tourism development requires constantly reconciling competing interests, and this is as true for the planning process as it is for implementation. Tourism destinations planning should be guided by multi-stakeholder debate and participation, but unlike the **democratic institutions** discussed previously, which are permanent mechanisms for inclusion and feedback, destination governance structures in the planning phase are typically temporary and *ad hoc*, meaning put together for a specific and limited purpose. Private sector representatives and development organizations may be tempted to ignore the often messy and difficult process of establishing destination governance structures for tourism planning and instead rely on a small group of technical specialists to formulate a plan. However, this is a terrible corner to cut, as the resulting 'expert' plan will lack local knowledge, undermining its usefulness, and will have limited buy-in by the local government and community, undermining its political strength. Moreover, there is no reason to believe that a plan formulated solely by tourism experts will be successful, especially given the intensely local, non-generalizable nature of sustainable tourism development. There are also broader objectives to consider: sustainable tourism can act as a catalyst for social inclusion and environmentally sound economic development only if proposals and policy decisions reflect a shared vision and shared responsibilities. Destination planning

should bring together stakeholders representing different sectors of the economy and society; planning processes should engage minorities and members of vulnerable groups, promote dialogue and facilitate collaboration, even when it is inconvenient or costly, so that the responsibilities and commitments involved in the development process are publicly undertaken and shared.[86] In some cases this may require first undertaking capacity-building efforts amongst groups that lack expert knowledge or necessary skills, so that every affected person can make a meaningful contribution to the development plan.

3. **Strong analytical foundations**: Reliable data are essential to sound policy, and tourism destination plans must be evidenced-based in order to be effective. Market analyses, environmental impact evaluations, poverty mapping and the establishment of social economic baselines should be augmented by assessments of local culture and social resources. Ideally, comprehensive study would precede destination planning, providing a common analytical foundation for determining initial conditions and defining measurable objectives. However, collecting and analysing information is costly and time-consuming, and the quality of the final analysis may be uncertain. Before planning begins, it is critical to first assess the amount of data available to the planners, identify absent or outdated information, and then decide how best to establish a strong analytical foundation for the planning process.

Finally, tourism destination planning should be considered in the context of other national, provincial and local policies, programmes and objectives, including national development plans, environmental policies, land, water and energy schemes, infrastructure investment agendas, the cultural orientation of the political leadership, and any current or pending legislation that may affect the destination's social or economic conditions.

---

86 For more on destination governance see Chapter 3.

THE PLANNING PROCESS

Broadly speaking, there are two ways in which policymakers may view tourism development: (i) as a single local industry operating within a distinct local economy; and (ii) as a national economic sector comprising multiple local industries spread throughout the country. Both perspectives are valid, and both should be considered during any planning process. The most successful national tourism plans work to integrate a diversity of local destinations into a nationwide network, capitalising on the unique characteristics and competitive advantages of different areas, investing in integrated tourism infrastructure, and balancing the interests of the tourism industry against other national-level priorities. However, for the purpose of the present chapter tourism will be regarded from a local economic development perspective, i.e. as a local industry rather than a national one.

Before delving into the details of tourism planning, a clear distinction should be made between tourism **development plans**, **marketing plans**, and **strategic plans**. The first step in tourism planning, especially for new destinations that do not already have an established tourism industry, is typically to formulate a:

- **Development plan**. The objective of the destination development plan is to mobilise public and private resources to create a business climate, infrastructure base, and regulatory framework conducive to the growth of the tourism industry. The development plan must accurately identify weaknesses in the provision of public goods and services critical to tourism, including efficient transportation and utility networks, an environment of public safety and security, and sufficient administrative capacity to cope with a large influx of tourists. The development plan should also account for the destination's social and environmental preparedness for tourism, and it is in this respect that participatory processes for the formulation of the development plan are especially critical. Are the people who will be directly affected by the industry ready to accommodate large numbers of foreigners with different customs, expectations and habits? Will the growth of the industry strain environmental resources, especially considering the food, drinking water and sanitation demands of a growing tourist population? Are the institutional foundations in place to efficiently and equitably resolve the conflicts that will inevitably arise with the growth of the industry? And are democratic policy mechanisms and participatory forums prepared to revise the development plan itself as the industry grows and conditions evolve? In this latter respect the development plan is closely related to effective destination governance. A successful tourism development plan will define and address the destination's readiness for tourism, establishing the necessary conditions for the industry to thrive, but it alone may not be sufficient to create that industry. In order for a new destination to establish itself, or for an existing destination to expand, the development plan should be accompanied by a:

- **Marketing plan.** The objective of the destination marketing plan is to determine how best to spur the growth of a tourism industry once the necessary groundwork is in place. Marketing plans frequently centre on publicity, raising the destination's profile in regional and international tourism markets. There are two elements to publicity: first, the destination must appeal to tourism investors, and second, it must appeal to tourists themselves. Efforts to boost a destination's investment appeal may range from advertising in industry publications and hosting industry events such as trade fairs and expositions to making specific offers available to investors, such as special tax terms for early investors or offering public land for development on favourable terms. Tourist promotion may include advertising in targeted source markets or offering public subsidies for tourism packages, especially air travel. The marketing plan should propose actions that both enhance and emphasise the value of a destination's tourism services, and it should be based on a single, consistent public image for the destination and a target position with respect to its source markets and customer base. The marketing plan should establish this vision of the destination's image and market position and define the specific public relations strategies necessary to make that vision a reality. The tourism development and marketing plans are bound together by the:

- **Strategic plan.** The destination's strategic plan is the sum of its development and marketing objectives, whether at the local or national level. The strategic plan is the set of comprehensive, overarching goals for the tourism destination held by the government and other stakeholders. It also reflects how the tourism industry is situated within the broader policy context, describing how tourism development will serve the broader economic and social interests of the destination. The strategic plan rarely guides specific, day to day decisions for either tourism development or marketing; instead, it provides a central statement of purpose that aligns the actions and expectations of stakeholders in both the public and private sectors. Formulating a strategic plan is essential to tourism policy mainstreaming, as the plan offers consistent guidance for public agencies; it also supports the development plan by prioritising tourism development as a matter of public administration and reinforces the marketing plan by serving as a public statement of the government's commitment to tourism, bolstering the confidence of the private sector. As with other elements of tourism planning, the process of successfully formulating a strategic plan is at least as important as the plan itself, if not more so.

BOX 7 VISIT SUNNY IRAQI KURDISTAN

In the mid-2000s it was rare to pick up an international newspaper and not find a story describing in harrowing detail the on-going violence in Iraq. Although Saddam Hussein had been ousted by American and coalition forces in 2003,

terrorist bombings, ambushes, and sectarian bloodshed re-
mained tragically common. A substantial share of Iraq's citizen-
ry had fled the country, and it often seemed as if only soldiers,
aid workers and combat reporters would willingly go the other
way.

Yet even as conflict raged across much of the country the
northern autonomous region of Iraqi Kurdistan was experiencing
an unlikely boom in what might seem to be its least-likely industry: tourism. Iraqi Kurdistan currently hosts over 140,000 tourists
annually, and nearly a third come from outside Iraq.[87] In 2007
there were just over 100 hotels in the entire region, now there are
more than 400. By some estimates there are currently more hotels
in the regional capital of Erbil than in Paris,[88] and these will soon
be joined by a 5-star Marriot currently under construction. The
region has signed its own bilateral tourism-promotion plan with
the government of Egypt, and Erbil has been named the Arab
Council of Tourism's 2014 tourism capital. But how was all this
possible for a relatively obscure region of a war-torn country?

Because diligent planning and steadfast commitment made
it possible. In the early days of Hussein's ouster the regional government of Iraqi Kurdistan began to consider how to open their
region to international tourism markets. The formulated a strategy that emphasised investment promotion, and integrated this
strategy into their broader agenda of business-climate reform.

---

87 Newton-Small, Jay (2012) "Destination Kurdistan: Is this Autonomous Iraqi Region
a Budding Tourism Hotspot?" *Time Magazine*
http://world.time.com/2012/12/31/destination-kurdistan-is-this-autonomous-iraqi-
region-a-budding-tourist-hotspot/#ixzz2WwNTGtU2
88 al-Shaher, Omar (2013) "Hotel Construction Explodes In Erbil To Keep Up With
Tourism" *Al Monitor*
http://www.al-monitor.com/pulse/originals/2013/06/hotel-construction-boom-
tourism-kurdistan-iraq-erbil.html#ixzz2X0gVQ7vK

The region was presented as the ideal place to do business in Iraq: politically stable, relatively safe and, perhaps most importantly, administered by a government that was committed to the interests of the business community.[89] The government's major obstacle was the near-universally negative perception of the situation in Iraq; a perception that was fundamentally inaccurate to the Kurdistan region but which nevertheless impacted its tourism prospects. This phenomenon is called a "reputation effect", in which a destination's reputation for volatility or violence continues to damage its tourism industry even when it is undeserved. The Government of Rwanda has faced similar problems in overcoming the legacy of the country's 1993 genocide, notwithstanding two subsequent decades of peace and stability.

In Iraqi Kurdistan the authorities worked to correct this perception by establishing a primary informational website (http://www.tourismkurdistan.com/) and revamping several other websites on specific subjects. They contracted outside public relations firms to publish advertisements for investment and tourism in the region and even launched television ad campaigns in the United States and elsewhere. This marketing plan was complemented by a development plan formulated by a Lebanese company, which identified 65 locations for tourism development, with proposed focus areas ranging from ski resorts to kayaking to places of historical and religious significance.[90] Erbil is now served by a modern US$400 million airport, with a second international airport at Sulaimany. Although much more remains to be done to link various attractions around the region to its major cities, Iraqi

---

89 Maher, Ahmed (2013) "Iraq 10 years on: Good times in Kurdish Irbil" BBC News, March 23 http://www.bbc.co.uk/news/world-middle-east-21900576
90 Newton-Small, Jay (2012) "Destination Kurdistan: Is this Autonomous Iraqi Region a Budding Tourism Hotspot?" *Time Magazine*
http://world.time.com/2012/12/31/destination-kurdistan-is-this-autonomous-iraqi-region-a-budding-tourist-hotspot/#ixzz2WwNTGtU2

Kurdistan's success in the tourism industry and its considerable potential for further growth are undeniable. Today the region is a beacon to potential destination markets around the world, and a testament to the idea that there is no obstacle to tourist development that cannot be overcome by sound planning, responsible governance, and a steadfast commitment to the growth of the tourism industry.

At the outset of the planning process it is prudent to consider to what extent the government's involvement in the development of the tourism industry should be active or passive. Active involvement means undertaking specific policy actions designed to initiate or accelerate the growth of tourism. This includes tourism-specific infrastructure investment, tax incentives for tourism development, publicly supported hospitality training programs, tourism promotion campaigns, or any other measure that either requires fiscal spending on the tourism sector or distorts economic incentives in ways that favour tourism development over other forms of economic activity. Some policies, such as tax exemptions for tourism investment, may do both.

Passive support for tourism refers to actions by the government that do not directly encourage tourism, but which seek to establish the conditions for its growth. Passive support involves building an economic and regulatory environment that is conducive to investment in tourism, but which does not specifically favour tourism over other industries. This may include improvements in the overall business climate, such as reducing the bureaucratic costs of starting a business or facilitating trade across borders, or general infrastructure improvements, such as rural electrification or upgrades in road quality.

There are pros and cons involved in both approaches. Active support for the tourism industry is more likely to be effective than passive support, insofar as it will likely result in the growth of the tourism industry, but it typically entails considerable costs and there is no guarantee that the results will be sustainable. The costs of using economic policy to actively support any specific industry or sector are numerous and no always obvious. Beyond the explicit fiscal cost of spending on sector-specific infrastructure, tax incentives, training and promotion campaigns, etc., there is also the opportunity cost of not spending those resources elsewhere, for example, on public health, primary education, or development programming in non-tourism-related areas. Finally, it is well worth considering the economic efficiency costs of active support. By establishing policies that favour one industry over others the government skews the allocation of private capital. In the best-case scenario, these policies jump-start the growth of the target industry, which then continues to expand under its own momentum; in the worst-case scenario, however, these policies create an artificially profitable industry that is dependent upon government support and cannot exist without it. One should also reflect on the political implications of creating a favoured constituency with a strong interest in maintaining its economic support (see Chapter 3).

Passive support carries its own advantages and risks. On the positive side, passive-support policies are less distortive and are likely to have broad benefits for the economy as a whole. Business-climate reforms, infrastructure investment programs and other policies that benefit the tourism sector will benefit other sectors as well. Passive-support policies may also have lower explicit costs, especially "stroke-of-the-pen" reforms to reduce the administrative burden and facilitate trade, though similarly low-cost measures such as streamlining visa procedures or enabling a competitive air travel market are available to support the tourism industry specifically. Explicit costs are often a major issue in garnering political support, as these tend to be the most politically "visible" costs associated with economic policies. On the downside, passive support is less likely to achieve specific objectives, such as fostering the growth of the tourism industry, as other economic activities may gain greater traction in a more hospitable economic environment. There is also a considerable risk associated with a potential lack of **tourism policy mainstreaming** in passive-support policies. Active support by definition requires a clear policy focus on tourism development, but passive support does not. Passive-support policies may be undertaken without any particular attention to the tourism industry, and consequently they may encourage the haphazard growth of tourism and the inefficient or even unsustainable exploitation of tourism-related resources.

PARTICIPATION IN THE PLANNING PROCESS

Whilst governments typically take the lead in destination planning—often in close collaboration with the private sector and in many cases with the active involvement of the NGO or donor community—the process of planning involves a wide range of diverse interests, each of which must be taken into account.

Private sector stakeholders alone may include at least three types of commercial interest: (i) those directly involved in the industry, such as tourism firms and investors; (ii) those indirectly involved in the industry, such as suppliers of tourism-related goods or services including transportation and retail; and (iii) those that compete with an existing or potential tourism industry, such as firms in resource-intensive sectors including mining, logging and fishing, whose interests are in direct conflict with those of the tourism industry. It is not enough to include members of just one or two of these groups in the planning process and claim that the private sector is represented. All have a legitimate stake in tourism planning and all deserve to participate in the planning process.

There is generally even greater diversity among civil society groups, and the planning process should not only include the tourism industry's initial supporters, but also those that oppose it or that favour alternative development policy options. Resolving these interests into a consensus vision of the quality of tourism development and the industry's place in the broader economy and society is an essential first step toward long-term sustainability, and is especially critical to ensuring policy continuity. Particular attention should be paid to ensuring the participation of marginalized or disadvantaged groups, such as ethnic or religious minorities, or those whose economic benefit has especially strong spill-over effects on social indicators, such as women and youth.

Non-governmental organisations and bilateral and multilateral aid agencies may also have a strong stake in the tourism development planning process, as they often have policy objectives that are directly impacted by tourism development. Incorporating these groups requires an understanding of their highly valuable competencies and equally critical limitations. NGOs and aid organisations frequently offer detailed knowledge and expertise that may otherwise be in short supply, even among government agencies, and the depth of their understanding is frequently informed by international experience. However, the local knowledge of these groups is highly variable, and they suffer from a number of serious incentive problems associated with the international development industry.[91] In most cases, the appropriate role of NGOs and aid agencies is organisational and advisory. These groups have the connections and resources necessary to organise planning forums and ensure broad-based participation. They can also bring the benefit of their experience to bear in determining on how the planning process should be structured and may offer specific guidance on the benefits and liabilities of alternative strategies. However, it is imperative that these agencies should not overwhelm the planning process or guide it to outcomes that violate the will of the participants.

It is important to recognize at the outset of the planning process that all of these stakeholders are guided by fundamentally positive impulses that reflect their desires for both private and common gain. Stakeholder objectives typically include: (i) *economic development*, as the local economy's capacity to generate wealth and contribute to positive social outcomes is progressively enhanced; (ii) *job creation*, as thriving private enterprise enhances economic

---

91 These have been detailed extensively in the large and growing body of literature critical of development practice. This subject is far too complex to be dealt with adequately here, but the contributions of William Easterly and Dambisa Moyo merit special mention, as do the more positive arguments of Jeffrey Sachs and the nuanced conclusions of Paul Collier.

security and presents new opportunities for employment; (iii) *income and profit*, as the growth of a new industry raises aggregate wage rates and boosts the returns to investment; (iv) *visitor satisfaction*, as tourists enjoy their vacation, return home and recommend the destination to others, enhancing its international profile and supporting the destination's long-term competitiveness; (v) *environmental quality*, as the conservation and promotion of a strong, productive and bio-diverse environment leads to increased general utility along with positive public health and livelihood effects, (vi) *cultural protection*, as this and future generations are able to experience and enjoy their cultural patrimony, taking pride in the traditions and accomplishments of their community; and (vii) *general wellbeing*, as the growth of the tourism industry contributes to a more favorable socioeconomic equilibrium. Although the process of tourism destination planning may be conflicted and even acrimonious, it is essential to recall that all participants want one or more of these outcomes to be realized.

Figure 3: Tourism Planning Participants, Contributions and Objectives

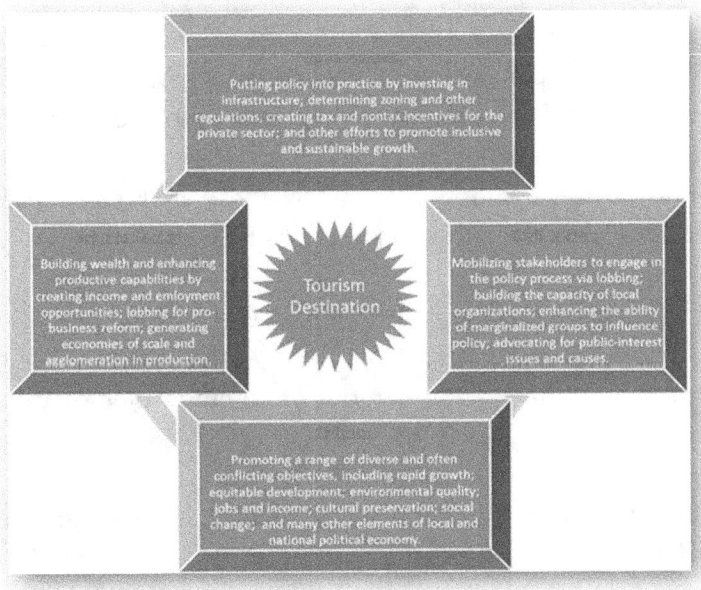

Source: Adapted from Burns (2015)

As always, the major challenge is to ensure that destination planning is conducted through participatory multi-stakeholders processes that encourage long term commitments to development.[92] Economic growth and commercial gain are not the only relevant measures of success in tourism destinations planning. Failure to preserve and protect the natural resources of the destination will diminish its capital base, reducing its drawing power for tourists and likely damaging the quality of life of the local population, while ignoring the value of cultural and social integrity can rapidly create negative attitudes towards the tourism industry, and even towards tourists themselves. An unfriendly or outright hostile attitude towards tourism on the part of local residents can destroy the economic value of a tourist destination as swiftly and surely as environmental degradation or cultural debasement.

Leadership in tourism destination planning must focus not only on the end result of the process but also on building the capacity for collaboration between stakeholders. This indirect but crucial objective of a participatory destination planning process will enable the efficient and productive resolution of conflicts as the industry continues to expand and new concerns emerge. A simple definition of the common goals of all stakeholders involved in tourism destinations planning, quite simple to endorse but very hard to achieve, is: (i) economic viability; (ii) social and cultural acceptability; and (iii) environmental integrity. Ultimately, these are in the interests of all parties involved, however different their positions may appear.

ELEMENTS OF TOURISM PLANNING

Although different destinations will have widely different agendas for tourism planning, there are a number of common themes to consider. These include:

- **Territoriality**: It is necessary to identify clear geographical areas within which tourism development will occur. This may be a single

---

92 Vignati, Federico (2008) Gestão de Destinos Turísticos: como atrair pessoas para polos, cidades e países. Sao Paulo: SENAC

locality, a contiguous region or a set of multiple locations connected by a common, integrated development plan. In the case of the latter, it is important to understand the relevance of so-called "inter-destination bridge ties,"[93] the opportunity to capitalise on one destination's advantages through collaborative efforts with other destinations in the region. Developed destinations may assume an anchor role for regional development, which emerging destinations may use to leverage competitive advantage. Over time, the success of subsidiary destinations may even help to reinforce the position of the anchor destination. The objective of territoriality is to link specific areas to specific tourism modes and objectives and to limit the parameters of tourism development to a manageable focus, but this focus must allow for inter-destination synergies. A territorial perspective is crucial for the identification and analysis of potential economies of scale, scope and agglomeration in tourism, which may be developed within the destination. These issues will be discussed in detail in Chapter 9.

- **Quantitative assessment**: Planning is a process of selecting from a variety of possible alternatives. To guide this process, reliable data are essential and rely on the strong analytical foundations discussed above. Specific areas of assessment include environmental impact analyses, multi-sector economic studies encompassing pro-poor and equity effects, and evaluations of the social development implications of the prospective tourism industry. In order to achieve sustainability it is critical that quantitative assessments go beyond simple economic viability to include an accounting of the stock of environmental and cultural capital, and identify ways in which this capital stock can be preserved and expanded.
- **Comprehensiveness and coordination:** A major threat to the efficiency and sustainability of tourism is the potential for overlapping, unsynchronised or inconsistent actions, whether by public

93 Haugland (2011) "Development of Tourism Destinations: An Integrated Multilevel Perspective," *Annals of Tourism Research* (38)1: 268-290

policymakers or private developers. Tourism planning should be comprehensive and coordinated, both internally (harmonising all tourism projects and policies) and externally (harmonising tourism projects and policies with projects and policies in other economic sectors). Pains should be taken to ensure that tourism development plans are also consistent with relevant local, regional or national environmental plans, land-use plans and infrastructure plans or broader national development master plans.

- **Feasibility:** There is always a tendency in any form of development planning to mistake aspirational goals for achievable ones, to confuse idealism with practicality. In order to be effective a plan must be feasible, even if it is flawed. The actions required by the plan must remain within the bounds of available resources; they must be incorporated into relevant budgets and provided for in the financial planning of the destination government and other funding agencies. They must take into account the limitations of the implementing agencies and the vicissitudes of political circumstances. Moreover—and this is too-frequently overlooked—adequate resources must be available to sustain the commitments of the plan over time. As the American novelist Kurt Vonnegut once wrote, "Another flaw in the human character is that everyone wants to build but nobody wants to do maintenance."[94] This tendency is unfortunately common in international development, where excellent plans are often undone by inadequate concern for their long-term demands.

- **Flexibility and continuity:** Any development plan will inevitably require modifications and reappraisals over time. The planning process must create permanent structures and instruments for incorporating feedback and enabling negotiation, allowing the plan to adapt to changing circumstances, counter new risks and take advantage of emerging opportunities. However, an adequate commitment to the execution of the plan is equally important; a

---

94 Vonnegut, Kurt (1990) Hocus Pocus New York: Putnam and Sons

plan is of little value if it is abandoned with ease. In this respect, destination governance bodies play an essential and complex role: the must adapt to allow for flexibility in the plan while at the same time ensuring its continuity.

PRIMARY OBJECTIVES OF DESTINATION PLANNING

The international tourism industry was not always as accessible as it is today. Globalisation and rising incomes in developed countries have brought tourism to the middle class, but for decades (even centuries) international leisure travel was the province of the wealthy. Modern tourism planning remains largely rooted in the luxury resort model developed in high-end tourist destinations in the Mediterranean, the South Pacific, and the Caribbean, and as a result tourism policymakers often demonstrate an implicit bias in favour of this type of "upscale" tourism, believing that their destination should attempt cater to only the wealthiest tourists. Policymakers may even consider the development of mid-range or budget tourism to be a failure on their part, and possibly in the eyes of their constituents, as these forms of tourism may be perceived to be less valuable or prestigious than "top-end" luxury tourism. In reality, however, the spending power of each tourist is hardly the most reliable metric for the value of the tourism industry, and high-end tourism may not be feasible or even desirable in any given circumstance. **Comparative advantage** and **market segmentation** in international tourism will be discussed in greater detail in Chapters 7 and 9.

Tourism destinations planning seeks to attract targeted tourists, penetrate certain markets, improve the quality of tourism services, expand job-creation capacity, increase of per capita income and build social, cultural and environmental capital. A sound planning framework should be shaped by sustainability issues, market trends and mid-long-term thinking. Planning is one of the main tools available for stimulating the development of tourism and creating the basis for proper destination management.

MONITORING AND EVALUATION

Any plan, no matter its scale, requires an information system to control its execution and evaluate outcomes and impact. Performance indicators and systems for monitoring and evaluation must be incorporated into any development plan. The inclusion of sustainability variables is a more recent sophistication, one born of experience and necessity. The use of measurable indicators in development planning is essential to determining the effectiveness of specific program and policies and to generating new data to inform other planning efforts, either within the country or beyond it.

Tourism plans must therefore include performance indicators and monitoring systems to gauge the effects of their implementation. SNV Netherlands Development Organization and the World Tourism Organization provide a particularly valuable set of sustainability-focused guidelines for monitoring and evaluation:[95]

- Each indicator should measure a specific aspect of sustainability, including its economic, social, cultural and environmental dimensions;
- All indicators should be clearly defined, statistically measurable and comparable over time;
- Indicators should be simple to interpret and relevant to priority areas;
- There is no universal set of sustainability indicators, and indicators for each destination should reflect its unique circumstances and development objectives.

Monitoring and evaluation systems are critical to determining the effectiveness of tourism policies, remaining abreast of changing conditions in the destination and incorporating lessons learned into future

---

95 SNV & UNWTO (2010)

strategies. These issues, as well as more detailed methods for effective data collection and analysis are discussed further in Chapter 8.

CONCLUSION

Strategic planning is a complex process, but it is absolutely indispensable to sustainable tourism development. Because of the tourism industry's exceptional dependence on social, cultural, environmental and other non-traditional forms of capital, it is essential that destination managers form a clear and consistent plan for how these resources may be exploited responsibly and sustainably, enabling tourism firms to generate important economic gains without damaging and depleting the local assets on which the industry's long-term viability depends. Planning can help to identify and resolve potential conflicts in advance, allowing destination managers to negotiate trade-offs between different interests and values in a way that produces the best possible outcomes for destination stakeholders.

In many ways the planning process is as important as the plan itself. A transparent, participatory planning process will encourage popular support and ownership of the resulting plan, increasing its chances for successful implementation. Conversely, plans that are formulated 'behind closed doors' with limited involvement from the private sector and civil society may be viewed as illegitimate or contrary to the interests of key stakeholders. The use of broad consultative mechanisms to incorporate a range of input will produce a plan that more accurately and comprehensively reflects destination conditions and more directly addresses the needs, objectives and aspirations of the diverse stakeholders involved in tourism development. Participation and consultation should be central to all aspects of tourism planning, including the formulation of sector development plans, marketing plans and the destination's overall strategic plan.

Destination managers must always bear in mind that planning is a matter of balancing and aligning the varied interests and goals of numerous actors from the public sector, the private sector and civil society, as well as individual citizens. The objective of the planning process is not merely to incorporate these interests into a single coherent plan; its larger, long-term aim is to increase stakeholders' capacity for productive collaboration. Building and routinizing systems for participation, consultation and cooperation between diverse groups and individuals will not only yield more accurate, comprehensive and popular plans today, but will build the foundation for even better and more sophisticated plans tomorrow.

EXERCISES

1. What is the value of creating a tourism development plan? Why shouldn't tourism industries be allowed to form spontaneously and develop on their own? Or should they?
2. Which public agencies might be expected to take the lead in the planning process, both at the national level and at the local level?
3. In a participatory planning process, what public agencies, private-sector organizations, civil-society groups or other stakeholders might destination managers attempt to organise first?
4. How can destination managers attempt to maximise participation while keeping the planning process manageable?
5. How do participatory planning processes support policy continuity in tourism development? What is the role of democratic institutions in the planning process?
6. Explain the key differences between the "development first" model and the "growth first" model described in the chapter. What are the advantages of each perspective?
7. The chapter lists seven typical stakeholder objectives. What are they? Can you think of any others that might be included?
8. The chapter also lists five elements of a well-designed tourism development plan. What are they? Can you think of any others?

CASE 8 – PUTTING THE BULGARIAN DANUBE ON THE TOURISM MAP.

By Manuel Bollmann and Knut Gerber and Hristomir Hristov from GIZ

A LOOK INTO THE PAST.

Danube - the great European river forms Bulgaria's 480km long northern border to Romania.

In this part of Europe, the Danube has retained its wild charm, biodiversity and intact ecosystems. Forests and wetlands dominate its entire length. Deserted islands enlivened only by birds, riverside marshes and lakes, fishing villages, several towns of around 30,000 inhabitants and only one city of 145,000 – this region has always been far removed from major investment projects or any kind of tourism- The authenticity of its cultural landscape has been preserved. Even for many Bulgarians, the Lower Danube is something of a mystery and land's end. It is definitely time to discover the Bulgarian Danube with its remains of Roman towns, which once guarded the northern frontier of the Empire; ancient Bulgarian and Turkish castles; the best preserved painted rock churches from medieval times; impressive Thracian tombs and Muslim mosque complexes. A number of these monuments are listed as UNESCO World Heritage Sites.

The north-western section of the Bulgarian Danube is often referred to as Bulgaria's least developed region, while its population is characterized by high percentage of cultures with nomadic traditions and other ethnic minorities.

The central section is in all social and economic fields dominated by agriculture and the biggest Bulgarian Danube Municipality Ruse. Here stands also the second and last Bulgarian bridge, which crosses the Danube into Romania.

The eastern part of the Bulgarian Danube region is also still far from being wealthy, but has already been partly influenced by the more developed Bulgarian Black Sea coast economy.

THE TURNING POINT

After a long lasting absence of the Danube as a destination on the Bulgaria and international tourism map, two recent developments have heralded its rebirth: The beginning of the implementation of Europe's macro regional strategy for the Danube basin of 2011 and the adoption of a new Tourism Law in 2013, which demanded the integration and restructuring of country's tourism zones.

In the beginning neither administrations nor NGOs were yet equipped with the capacity to properly adopt and launch the measures proscribed in the strategy and legislature, to absorb the relevant funds for their implementation or to form any kind of organizational structure for managing the newly exclaimed destination (Danube). This changed only after a stakeholder awareness building process was launched and further developed through 2012x and 2013.

Before that relevant action, public and private stakeholders in the region neither shared any kind of information, network nor even communicated bilaterally. A major cause for this were heavily centralized political and economic structures in Bulgaria, which included the tourism industry. Thus the public sector had to initiate change and take the first lead.

The Bulgarian Ministry of Economy and Energy (until 2013 called Ministry of Economy, Energy and Tourism) began to lead the awareness and (pre)implementation process in the Danube region. In addition, it was appointed as co-coordinator of the Priority Filed 3 of the EU Danube Strategy "Culture, Tourism and People to people contacts".

Then in 2012 the German government was asked to support the implementation process of EU Danube Strategy in the tourism sector and on its behalf, was commissioned to advise and support the Ministry on these issues

CHALLENGES.

The GIZ project began its work in 2012, forming first advisory units that would link the Ministry in the capital Sofia with the region via 2 office structures, one in Sofia and another in Ruse. These offices' main tasks were to assess communication gaps between the different public, private and NGO stakeholders, to link EU Danube Strategy and policy issues with the recipients at Danube, to initialize and support awareness campaigns and to improve advocacy and promotion of the Danube region.

Due to limitations provided in Bulgarian Law, these newly formed units, called Focal Point Destination Danube (FPDD), could not be registered as legal entities. However, this did not turn out to be a real disadvantage because it provided an opportunity to initiate a participative process, which ultimately led to acceptance and a sense of ownership among all of the involved parties.

It also presented a better opportunity to proceed logically towards the FPDD structures, which would ultimately be able to become the foreseen destination management structure, or at least to be recognised as the incubator for an upcoming structure - responsible for tourism management in Danube region.

Within a still ongoing – more technical discussion about the best way forward, the FPDD has argued in favour of establishing a form of Destination Management Organization (DMO) for the Destination Danube. Beyond this, the FPDD still identified a lack of interest, anticipation and feedback in general. A "bottom-up" process to raise awareness among the local population would be needed in order to change this situation, but has yet to be equipped with the necessary resources. FPDD also identified another huge bottle neck – a lack of management capacities to lead such a process – in both the private and the public sector.

At some point in the near future a general decision about a future tourism structure will be necessary. But in order to improve awareness and knowledge among public and private stakeholders about typical DMO roles and tasks and to lay a foundation for building a sense of ownership among the broader Bulgarian society, the most relevant stakeholder group needed to be given special attention.

To cover the main knowledge gaps the FPDD started awareness and Human Capacity Development (HCD) measures with responsible civil servants from municipalities and municipality-owned (outsourced) and with relevance for the region institutions located in. Parallel actions with business representatives were locally/ partly initiated to support the ownership idea, but that will not be reflected in this case study.

OVERCOMING THE CHALLENGES

Unexpectedly two different events occurred. At the GIZ Headquarters in Germany, the specialized division on Sustainable Development through tourism had, independently from explicitly expressed partner demands in Bulgaria, internally developed an innovative multi-module training program on sustainable tourism. The technical content and methods of which were developed together with academic and consultancy partners.

Reflecting the above mentioned gap regarding bottle necks within the Bulgarian project, GIZ advised FPDD to elaborate a capacity building program for the identified first target group. Clear demands on which capacities in particular where needed, had at this point in time not yet been expressed by them.

At GIZ Headquarters, there was a clear objective to conduct a first pilot testing of the training modules so it could later be adequately promoted. In turn the Bulgarian stakeholders were informed about the availability of the different training modules in question and that the training providers were prepared to adopt its content and time frame in a pilot project, and to focus them on the Bulgarian target group's individual demands.

PROBLEMS AND DIFFICULTIES

One of the main challenges was how to approach, identify and select the right participants. In order to maximize positive impacts and sustainability of the training, participants had to fulfill three basic criteria: They had to have certain language capacities in English or German, which would help direct communication with the trainers beyond the basic support that was given by the interpreter. They needed to have a certain scope in their current job-description and carrier perspectives, which would allow them to implement change by applying the new capacities they would learn in the trainings. And finally, their superiors at their respective institutions had to both grant them the time off needed for the training and agree that their employee would have a limited degree of leverage after his training, which would allow for practically applying learning outcomes.

RESULTS

The main results of the project so far include an increased visibility of critical issues in tourism policy, planning and development and a higher awareness of benefits of tourism in Danube region in general. The mayors of different Danube municipalities benefit from the learning outcomes and increased capacities of their employees, which they can now make use of to the benefit of their communities.

Mayors and Nature Park Directors have realized that they now have a group of young experts at their disposal, who are available and able to deal with critical tourism policy issues.

FPDD now has a stable and active group of partners in a network and a better access through them to administrations and other tourism stakeholders.

FPDD has gained a respected voice for addressing Danube tourism related issues to regional and local authorities. Follow up activities include individual trainings (such as two of the training's graduates gaining additional capacities in the "Project Management for Sustainable Development" (PM4SD) funded by the European Union), regular group meetings among the group and with their stakeholders and common regional activities lead by group spirit,. Internationally within other GIZ programs, the new HCD training module and its successful piloting in Bulgaria have resulted in increased demand for implementing the training modules also in other project contexts.

Six

Collaboration and
Competiveness

The highest reward for man's toil is not what he gets for
it, but what he becomes by it.

— JOHN RUSKIN

OBJECTIVES OF THE CHAPTER:

- Explain the importance of collaborative processes in economic
  policy in general and tourism development in particular, and situ-
  ate these processes in the context of competitive markets.
- Assess the specific ways in which multi-stakeholder collaboration
  can contribute to sustainability.
- Present collaboration strategies designed to improve the competitiveness of tourism destinations at the local, national and international levels.

INTRODUCTION

The success of free-market competition as an engine of broad-based
economic growth and sustained poverty reduction has been dramatic,
yet too often it has led policymakers to adopt an oversimplified view of
the virtues of competition and individual self-interest. While the market is

an extraordinary tool for aligning private incentives to serve the common good (see Chapter 1), it is naïve to assume that unfettered competition is always and everywhere the best strategy for achieving superior outcomes, either personal or social. On the one hand, competitive organizational and professional objectives can stimulate learning and adaptation, promoting technological progress and enhancing the economic productivity. On the other hand, competitive forces can be deeply destructive, particularly in non-standard markets that do not conform to the traditional rules for efficient competition, or in situations where the fundamental political and administrative prerequisites for efficient competition have not been met.

Unregulated economic competition has proven especially ill-equipped to promote social cohesion, protect cultural values, or tackle issues of environmental quality and the conservation of biodiversity. A growing awareness of the limitations of competition has led to a new appreciation for collaboration and the virtues of cooperative solutions, perspectives which are currently gaining ground in the literature of international development. Due to the unique characteristics of the tourism industry and the complexity and diversity of objectives at stake, multi-stakeholder collaboration is increasingly recognised as vital to sustainable tourism development, both in advanced and developing economies.

An essential difference between collaboration and competition, and a major determinant of their respective advantages, is the way that the objectives of the participants are defined. In some situations different interests attempt to allocate a limited quantity of resources between them. This is called a **zero-sum game**. In these situations, competition can ensure that finite resources are allocated to those who value them the most, and who can make the most productive use of them. However, in certain circumstances pure competition over limited resources can lead to less-than-optimal outcomes for some or all of the participants. Collaboration, by contrast, allows participants to transform the nature of the contest itself. By working together, and in some cases even voluntarily deferring their immediate interests in the service of a greater objective, competitors can convert a zero-sum game into a **positive-sum game**, generating greater benefits for themselves as a group than they could possibly achieve as individuals.

Some real-world situations are either purely competitive or purely collaborative, but many combine elements of both. Although they may appear contradictory, competition and collaboration frequently operate in harmony, each supporting and promoting the other; but this harmony is not achieved by accident. Consider, for example, a professional football player. He and his team are locked in a purely competitive struggle with the opposing team. A football match is a zero-sum game: if one team is to win, the other must lose, and no superior outcome can be achieved through collaboration. The player, meanwhile, collaborates with his team in a joint effort to win the match: no player, no matter how skilled, can win without the support of his team, and his objective in the match is not severable from that of his teammates. Either the entire team wins, or the entire team loses; the outcome for one is the outcome for all.

But even as the player collaborates with his team to win the match, he is also involved in a longer-term competition with his own teammates. Players face strong incentives to stand out from their teams as they strive to achieve superior statistics and attain recognition as "star players". If the players' individual incentives to excel in the sport are well aligned with their group incentive to win the match, the team will be greatly strengthened and the players will benefit both as individuals and as a group. If, however, their competitive incentive to excel personally overrides their collaborative interest in winning the match, a group of star players may fail to cohere as a team and lose despite their individual prowess. Conversely, team members that care about winning the next match, but not about their personal development as players may collaborate well, yet fail to improve their individual skills over time, ultimately weakening their collective ability to win.

Economies function in much the same way. They are driven by competitive contests over scarce resources, but these contests occur within a framework of rules, institutions and social norms that align individual incentives to further common interests and achieve joint objectives. This is true at the national level—where robust competition between firms, undertaken within a well-designed legal and regulatory framework, produces wealth for the firm and economic strength for the nation—and it is often true for specific industries as well. Even firms that directly compete with one another in the same market typically share a common set of interests and objectives, and they can often achieve superior outcomes by working together in some areas while competing in others.

BOX 8 - AIR UNFAIR: COLLABORATION AND CARTELISATION

So strong is the power of collaboration in private markets that many of the most essential business regulations exist solely to prevent firms from collaborating, rather than competing. Firms often attempt to collaborate in order to achieve superior outcomes as a group than they could as individuals, highlighting the considerable advantages of collaboration even, or indeed especially, in competitive systems. However, in many cases these positive outcomes for the collaborating firms would be realised at the expense of the public and at a net loss to the economy.

This phenomenon is known as "cartelisation". It occurs when firms in a given market join together to form a cartel—a kind of cooperative group—which allows them to manipulate prices ("price fixing"), divide up control of markets ("local monopolisation"), or otherwise subvert competition in order to generate increased profits at the expense of consumers, other firms, and the efficiency of the economy as a whole. Cartelisation is not always possible: it requires that there be a limited number of firms operating in the market, with barriers to the entry of new firms, and that the firms which form the cartel are able to observe each other's behaviour and ensure that no member is violating the cartel's agreements.

The airline industry fits these criteria, and as a result airlines are frequently charged with cartelisation. A limited number of carriers fly any given route, and the finite supply of available terminal space creates a structural barrier to the entry of new competitors. Airfares and schedules are clearly publicised and readily available to anyone, making it easy for airlines to keep tabs on one another. Imagine two cities, City A and City B, each with one airport; flights between them are offered by four competing airlines, which together lease all the terminals at both airports. Competition between airlines has pushed ticket prices all four airlines to around US$100 for flights between City A and City B.

Now, imagine that you are the CEO of one of these airlines. One day you're invited to an industry meeting attended by the CEOs of the other three. The conversation soon turns to the City A – City B route and how you're all just barely squeaking out a profit, what with ticket prices so low. Then, one of your colleagues suggests that the route would become far more profitable if you all just agree, right then and there, to raise ticket prices to US$150; you would all lose some business, as fewer customers would be able to pay the higher ticket price, but you would more than make it back in revenues from the remaining sales. This is price fixing.

Alternatively, one of you might suggest that the group agree to cede control of the all airport terminals on the A – B route to one of your four airlines in exchange for that airline giving up its terminals on other routes, turning a competitive market into a patchwork of local monopolies. In either case the agreement would be easy to enforce, since you all know each other's ticket prices and flight schedules, and as long as your four airlines hold leases on all of the terminals involved no new competitors can upset the balance. This is local monopolisation.

The propensity of firms to collaborate at the expense of the general interest has long been recognised. In <u>The Wealth of Nations</u> (1776) Adam Smith famously noted that "seldom do members of the same trade gather together for any purpose but that it ends in a conspiracy against the public". Though more than a century and a half separated Adam Smith from commercial air travel, he is referring to exactly the situation outlined in the example above. Since the increased profits of the cartel are achieved by subverting competitive forces, the cartel's existence damages the interests of consumers, reduces the efficiency of the airline industry as a whole, and may have deeply negative consequences for other industries that rely on air travel. It is, in effect, a conspiracy against the public, and for this reason virtually every country has laws designed to prevent this type of collaboration. However, these are not always successful, and maintaining competition in cartelisation-prone markets is a constant challenge. In designing systems for productive collaboration between stakeholders in the tourism industry it is important to guard against the possibility of excessive, even illegal, forms of economic collusion.

A similar competitive/collaborative dynamic operates in democratic systems. Politicians compete with each other in elections—a zero-sum game, as only one candidate can win—but in an effort to ultimately collaborate on the joint endeavour of promoting the welfare of the nation. Interest groups within civil society also function this way, each attempting to advance its objectives, often at the expense of other groups, but all benefit collectively from the collaborative framework of democratic processes. Competition and collaboration within political systems is a positive-sum game: even if one party or interest group would benefit dramatically from the elimination of political competition that advantage would come at an enormous cost to all others. Subordinating one's individual interest in dominating the political system and instead agreeing to operate within its rules and competitive structures greatly advances one's interest as a member of a group. While democracies must be constantly vigilant against corruption, patronage and undue influence, the general recognition that people and associations gain more by collaborating with one another within a competitive democratic framework than they would by subverting that system is what enables democracies to sustain themselves over time.

But democracy is about more than zero-sum games between competing interests. As democratic processes become more sophisticated competing interests will build their capacity for productive collaboration, achieving more as a group than they could as individuals. Advancements in consensus-building and participatory decision-making techniques are reflected in the growing literature of collaborative process and in the establishment of new forms of social, political and economic organisation. On particular, numerous innovative systems for public-private collaboration have been developed in recent years, many of which have proven remarkably successful in areas such as social-service provision and environmental protection.

Public agencies, private firms, civil society groups, local and international NGOs and other stakeholders are perhaps best understood as elements of an integrated system, cable of coordinating with one another in order to achieve commonly held objectives while at also competing with one another to maximise technical and distributional efficiency. The institutions, processes, rules and norms to guide collaborative efforts are as essential as those that regulate competition. Building the foundation for collaborative systems, and establishing the atmosphere of reflexive trust and cooperation that enables them to thrive, cannot be accomplished overnight. Although effective multi-stakeholder collaboration is initially a matter of legal, regulatory and organizational systems, ultimately it is the habits and values created by these systems that yield the greatest benefits, as participants become increasingly accustomed to formulating collaborative solutions to joint problems rather than automatically viewing any conflict as a zero-sum game to be either won or lost.

The economic and social costs of zero-sum competition are often very high. In pure economic terms unfettered competition without sufficient collaborative processes in place may be subject to "market failures" including the collective action problems described in previous chapters as well as the more common efficiency issues associated with **positive and negative externalities**. Externalities occur when the private decisions of certain individuals or firms impact other individuals or firms, either positively or negatively, creating costs and benefits that are not subject to market mechanisms. Externalities are extremely important in the tourism industry, in which so much economic (as well as social, cultural and environmental) value is fundamentally dependent on the decisions of multiple uncoordinated actors. Those affected by externalities cannot either reward or discourage those decisions through the market itself, which results in the systematic overproduction of negative externalities and the underproduction of positive ones.[96] While laws and regulations can help to combat negative externalities, increasing positive externalities frequently requires collaboration, not merely between firms, but between firms, public sector agencies, civil society groups and a range of other stakeholders.

This is the broader challenge of collaboration: to establish systems for deliberation and joint action not only within any given sphere of activity—the economy, the government, civil society—but between these sectors as well. Going forward, we will examine collaboration in sustainable tourism development from the perspective of stakeholders cooperating both within and between these broad sectors of society, examining opportunities for productive cooperation and the harmonization of incentives.

---

96 This definition is adapted from the classic article by James Buchanan and Craig Stubblebine (1962) "Externality" *Economica* 29(116): 371–384.

PRINCIPLES OF COLLABORATION

The process of collaboration is based on several fundamental criteria which are critical to its success. A collaborative process that fails to meet one or more of these criteria will likely be abandoned by some or all of its participants and consequently fail to meet its objectives. Although it may become easier over time, as systems become more firmly established and participants become habituated to them, ensuring that collaborative processes are satisfactory to all participants is itself a continuous process. The specific criteria for satisfaction may be different in different social contexts, but their most basic elements include:

Mutual benefit, as all participants must be aware of the potential gains that can be achieved through collaboration and how their individual interests relate to those of other stakeholders. In order to sustain a voluntary collaborative process all participants must believe that they can accomplish more in partnership with other stakeholders than they could on their own. The perception of mutual benefit depends a great deal on the past experiences and expectations of the participants, as well as organizational cultures and prevailing social norms. Collaboration requires that stakeholders suspend their immediate interests as individuals in order to serve their broader interests as members of a group, and their willingness to do so reflects the extent to which they trust their fellow stakeholders to do the same. Participants that have a history of mutually beneficial collaboration will be likely to appreciate the advantages of working together; while participants who are not used to collaboration, who have an acrimonious history, or who have had negative experiences with similar cooperative efforts in the past may tend to focus on its downside risks. Demonstrating the mutual benefits available to all participants in a collaborative process is the first step in building a set of long-term relationships based on trust. Developing these relationships and maintaining them over time requires a high degree of:

Transparency, as the participants must have confidence in the fundamental fairness of the collaborative process and in the compliance of their collaborating partners. Procedures for offering input and making joint decisions should be simple and straightforward, and care should be taken to ensure that all participants fully understand how the collaborative process works. Monitoring is also important to transparency, and participants should be satisfied that the other stakeholders are adhering to the collaborative process and honouring their obligations to it. It is not necessary that each participant should know all about the others, but all participants must have essential confidence in their common interests and trust in the commitments they undertake together. Transparency helps to ensure that no one is gaining undue advantage at the expense of their collaborating partners, and is consequently vital to maintaining their:

Equality, as no participant should have excessive influence over the process or its outcomes. An effective collaboration should be based on impartial systems for discussion and decision-making that implicitly recognizes and respects the equal rights of all participants. This requires establishing mechanisms to ensure that relations are established on the basis of common interest, and that no participant or stakeholder group is able to exercise power over others solely because of their political or financial resources, or the social clout of one group over another. This is no easy task, and the power dynamics of the broader society will tend to replicate themselves despite the best efforts of those organising the collaboration. Fortunately, there is a large and growing literature on establishing democratic processes for multi-stakeholder collaboration, which can be drawn upon to help ensure that the fundamental equality of all participants is respected.[97]

Multi-stakeholder collaboration can be a decisive factor in the development of a tourism destination due to the unusually high returns to coordinated decision-making inherent in the tourism industry. The success of tourism, how the industry evolves and shapes itself in any given destination, is a combination of numerous interrelated factors, why are

---

97 See, e.g., Hemmati, Minu (2002) Multi-Stakeholder Processes for Governance and Sustainability: Beyond Deadlock and Conflict London: Earthscan Publishing

beyond the control of any individual stakeholder. Multiple economic sectors are vital to the industry, including international and local transportation, hotels and restaurants, and tours, activities and attractions. These services are typically offered by a range of different firms, which compete with one another while also sharing a common interest in the success of the tourism industry as a whole.

Meanwhile, a number of non-economic assets (or assets that are not commonly viewed in economic terms), such as the social and political stability of the destination, the cultural affinity of the population for tourism, local rates of crime and violence, and the quality of both the natural and man-made environments all exert a powerful influence over the development of a tourism destination. Ensuring that the contribution of these factors is positive requires the involvement of far more stakeholders from not just the private sector, but also the government and, especially, civil society. A robust and sustainable tourism industry is the result of simultaneously competitive and collaborative work between tourism firms and between those firms and the wide range of other public and private interests at work within the destination.

COLLABORATIVE STRATEGIES TO IMPROVE COMPETITIVENESS

The competitiveness of tourism destinations depends not only on their absolute and comparative advantages, subjects which will be discussed further in Chapter 7, but also on their ability to adapt to dynamic market conditions. A successful tourism destination must continuously confront five competitive challenges. These are: (i) the threat posed by rival tourism destinations; (ii) the threat posed by alternatives to tourism; (iii) the bargaining power of suppliers; (iv) the bargaining power of customers; and (v) conflict among competitors. Collaborative strategies can strengthen the position of the tourism destination, addressing the unique challenges associated with each of these dimensions of competiveness. You should know six strategies for collaboration to improve the competitiveness of tourism destinations:

Collaboration and overall destination competitiveness: The total number of tourism destinations worldwide is steadily increasing as a result of the ever-expanding international physical and economic infrastructure that is at the heart of the globalisation process. Investment reaches new destinations and builds their tourism capacity, stronger transportation networks make remote areas more accessible, rising wage rates in emerging economies boost global demand for tourism,[98] and ever more local and national governments come to recognize the economic potential of tourism and work to promote new destinations or expand existing ones. Since at any given time demand for tourism services is finite, all tourism destinations are, to a greater or lesser extent, competitors with one another; the performance of one destination can have enormous implications for others, especially if they both draw from the same source markets. Recall, for example, the impact of political instability in North Africa on Cape Verdean tourism discussed in Chapter 3.

In this respect all tourism firms operating in one destination, though they compete with one another within their destination market, also share a common interest in the success of their destination. There a number of ways in which collaboration can serve this interest; however, it must be borne in mind that this collaboration should not take place exclusively between tourism firms, but must also involve the active engagement of representatives from the government, civil society, and the affected communities. In some cases NGOs, international aid agencies or other relevant stakeholders should also be included, especially where they can offer specific knowledge or experience that may not otherwise be available.

One strategy to improve the competitiveness of the destination as a whole is to encourage large-scale infrastructure investment. Increasing

---

98 In 2012 China became the world's top tourism source market in terms of total expenditure. See UNWTO (2012) "China – The New Number One Tourism Source Market in the World" *World Tourism Organization Press Release No.13020* Madrid: UNWTO http://media.unwto.org/en/press-release/2013-04-04/china-new-number-one-tourism-source-market-world

the availability of transportation and decreasing transportation costs, enhancing basic services such as electricity, water and sanitation, as well as more sophisticated infrastructure such as internet bandwidth, and investing in the development and/or rehabilitation of tourism-related cultural, historical or environmental assets can enhance the market position of an entire destination. This can increase the profitability of all tourism firms operating in the destination without diminishing or distorting the competitive incentives between them. For example, Brazil's Tourism Development Program has invested US$1.47 billion in tourism infrastructure in the country's northeast, with the objective of facilitating access to the region and improve the quality of public services of its main tourism destinations. This approach has been highly successful, and improvements in infrastructure can have important spill-over effects on non-tourism-related employment and social indicators.

Large-scale investment in regional development is note restricted to countries with infrastructure deficits. In Europe, where basic infrastructure is already extensive and high-quality, the governments of Germany, France, England and Spain established a consortium with the airplane manufacturer Airbus to build the largest passenger plane in history, the A380, which carries up to 555 passengers. It is expected that the A360 will reduce operating costs and air-traffic congestion while enhancing the experience of air travel. This strategy is especially notable for being a multi-country collaboration designed to benefit "Western Europe" as an integrated tourist destination. Countries in many other parts of world may benefit from a similarly collaborative approach, a subject which will be discussed in greater detail in Chapter 7.

Collaboration and corporate brand identity: Much like individual firms tourism destinations often strive to cultivate their own particular brand. The destination's collective ("corporate") brand can benefit all tourism firms simultaneously, much in the same way as large-scale infrastructure investment. Corporate branding can also help to coordinate private investment around a common vision of the destination's "identity". How this identity is defined has very important implications for the local population and public agencies, and again it is extremely important that this identity is determined through a broadly consultative multi-stakeholder process.

Consider, for example, one of the most successful corporate branding efforts in recent memory, the now-famous slogan of Las Vegas, Nevada, "What Happens in Vegas Stays in Vegas". More than a catchy motto, this brand identity capitalised on the destination's pre-existing reputation for licentiousness. As such it could have proven highly controversial among local residents had it not come at the end of a decade-long campaign to clean-up Las Vegas' image and promote it as a family-friendly destination. In this context the slogan came across as a winking allusion to the city's reputation without constituting an endorsement of seediness or criminality.

Corporate branding can also be applied at the national level. In an effort to promote international tourism in Ethiopia the national air carrier, Ethiopian Airlines, adopted the much-beloved slogan "13 Months of Sunshine" as way to emphasise both the country's warm climate and its cultural uniqueness. The Ethiopian Ge'ez calendar has 13 months, and it is the liturgical calendar for the Ethiopian Orthodox Church. Orthodoxy is both a central element of the country's cultural identity and a major tourism draw: many of the country's most-visited attractions (both for domestic and international tourists) are religious sites, including the island monasteries of Lake Tana and the rock-hewn churches of Lalibela. This slogan is not only well-designed from a marketing perspective, it is also highly popular in Ethiopia and among the Ethiopian diaspora,[99] as it emphasises two national features that are uncontroversial sources of pride for the majority of Ethiopians.

---

99 "13 Months of Sunshine" is the title of both a 2007 Ethiopian hit film and an enduringly popular song by Ziggy Marley.

The benefits of a strong corporate identity are numerous and will be discussed further in the following chapter. It may not be feasible to produce a tourism slogan through collaboration (this is a creative process that in most cases should be contracted to a professional public relations firm) multi-stakeholder collaboration can be used to ensure that the destination's corporate identity reflects the aspirations of policymakers, tourism firms, and the public as a whole. A brand identity that conflicts with the interests and objectives of one or more of these groups will likely meet significant resistance and may prove unsustainable over time. Tourism destination governments should formulate marketing policies for the sector jointly with private firms and civil society representatives so that the destination can transmit an image that is both economically and socially successful.

Collaboration and tourism information: The internet has proven to be an enormously powerful tool for publicising tourism destinations and disseminating information about tourism-related services. Although many private information service providers may already offer information about a given destination and the firms operating there, there are nevertheless considerable benefits to establishing a common web portal for the destination as a whole. A common web portal can help to reinforce corporate identity—website development played a critical role in the growth of tourism in Iraqi Kurdistan, as described in the previous chapter—but its most immediate purpose is to aggregate information for ease of use.

Tourism is subject to "search costs" in much the same way as other industries. Prospective customers will only spend so much time attempting to access information about the products on offer at a given destination and comparing that information with potential alternatives. Facilitating access to information boosts the competitiveness of the tourism industry as a whole by cutting search costs. There are also economic benefits to aggregating diversity: presenting a wide range of products and services in the same place can attract more total customers than each of the various product and service providers could attract on their own.

Like infrastructure investment plans and corporate branding campaigns, tourism portals can be established at the local, regional, national or even international level. The city of Sydney, Australia has its own tourism portal (www.sydney.com.au), as does the Cusco region of Peru (www.cuscoonline.com), the US State of Hawaii (www.hawaii.com), the nation of China (www.cnto.org) and the 32 nations and territories that make up the Caribbean Tourism Organization (www.onecarribean.org). Each emphasises the diversity of tourism experiences on offer in the destination and facilitates access to both public and private resources related to the tourism industry. The accuracy of this information, the ease of accessing it, and even the attractiveness of its presentation all contribute to enhancing the competitiveness of the destination.

Collaboration and local sourcing: As tourism destinations develop they consume larger and larger volumes of goods and services. Large-scale tourism firms in particular may have difficulty satisfying these demands within the local economy, and they may consequently fill the gap with imports. This is especially true of food and beverage purchasing in large, all-inclusive resort hotels, and though it also occurs in many other areas of the tourist trade, this particular case provides an especially clear example.

Large resorts that provide food and beverage service as part of their all-inclusive packages often have difficulty either obtaining sufficient quantities of basic ingredients, or ensuring that what they do buy is of adequate and consistent quality and reliable availability. This is because local foodstuffs markets in tourism destinations—and especially in small islands or other remote locations—tend to be small and designed to serve individual customers. Numerous producers, in many cases family farmers or artisanal fishermen, each market a small quantity of goods, either selling them directly to consumers or via intermediary traders. This distribution model may be well-suited to the demands of the local food market, but it is ill-equipped to handle the needs of large-scale purchasers such as resort hotels. Consequently, large resorts frequently import basic foodstuffs even when these goods are available in the local market.

It is important to note that, all other things being equal, resorts and other tourism firms generally want to buy locally, as local goods are almost invariably less expensive than comparable imports. The inability of the local foodstuff supply model to meet the demand of large-scale buyers is due to the presence of one or more market failures in the destination economy, failures which arise because the private linkages between producers, and between producers and purchasers, are not sufficiently strong to allow for efficient scalability in production and marketing. Structural costs associated with limited information about available produce and the difficulty of establishing long-term relationships between producers and purchasers undermine the ability of tourism firms to procure goods and services locally, forcing them to rely on more expensive imports. Consequently, assisting tourism firms in sourcing their goods locally can not only help to boost local livelihoods and minimise the import **leakages** discussed in Chapter 4, it can also increase the competitiveness and overall economic efficiency of the destination by rectifying the underlying market failure that prevents buyers from making large-scale purchases with confidence in the consistent quality and ready availability of locally produced goods.

Local sourcing initiatives provide an opportunity for collaboration both between the government and the private sector and between multiple individual firms, including both producers and consumers. In the case of local food and beverage supply, the first step is generally to organise producers into one or more marketing groups. These are voluntary associations that allow farmers, fishermen, ranchers and other producers to pool their produce and market it collectively to large-scale buyers in exchange for higher prices and/or more favourable terms then they could expect in the traditional small-scale food market. Local marketing groups are able to attenuate market failures by providing prospective buyers with information on the quality, availability and price of locally produced goods and by negotiating purchasing terms on behalf of their constituent producers. However, it is essential to recognise that the effectiveness of a marketing group is directly dependent on the reliability of its information and on the credibility of its agreements. Much like a private firm, a marketing group that cannot meet its commitments and build trust with its clients will swiftly fail.

Addressing market failures is rarely easy, and improving local sourcing through marketing groups involves a number of important challenges. These obstacles, and strategies for overcoming them, are described in a growing body of literature on public policy and development microeconomics. In broad terms, a local-sourcing initiative should begin by identifying which tourism-related imports could potentially be supplied by the local market. It should then determine precisely why the local market is failing to meet the needs of purchasers and then assess the feasibility of alternative strategies for building stronger linkages between tourism firms and the local market. The active cooperation of tourism firms and local producers is essential at every step of the process.

Collaboration and the quality of tourism policy: As described in Chapters 2 and 3, tourism firms can unite to form a powerful political interest group, and like all interest groups these firms will tend to encourage policies that favour themselves, even at the expense of the broader public good. In some cases, tourism firms may even lobby for policies that actually reduce the competitiveness of the tourism industry itself. This may appear self-defeating, but it reveals the extent to which the tourism firms operating in a given destination do not represent the interests of the destination's tourism sector as a whole, but merely their own joint interests as individual firms. For example, tourism firms may use their political influence to advocate for strict land-use policies, restrictions on foreign property ownership, local content requirements for new investment projects, or other laws designed to protect existing tourism firms from new entrants into the market. Political measures that create barriers to entry in the tourism sector will decrease competitive pressures, enhancing the profitability of existing firms at the expense of economic efficiency and overall destination competitiveness.

This is just one example of the many ways in which tourism firms may collaborate in an effort to make the destination's tourism policies serve their own narrowly construed interests. Yet in most cases the solution is more collaboration, not less. Encouraging tourism industry associations to incorporate representatives of the government, civil society and the NGO sector and establishing regular forums for dialogue between multiple tourism-related advocacy groups reflecting a range of policy interests, can greatly improve the quality of the policies advocated. Collaboration will not change the fundamental self-interest of tourism firms—nor should it—but these firms will realise that their policy advocacy will be more effective if they have the support of a coalition of interest groups, and that they can form such a coalition by adapting their public policy agenda to serve a wider range of objectives that more accurately reflect the public interest. Efforts to broaden public policy collaboration can be complemented by establishing or reinforcing mechanisms for independent oversight of the public policy and advocacy processes in order to ensure their integrity, transparency and impartiality. As with nearly all aspects of collaboration in tourism development, broad public policy collaboration and effective oversight depend on strong civil society associations and the **democratic institutions** that make a strong civil society possible.

THE INSTITUTIONAL FRAMEWORK FOR COLLABORATION

Many tourism destinations have created institutions, organisations and public forums specifically designed to facilitate collaboration between the public sector, the private sectors and civil society on issues related to the tourism industry. In countries with that enjoy political stability and a healthy civil society, these collaborative institutions are often complemented by a range of formal and informal associations and networks, which may arise spontaneously without the need for any explicit attempt at fostering collaboration. Countries with sophisticated and well-established tourism industries often have a large number of these institutions and associations. Some common forms include:

Tourism Councils: These organizations are typically established under the auspices of a government agency but comprise representatives of the private sector, civil society and, in some cases, a country's development partners.[100] Tourism councils can operate at the national, regional or local level, and while they may be officially sanctioned, they are not generally considered organs of the government and are distinct from tourism ministries or other government agencies. Tourism councils are primarily devoted to promoting a shared vision for the development of tourism; they often take the lead in organising multi-stakeholder dialogue on tourism issues and frequently play an important role in defining tourism policies and in promoting the destination in source markets. The responsibilities of the tourism council encompass all the dimensions of collaboration described above, but are particularly relevant to corporate brand identity, tourism information, and the quality of tourism policy. Tourism councils are often responsible for a wide range of support services, from tourism knowledge exchange to policy advice to advertising, outreach and advocacy.[101] There is a great deal of varia-

---

100 This includes domestic and international NGOs as well as bilateral and multilateral aid agencies. These groups are often included in a technical or advisory capacity, which helps to ensure local control while taking advantage of the skills and experience offered by these groups.

101 The Tourism Council of Thailand is an excellent example of how tourism councils are often organised and the diversity of issues they are tasked with. The Tourism Council of Thailand was established by the Thai government under the Tourism Council Act, BE 2544 (2000) as a private corporate entity authorized to pursue a set of specified activities. The Tourism Council is charged with organizing representatives of the public and private sectors, promoting the growth of the tourism industry, preserving Thailand's heritage and cultural identity, monitoring the quality and ethical integrity of the tourism industry, contributing to education, research and training on tourism-related issues, providing advice on tourism policy, and encouraging the integrated participation of local governments in national tourism, among other functions and objectives. For more, see: http://www.thailandtourismcouncil.org/th/about.php.

tion in how tourism councils are organised, but whatever their structure, a formal collaborative platform is essential to any tourism destination committed to inclusive and sustainable development.

Research Agencies: These are statistical and analytical groups tasked with compiling essential information on the tourism industry. Tourism research agencies may be specially designated offices of the government's national tourism authority or its national statistical agency, which focus on the data needs of government policymakers; academic institutions that work in partnership with the government, the private sector or civil society groups to execute specific research assignments or monitoring and evaluation activities; or they may be private firms that provide market intelligence on tourism to the government or private firms. Tourism research examines prevailing market conditions and helps to identify constraints that can be addressed through public policy. They also analyse the impact of tourism on local populations and estimate its contribution to employment, gross domestic product, export revenues and other micro- and macroeconomic indicators. The work of tourism research agencies produces market intelligence that is valuable to the private sector and social assessments of the tourism industry that are relevant to civil society groups; these agencies serve an important function in multi-stakeholder collaboration by providing a common frame of reference for discussions of the nature, impact and future prospects of the tourism industry.

Industry Associations: These are formal or informal networks of tourism firms and other private sector organisations that focus on advancing the shared interests of firms operating in the tourism sector or those with a strong stake in it, such as transportation providers, importers and retailers. Industry associations share information on common obstacles and opportunities in the tourism sector and advocate for favourable policies at the national, regional and local levels. As described above, these policies do not always accord with the national interest, and may focus on short-term economic gains over long term sustainability. This makes industry associations a prime target for inclusion in collaborative processes. Encouraging industry associations to incorporate more diverse views and welcoming the participation of industry associations in larger consultative forums can help to broaden their perspective, introducing issues and concerns that are relevant for the sustainability—and ultimately the profitability—of the tourism industry, but which might otherwise receive insufficient attention. For example, shifts in public opinion either in favour or against tourism development can have crucial implications for firms in the sector, but industry associations that fail to incorporate government and civil society representatives may be unaware of key social and political developments. Conversely, industry associations may be uniquely suited to improve the quality of tourism policy, as they often have highly accurate knowledge about both local and international tourism markets. For example, they can alert policymakers and civil society representatives when they attempt to undertake measures that are well-meaning, but economically infeasible. Government agencies and civil society groups should work to form bonds of trust and transparency with tourism industry associations as a central objective in their collaborative development strategy.

CONCLUSIONS

Like many other industries, the political economy of tourism is highly complex, and what serves the interest of any one stakeholder does not necessarily serve the interest of the public at large. Moreover, the myopic pursuit of narrowly construed self-interest can prove counterproductive if it undermines larger shared objectives. Continuous dialogue and active cooperation between the government, the private sector and civil society are essential elements of economic, social, cultural and environmental sustainability, as collaboration enables individual stakeholders to balance their personal and collective interests, achieving better outcomes as a group than they would be capable of as individuals.

The tourism industry is unusual in many ways, but one of the most important is that tourist satisfaction does not depend solely on the quality of services provided by a single firm; rather, it is a function of the overall experience offered by multiple firms across a range of sectors—accommodation, transportation, food service, retail, and many others—as well as the sum of the interactions, both economic and noneconomic, that take place between the tourist and the host community.

Collaboration between different public, private and civil society actors can allow firms to better address the demands of their customers, and help to ensure that all forms of local capital—economic, social, cultural and environmental—are preserved and enhanced. Building a consensus among destination stakeholders that they are participants in a positive-sum game and fostering an awareness of their shared interests requires understanding the local tourism industry as a single cohesive, integrated unit. This will be the subject of the following chapter.

EXERCISES

1. Explain the difference between a zero-sum game and a positive-sum game. Think of at least one real-world example of each.
2. Define externality and explain its relevance to collaborative decision-making.
3. Describe a situation in which collaboration between private enterprises can lead to negative economic and social outcomes. Define the terms "price-fixing" and "local monopoly".
4. Describe a situation in which collaboration between the government, the private sector, and civil society groups can allow them to solve a problem together that no one group could solve on its own.
5. Discuss the role of democratic institutions in multi-stakeholder collaboration and identify mechanisms for collaboration, whether discussed in the chapter or not.

6. Identify at least two tourism destinations that have a distinct corporate brand identity and discuss how those brands relate to their cultural identity.

7. Discuss the obstacles and advantages to local sourcing of tourism inputs.

8. In your opinion, what are some of the main barriers to collaboration between the government, the private sector and civil society? How might they be addressed?

CASE 9 - DESERT TOURISM AS A VEHICLE FOR NATURE CONSERVATION: THE JORDANIAN EXPERIENCE

By Mohammed Zaarour, Director at RSCN - mohammed.zaarour@rscn. org.jo

SYNOPSIS

The Royal Society for the Conservation of Nature (RSCN), a long established Jordanian NGO, has been developing tourism ventures in its desert parks for over twelve years as a means of generating revenue, community benefits and awareness to support its conservation goals. Its first venture was in the spectacular Dana Nature Reserve, at the edge of the Jordan Rift valley, where an array of eco-tourism facilities and activities were developed that now attract over 35,000 visitors a year and provide enough revenue to cover most of the Reserve's running costs. Dana is widely considered as a regional model of sustainable biodiversity conservation and the RSCN has been applying 'Dana principles' to all its protected areas. This paper examines the effectiveness of these ventures in meeting conservation goals and presents the major lessons learned and hopes for the future.

BACKGROUND

Jordan is a small arid country, with a remarkable diversity of desert ecosystems, from extensive plains of basalt gravels and rocks, known as *Hamada*, to classical sand dune systems and dry mountain ranges. They include the grand desert of Wadi Rum, with its monolithic towering cliffs of sandstone; internationally famous as a tourist site and as the dramatic backdrop to sequences in the vintage film 'Lawrence of Arabia'. Along the western flank of the Kingdom runs a mountainous escarpment forming one edge of the Jordan Rift Valley, where the desert landscape gradually changes with altitude to dry steppe and open Mediterranean Forest. Some areas along this escarpment, where desert vegetation grades into more moisture-loving plant communities, are very rich in biodiversity and continue to support scarce large mammals like wolves, hyenas and ibex.

The protection and management of Jordan's special ecosystems is entrusted to a non-governmental organization, the Royal Society for the Conservation of Nature (RSCN). It is one of the few NGOs in the world given such a national mandate by government. The Society was formed in 1966 by a group of disillusioned hunters, worried about dwindling populations of game animals and was the earliest voluntary conservation organization to be established in the Middle East. It started its first conservation programme in the Eastern Desert, with the creation of the Shaumari Nature Reserve as a release site for the critically endangered Arabian Oryx and is now responsible for six protected areas, covering a land area of over 700 square kilometers. These protected areas represent some of the finest landscapes and ecological systems in the Kingdom and vary in size from the desert oasis of Azraq, at 23 square kilometers, to the mountainous wild lands of the Dana Nature Reserve, at 320 square kilometers (Figure 1).

For several decades, RSCN managed its protected areas as isolated sanctuaries, fenced and guarded from the general public and with little involvement of local communities.[102] This all changed in 1992 with the Rio Summit and the Biodiversity Convention. As a signatory of the Convention, Jordan was the first country in the Middle East to be awarded a multi-million dollar pilot project under the Global Environment Facility (GEF) to develop a regional model of integrated conservation and development. The project was focused on the Dana Nature Reserve in southern Jordan and its emphasis on linking protected area management to the socio-economic development of local people ushered in a new era in conservation thinking, which the RSCN continues to spearhead today. In particular, it kick-started the development of eco-tourism as a principal tool for sustaining the management of protected areas and for engaging local communities in nature-based livelihoods. Since 1994, when the project began, RSCN has been developing eco-tourism ventures in all of its protected areas and is now a significant player in Jordan's tourism industry. These ventures have revo-

---

102 The exception was the Shaumari Nature Reserve, which had a small animal collection and was open to visitors and school groups.

lutionized RSCN's image in the eyes of the Jordanian public and decision makers and they have made a major contribution to covering the running costs of protected areas, despite the fact that Jordan sits

Figure 1: Jordan has a wide variety of spectacular desert landscapes. Above, the "Wadi of the Teeth", Eastern Desert near Azraq. Below, the Dana Nature Reserve in the southern mountains of the Jordan Rift Valley.

in one of the most politically volatile regions of the world and has suffered from major oscillations in visitor numbers with each political crisis.

THE DANA STORY

The Dana Nature Reserve lies just north of the famous archaeological site of Petra and occupies a spectacularly beautiful slice of the Jordan Rift valley. Several thousand people from nomadic and settled communities live in and around the Reserve, many of whom are partially or entirely dependent on the reserve for their livelihood. Their use of the reserve, however, is causing serious ecological problems, stemming from excessive livestock grazing, hunting and fuel wood collection. These activities had little detrimental impact in the past, when tribal populations were smaller and Bedouins could practice their nomadic lifestyles without issues of national borders, settlement policies and major infrastructure developments. But now the pressure of these traditional livelihoods is concentrated in the last remaining areas of unspoiled landscape and is the major threat to their ecological integrity. In an attempt to solve this problem in the Dana and create more sustainable income sources, an eco-tourism operation was gradually developed under the GEF project mentioned above, building on the scenic, ecological and cultural assets of the protected area.

"Nature First"

The tourism concept for Dana was built on the premise that "nature should come first" and local people should be the prime beneficiaries. The first stage in realizing this concept was to develop a zoning scheme, identifying areas where tourism (and other) activities can be accommodated with relatively little serious environmental impact. There are currently three major zoning categories: 'intensive use', 'semi-intensive use' and 'core zones'. The first two categories are where all tourism activity is concentrated and the 'core zones' are where conservation needs are given priority and human access is restricted to enforcement rangers and occasional visits by researchers and other management staff. All the zone boundaries were derived from an analysis of baseline surveys of flora and fauna, including the known whereabouts of endangered species, and of existing patterns of local community use. While biodiversity conservation is a primary objective of the reserve, the zoning scheme now in place represents a pragmatic compromise between conservation priorities and local community needs

From campsite to guest house

Following the introduction of the zoning scheme, a range of visitor facilities were constructed over several years, including a campsite, visitor centre, hiking trails and a strikingly designed guest house. The campsite was the first to be developed, as a small camping area had already been created before the GEF project started, although it was discovered from the baseline surveys that the area fell into the core zone designation. The camp, however, was already known and used and was originally a favoured Bedouin camping area, occupied every summer season for goat grazing. Clear topographical boundaries were therefore defined for the campsite and all hiking routes out of the site were directed into the semi-intensive and intensive use zones. A shuttle bus system was also introduced to ferry visitors from the reserve entrance gate to the campsite, instead of allowing access by private vehicles, which had been allowed before the zoning scheme was finalized. With the shuttle system in place, number limits were then defined for visitors entering the reserve and for the trails and campsites, based on 'guestimated' carrying capacities and a simple monitoring programme devised to assess their impacts.

The success of the campsite in attracting visitors prompted the creation of a small guest house close to the edge of Dana Village. Originally intended as accommodation for researchers under the GEF project brief, the building was 'hi jacked' half way through construction and converted into a 9-roomed lodge for tourists. (The researchers were eventually housed in a restored village house). This decision reflected not only a gowning awareness of the potential of tourism in Dana to be a key conservation management tool, but also the dramatic location of the building, perched at the edge of the precipitous cliffs of Wadi Dana and close to a 'biblical-looking' village. The architect had also designed a simple building, merging elements of village vernacular architecture with more modern elements, to create a building with a definable Arabic character, unlike any other in Jordan. It was soon apparent that this mixture of good design, location and exceptional visual and cultural interest was a winning combination for attracting tourists and the Dana Guest House became – and remains – one of the most popular and viable tourist facilities in the nature reserve, despite having only 9 rooms, with just one en-suite bathroom[103].

Figure 2: the Dana Reserve tourist facilities

Local people on board

Throughout the development of the tourism and conservation initiatives outlined above, local people were part of the process at every stage and an extensive capacity building programme was undertaken to enable them to share in the benefits. Employment opportunities were one of their chief concerns and RSCN introduced a strict policy that all tourism

---

103 The lack of en-suite bathrooms reflects the origin of the Guesthouse as researcher accommodation. All RSCN's new facilities have en-suite bathrooms, as most customers clearly prefer this

jobs were to be filled by local residents. It also tried, wherever possible, to provide these opportunities to the families who were most dependent on the nature reserve for livestock grazing and other subsistence livelihoods. A range of small businesses was also developed to produce tourist souvenirs and other products and these provided additional employment and revenue, especially for the women of the communities.

When the project began in 1994, there were fewer than 100 visitors to Dana and by the year 2000, this had increased to almost 20,000[104]. The tourism and sales receipts over this period generated enough revenue to provide 55 full-time jobs and direct and indirect benefits to over 800 people in the surrounding communities. Moreover, by 1998, the level of revenue was such that all the running costs of the nature reserve were covered, making it totally self-sufficient financially. Since the reserve is large by Jordanian standards (320 square km) and of recognized global significance for biodiversity conservation, this is a remarkable achievement. In recognition of this achievement, Dana has won four international awards for sustainable tourism.

The first purpose-built eco-lodge

Buoyed-up by the success of the tourism enterprises, RSCN embarked on the construction of a purpose-built eco-lodge at the western gateway to the Dana Reserve during 2003. This was located in the remote Wadi Feynan, on the site of an old copper mining research base, and built with funds provided by USAID. Distant from roads and power supplies, the Lodge represented a brave attempt to create a unique tourism experience in Jordan and bring enhanced economic benefits to the Wadi Feynan Bedouins, who are among the most underprivileged tribal groups in the Kingdom and whose reliance on intensive goat grazing in the nature reserve is a cause of many ecological problems. Its location was also part of a strategic conservation initiative to use tourism to offset the threat of

---

104 These are people entering the Reserve and paying entrance fees. Many visitors stay in and around Dana Village and other areas on the periphery and do not pay to enter. These are not recorded in statistics

open-cast copper mining in the Feynan area. There is persistent pressure from government and private sector companies to rework the extensive, but very low grade, copper deposits surrounding the Lodge (which, ironically, provided the economic base of previous civilizations in the region, from Neolithic to Islamic) and the development of tourism provides an alternative and far more environmentally sustainable livelihood option.

The Feynan Lodge, like the Dana Guest House, is an exceptional building. Taking influences from ancient caravanserai and Yemeni architecture it provides 26 rooms, all organically shaped and different in layout (Figure 3). It incorporates several environment-friendly features, including solar power, high insulation and passive ventilation systems and, in the absence of mains electricity, it is lit at night by candle light, which gives a very special atmosphere to the building and creates an unusual attraction for tourists. It was opened in September 2005 and provides direct employment for 14 local Bedouins, as well as income for local service providers such as the village shuttle service, bread makers, vegetable growers, etc. By the end of 2006, it had already attracted sufficient visitors to cover its operational costs and make a small profit.

Figure 3: "Taking influences from ancient caravanserai and Yemeni architecture, the Feynan Eco-lodge provides 26 rooms, all organically

shaped and different in layout. It incorporates several environment-friendly features, including solar power, high insulation and passive ventilation systems and, in the absence of mains electricity, it is lit at night by candle light, which gives a very special atmosphere to the building and creates an unusual attraction for tourists".

With its array of tourist facilities and activities, Dana is now featured in several international tourist guides, including the 'Rough Guide', 'Insight Guide' and 'Lonely Planet', but despite its growing reputation and increasing visitor pressure, tight controls on the number, distribution and behaviour of visitors continue to be applied. So far, the site is showing little sign of excessive negative impacts from tourism; on the contrary, routine monitoring programmes show increases in the populations of several key species, like the Nubian Ibex, Griffon Vulture and Syrian Wolf. Another notable aspect of Dana is that it attracts a high percentage of Jordanian visitors, over 50% in most years, which not only helps to maintain income levels when international tourism fluctuates but also to create more in-country support for protected areas.

Income drivers and financial performance

The main income drivers operating in Dana are entrance fees, accommodation fees and activity fees (guided hikes mainly). A summary of the financial performance for Dana in 2005 is given in table 1 below and provides an indication of the source of revenues and overall balance sheet.

Table 1: Summary of Financial Performance for Dana Nature Reserve 2005

- No of overnight visitors   7,776
- No of day visitors entering the reserve   8,100
- Overall occupancy rate (Guesthouse, campsite
  and Lodge)   52%
- Revenue from entrance fees $24,250

- Total revenue from entrance, accommodation
  and activity fees $222,000
- Business plan target $239,930
- % of business plan target covered   92%

It is interesting to note from the Table that a relatively small number of visitors can generate enough revenue to maintain a large protected area, if this revenue is channeled directly into the site. Entrance fees, however, make a relatively small contribution to running costs at this level of visitor use (average of $3 per person[105]) compared to the accommodation (average $26 per person). It should also be noted that construction of the Dana facilities was financed by international donors and RSCN is not required to repay the capital outlay from revenue. While this confers a great financial advantage, RSCN regards the investment of donor money in tourism facilities as a major way of ensuring the sustainability of donor-supported conservation programmes.

Replicating the Dana approach

Building on the experience gained from the Dana tourism programmes, RSCN has been transferring the "Dana approach" to the other five protected areas under its jurisdiction. These areas are very different in size and landscape character, ranging from a restored oasis in the Eastern Desert to a large arid mountain system on the shores of the Dead Sea, deeply incised by wadis and flowing rivers. They also include two forest reserves in the north of the country that provide a great contrast to the desert areas of the south and east. Collectively, over the last 12 years, the Society has developed six permanent lodges/ guesthouses, three campsites, three visitor centres and many hiking / activity trails. The character of these facilities differs in each site and great effort has been made to take inspiration from the local landscape and human and cultural history in their design. There is, for example, a recently completed Lodge

105 Entrance fees have since been raised to $5 for Jordanians and $10 for internationals.

in the village of Azraq in the Eastern desert, created from a renovated British army field hospital of the 1940's. The design carefully maintains the character of the original buildings but creatively links them to a very modern, sculptural new wing, incorporating tent-like structures to hint at their military past. At Mujib, on the shores of the Dead Sea, the chalets have domed roofs painted silver to mirror the colour and shine of the surrounding seascape; while in Ajloun, wood has been used in the tented bungalows to reflect their forest setting (see Figure 4).

With this portfolio of projects and experiences, RSCN is now confident about the benefits of desert tourism for nature conservation. With careful planning and management, tourism has been shown to provide an affective vehicle for:

- Generating substantial income for biodiversity protection
- Creating jobs and revenue for local communities and, thus, more positive attitudes and support from local people towards conservation
- Helping Jordanians to appreciate and value their natural heritage
- Ensuring that conservation is seen as part of the "real world", with a clear economic value that government officials and other decision makers recognize and appreciate.

Figure 4: The tourist facilities recently completed by RSCN. Silver-domed chalets at Mujib on the shores of the Dead Sea.

ISSUES AND LESSONS LEARNED

Looking back over twelve years of experience, the main problems and issues affecting the development of desert tourism as a conservation tool in Jordan have largely been social and business-related, rather than ecological. As noted above, key ecological indicators in the Dana Reserve, which is the most developed for tourism, have not shown a negative relationship with increasing tourism activity. The one exception concerns local community livelihoods. It was envisaged that increasing job opportunities in tourism would reduce the dependency of local people on ecologically damaging land use practices, especially goat grazing. This does not, however, seem to be the case. A study conducted in Dana in 2001[106], five years after tourism began, concluded that RSCN's socio-economic strategy (including eco-tourism) had not significantly reduced the level of goat grazing in the reserve. The author notes, however, that RSCN [its socio-economic strategy] *"has been very successful in improving the attitudes of the local population toward conservation and the presence of the reserve"*

One of the main and very visible social impacts has resulted from local entrepreneurs capitalizing on the tourists attracted by RSCN. This is most evident in Dana Village, where resident cooperatives and business-oriented individuals have created small hotels from the old village houses to exploit the growing reputation of the Dana Nature Reserve as a tourist destination. This in itself is not a problem – indeed it would normally be welcomed and fostered by RSCN – but the proprietors have shown little regard for the architectural, historical and visual quality of the village and the resulting hotels and guest houses have become a visual eye sore. Apart from unsympathetic restoration, they have added intrusive signing, strings of neon lighting and a host of small 'kitsch' interventions that are seriously affecting the architectural integrity of

---

106 Combining Conservation and Development: An Evaluation of the Socio-economic Strategies of the Royal Society for the Conservation of Nature in Dana, Jordan. MA thesis, Amberley Knight, Brigham Young University, USA, July 2001.

this Ottoman village (Figure 6). The local cooperative hotel also started employing foreign women for housekeeping and waitressing, undermining the benefits of tourism for local employment. Developments such as these, as well as attempts to compete for customers, have led to rivalries and disputes between owners and families, and to criticism of RSCN for restricting development inside the protected area. RSCN is now planning a major project to involve the Dana Village community in creating a restoration and tourism development scheme for the whole village that will hopefully create more equity in benefit sharing and bring architectural quality back to the village as a driver for better tourism returns.

Another issue has been pricing for Jordanians. RSCN has pitched its pricing policy for entrance, accommodation and activity fees according to the need to cover all tourism operational costs *and* raise revenue for supporting protected area management costs. While the fees are not high by international standards (average rate for a double room is $60) they are expensive for a large proportion of the Jordanian population and RSCN is sometimes criticized for "pricing out" sections of society. This is an important philosophical issue for an NGO that has been given responsibility for managing natural heritage sites on behalf of the nation, since access to these sites is arguably the birthright of all Jordanian citizens. Indeed, the whole idea of RSCN becoming business-like and commercial in the interests of conservation is not always received favourably; and this, ironically, includes a proportion RSCN's own staff, who feel the Society is losing sight of its conservation and NGO roots. RSCN has tried to reduce the perceived inequalities in pricing by charging lower fees for Jordanians than for international visitors and it is also planning to introduce free 'open days' in all protected areas. As for bridging the philosophical divide between business and conservation, RSCN now makes sure that the conservation benefits of tourism are well promoted in its marketing and PR materials and it has created institutional mechanisms that encourage internal dialogue and cooperation between the staff of the business and conservation departments.

Figure 6: local entrepreneurs in Dana Village have capitalized on the tourists attracted by the nature reserve but the resulting hotels have little regard for village history and architecture and threaten to destroy the visual quality and social integrity of the Village.

The difficulty of convincing local tour operators to support RSCN's eco-tourism products was mentioned earlier and, while RSCN has made major progress in this (see 'Wild Jordan' above), there remains an important and unaddressed concern: the weakness of Jordan's search and rescue system. Tour operators are very reluctant to place their clients in remote locations without effective safety measures and search-and-rescue procedures. At present Jordan does not have a coordinated national system and rescue in the field relies on local coordination between the police, civil defence and air force, which are often ill-equipped for dealing with remote location emergencies. RSCN has taken it upon itself to train its guides and field staff in the required skills but some tour operators remain concerned that, without a national back-up system, their clients will be endangered and could potentially have grounds for law suits in the case of badly managed accidents.

The last significant problem RSCN has faced in its tourism ventures is related to maintaining operational standards and design quality. All RSCN's tourism staff are recruited locally as a mater of policy and capacity building for these staff is now a routine function of RSCN's work. In general, the staff perform very well and Jordanian hospitality is legendary but there are persistent problems of maintaining operational standards. There is a tendency to let standards slide, particularly in relation to the small, detailed service requirements that make the difference between a satisfactory service level and an excellent one, or between a service and an 'experience'. Examples include maintaining agreed menu choices, such as having fruit at breakfast, as preferred by Europeans, providing room information to visitors, folding down sheets carefully, offering 'touches' like pillow gifts, maintaining furniture layouts and repairing damaged and worn items in guest rooms. Some important environmental areas also tend to get overlooked such as segregation of garbage and maintaining 'back yard' tidiness. Much of this stems from the difficulty of finding key personnel with the right managerial approach, especially in remote locations. RSCN has experimented with bringing in hotel trained staff from outside to act as counterparts for local staff and develop capacity but none have been willing to stay in rural locations for an adequate period of time. For this reason, the idea of forging partnerships with private sector companies or developing private sector concessions is now being considered, as outlined below

Federico Vignati • Don Hawkins • Bruce Priedeaux

Figure 7: Search and rescue capability is still a major concern of tour operators. RSCN staff teams have been trained to handle most emergencies but there is no coordinated national system.

Seven

Economies of Agglomeration and the Cluster Approach to Tourism Development

Try not to become a man of success, but rather try to become a man of value.

— ALBERT EINSTEIN.

OBJECTIVES OF THE CHAPTER:

- Examine the positive externalities created by the tourism industry and how they can create an economy of agglomeration in tourism.
- Define the cluster approach to tourism development and explore the relationship between the formation of tourism clusters and the growth of tourism destinations.
- Analyse the advantages and drawbacks involved in organizing and managing tourism clusters.
- Examine several examples of tourism clusters and micro-clusters.
- Consider other issues related to the formation and management of tourism clusters.

INTRODUCTION

As our understanding of the international tourism industry continues to evolve, so too do the conceptual models and practical strategies on which tourism policy is based. In recent years the so-called **cluster approach** to tourism development has become increasingly popular as a framework for identifying, assessing and managing the growth of tourism industries in both developing and advanced economies. The cluster approach is primarily an analytical methodology used to describe how and why different industries develop in different regions, or fail to develop, and how these specialised regional economies interact with one another at the national and international levels.

An **economic cluster** is a group of related firms located in the same geographic area, which derive specific advantages from their close proximity to one another and from the connections and spill-overs that proximity allows. Clusters form organically on the basis of these mutual advantages, microeconomic benefits that profoundly influence the distribution of firms and industries in the local, regional or even national economy. From a public policy perspective a cluster encompasses the range of private and public sector actors involved in the same value chain, or a set of closely related value chains, including those in the tourism industry that add value to its final products—tourism services. The cluster approach allows policymakers to view the tourism not as an abstract national economic sector, but as an interconnected network of locally-specific economic clusters, each of which develops around a particular set of economic activities. Tourism clusters include firms and workers, both in the tourism itself and in related industries and services, as well as government policymakers, public administrative authorities, private sector associations, research, educational and vocational training institutions, NGOs, international donors, and a broad diversity of civil society organisations.

The cluster approach is based on leveraging the positive spill-over effects that successful tourism firms generate for one another and for society as a whole. These include facilitating access to information and the transfer of knowledge between firms, expanding access to new technologies, improving the destination's reputation in international tourism source markets, boosting the availability of financial and human capital, strengthening supply and demand linkages within the private sector, enhancing the quality of the business environment, and adding to the stock of public goods, along with a variety of other benefits, all of which have a significant impact on the development of tourism industries and on the long-term viability of destinations. Taken together, these benefits form an **economy of agglomeration**, in which the mere presence of successful firms in a given area increases the competitiveness of other firms in the same area, improving the efficiency of the industry as a whole; this phenomenon is the basis of the cluster approach to tourism development.

As with many other industries, successful tourism firms operating in a given area generate **positive externalities** that reduce production and transaction costs or otherwise improve the competitive position of other firms in the same area.[107] Efficient information access and knowledge transfer allow firms to respond to unpredictable change; they enable innovation and creativity and promote the rapid adoption of new organisational techniques and new productive technologies. Flexibility, responsiveness and a high rate of technological are important in any industry, as all forms of economic activity are subject to both unexpected short-term shocks and to long-term shifts in market dynamics.

Firms and industries that can rapidly adapt to new circumstances and exploit emerging opportunities have a significant advantage over their more intransigent competitors; while firms that continuously strive to improve their efficiency by revising their business models and incorporating

---

107 The concept of positive and negative externalities was defined and discussed in Chapter 6. While externalities can involve either monetary or non-monetary utility and may reflect social, cultural and environmental costs and benefits that are not easily quantifiable, in this chapter examines externalities in their traditional economic sense.

new operational methods will gradually supplant those that rely on obsolete systems. These qualities of swift adaptation and continuous improvement are especially important in the tourism industry, in which "serious obstacles to innovation processes and knowledge transfer" give a competitive advantage to enterprises with strong horizontal connections;[108] that is, to those which are most able to learn from other firms facing similar circumstances. The presence of successful tourism firms in a destination generates critical **market information**, facilitating innovation, promoting the transfer of knowledge and speeding the adoption of new technologies by other firms in the same destination; and this is just one example of the many benefits produced by an economy of agglomeration.

Another example is the positive **reputational effects** produced by successful firms. As described in Chapter 2, the reputation of a tourism destination, whether accurate or not, has enormous economic value. Successful tourism firms generate positive publicity for the destination, raising its international profile and attracting more tourists, which ultimately benefits all firms operating in the same destination. This is a classic externality because many of the firms that benefit from the destination's improved reputation had nothing to do with creating it, and the market cannot efficiently reward the firms that did. As with the other positive externalities that combine to create economies of agglomeration in tourism, the purpose of the cluster approach to tourism development is to better incorporate these effects into market mechanisms and to use public policy to magnify their contribution to the destination's competitiveness.

A number of related benefits produced by economies of agglomeration involve increasing the availability of human and financial capital. Successful firms both enhance the human capital of the existing workforce—either by training local workers or simply by giving them an opportunity to build their experience—and attract skilled workers from

---

108 Hjalager, A. (2002) "Repairing Innovation Defectiveness in Tourism." *Tourism Management*, 23(5): 465-474

other areas. This greatly improves **the quality of the local labour force**, which can significantly reduce operating costs for firms that employ similar types of workers. For instance, a large hotel may employ numerous skilled and semi-skilled workers, from chefs to groundskeepers to accountants to highly specialized professionals (e.g. scuba instructors), a hotel that can easily find (and replace) these workers from within the local labour force has a definite advantage over firms that have to attract or train skilled workers themselves. As the number of hotels in an area grows, so does the local pool of skilled hotel workers, making it easier for new hotels to enter the market.

Successful firms enhance local **access to financial capital** in much the same way. Financial infrastructure develops to meet the needs of a growing industry: as successful tourism firms demand financial services and utilise them effectively, these services become more readily available to all firms in the destination. Other tourism firms are especially well-positioned to benefit from the expanding financial sector, as financial service providers are already familiar with their industry and are better able to gauge their creditworthiness. Just as successful tourism firms attract and train workers to suit their labour needs, increasing the sophistication of the local workforce and enhancing its value to similar firms, successful tourism firms also attract financial service providers and build their capacity to serve the needs of the tourism industry, increasing the sophistication of the local credit market and enhancing its value to other tourism firms.

Beyond access to labour and capital, successful firms further reduce transaction costs for one another by strengthening their industry's local **upstream and downstream linkages**. Firms in virtually every industry purchase inputs from other firms (upstream linkages) and sell their goods and services to still other firms or to consumers (downstream linkages). For example, a clothing company may buy cloth from a wholesaler, turn it into finished clothes, and then sells those clothes to a retailer. The cloth wholesaler is the company's upstream link and the clothing retailer is its downstream link. All other things being equal, the more access the clothing company has to upstream linkages (the more wholesalers are available to supply it), the better the price and quality of the inputs it can buy; similarly, the more access the company has to downstream linkages (the more retailers are available to buy from it), the better the prices it can command and the greater the quantity of clothes it can sell. Tourism firms are much the same: the presence of multiple firms increases the number of input suppliers operating in the local market as well as the number of consumers, both individual tourists and downstream tourism firms, available to sell to. As the tourism market becomes more diverse and sophisticated the upstream and downstream linkages of each firm increase and the market as a whole becomes more efficient.

A business can also benefit from being located near other firms that provide **complementary goods and services** to the same customer base. For example, along many of the world's highways it is common to find fast-food restaurants situated next to gas stations. This is no coincidence, as each firm benefits from its proximity to the other: drivers who stop for gas will often buy food as well, and drivers stopping to eat will buy gas. The efficiency of this arrangement saves the consumer time (no need to make two stops for food and gas) and boosts the sales of the firms. In many cases other firms that also target passing motorists as prime customers will choose to locate in the same place, further expanding the range of goods and services offered by the roadside micro-cluster. Tourism firms experience the same efficiency gains from locating near one another: hotels, restaurants, transportation providers, souvenir shops, recreational facilities, local guides and international tour companies all target the same customer base—tourists. Establishing themselves within the same cluster allows each firm to reach far more potential customers that it would be capable of on its own. Tourists also benefit from easy access to a range of goods and services, and the greater the diversity of options the more the tourists value their abundance of choice, which further boosts the competitiveness of the destination.

Meanwhile, on the public policy side, successful firms can contribute to improving the overall **business climate** by promoting administrative reforms which benefit all firms in the same area and especially other firms in the same industry. The "business climate" is a catch-all term for the costs (both in time and money) involved in opening, operating and liquidating a business. Successful firms typically push for improvements in the administrative and regulatory efficiency of their industry, encouraging government agencies at the local and national level to undertake reforms that reduce the cost of doing business.[109] This may include simplifying business registration and licensing procedures, streamlining tax structures and payment systems, and working to curtail corruption and rent-seeking among public officials. Strong private-sector advocacy can be an enormously powerful tool for reforming inefficient regulatory structures and improving the business environment. Each new firm adds to this constituency, strengthening it. Business climate reform produces further positive externalities, as firms that did not bear the costs of lobbying for reform are still able to enjoy its benefits.

Finally, successful firms can contribute to the local economy's overall stock of **public goods**, boosting the productivity of all firms in the market. Successful firms pay taxes to local and national governments, and they lobby those governments to provide infrastructure and services that benefit their business. This includes basic utilities (power, water, sanitation and solid waste management systems, etc.) and essential transportation networks (roads, railways, commercial seaports), as well as more

---

109 It should be noted that this is not always the case. In some instances firms may lobby to *increase* the regulatory burden in an effort to create barriers to the entry of new firms (see Chapter 6) or otherwise establish a structural advantage for existing firms, while collusion between existing firms and corrupt regulators, often undertaken for similar purposes, can take a number of different forms and its instance varies greatly from case to case.

sophisticated forms of public capital (international airports, broadband internet, advanced medical services, etc.), and may also include highly specific services (tourism information offices, tourism police forces[110], national park services, public museums, etc.). As with business climate reform, the more firms in a given industry that enter a local market, the stronger the tax base and the constituency for public investment. Firms that enter the market later can benefit from the infrastructure and services that established firms paid and lobbied for; these benefits are therefore yet another positive externality associated with a growing economy of agglomeration.

As this pattern suggests, the order in which firms enter the local area is critical to developing economies of agglomeration. *The first entrants bear the greatest costs.* They face a serious lack of practical operating knowledge and they bear the full risks associated with adopting new business models and new technologies, while firms that enter the market later can benefit, second-hand, from their experience. The first firms to establish themselves in a new market have to build its reputation from scratch; they must attract or train skilled workers themselves and may have limited access to financial service providers; they may have to cope with a cumbersome bureaucracy and overcome a lack of basic public goods. However, the success of the first entrants into the local market will improve all of these conditions over time, making the local economy progressively more attractive to similar firms. This process, in which each new firm to enter the market generates positive externalities that benefit all other firms, is the basis of an economy of agglomeration.

---

110 For example, Thailand's Tourist Police is an auxiliary force created specifically to handle administrative work associated with minor crimes in the tourism industry, especially petty theft and fraud committed against tourists. The Tourist Police lacks normal police powers, but has a multilingual staff that takes and translates reports for the regular police force, as well as providing information and other forms of assistance to foreign crime victims.

THE THEORY OF ECONOMIES OF AGGLOMERATION

Economist Alfred Marshall was among the first to recognise the considerable benefits that multiple firms operating in close proximity generate for one another, noting in particular the advantages of accessing a common labour market full of workers that specialise in the same industry.[111] So important was Marshall's contribution to this area of economic theory that the benefits derived from economies of agglomeration are sometimes referred to as "Marshallian externalities".[112] An extensive literature has grown up around Marshall's theoretical framework, and new evidence continues to highlight the impact of market access, industrialisation, technological innovation, the development of workforce capabilities and other benefits achieved through the clustering of similar firms.[113] The efficiency gains associated with the clustering of related economic activities are in many cases so strong that economies of agglomeration have been identified as a main contributor to the persistence of vast economic disparities between advanced and developing countries. This view holds that lower factor prices and structurally higher marginal returns to investment in developing countries should be shifting global capital towards the developing world, but this effect is not occurring as quickly or as uniformly as it should because the world's most advanced nations enjoy entrenched economies of agglomeration in numerous industries. The benefits produced by the dense clustering of firms in wealthier nations offset the competitive advantages of

---

111 "[A] localized industry gains a great advantage from the fact that it offers a constant market for skill." Marshall, Alfred (1920) <u>Principles of Economics: 8th Edition</u> London: Macmillan and Co. See also: Overman, Henry G. and Diego Puga "Labor Pooling as a Source of Agglomeration: An Empirical Investigation" in <u>Agglomeration Economics</u> Edward L. Glaeser (ed.) Chicago: The University of Chicago Press/The National Bureau of Economic Research http://www.nber.org/chapters/c7981.pdf

112 See, e.g., Andres Rodriguez-Clare (2007) "Clusters and Comparative Advantage: Implications for Industrial Policy" *Journal of Development Economics* 82: 43-57

113 For more on recent developments in the academic literature see www.cluster-research.org, an online research project exploring the cluster approach and its impact on microeconomic competitiveness throughout the world.

poorer ones, discouraging industrialisation in developing countries and perpetuating their relative poverty.[114]

Contemporary economists continue to strengthen the theoretical framework behind economies of agglomeration and Marshallian externalities by explaining what causes the clustering of companies and how clustering determines **economic geography** and by assessing the impact of clustering on firms and regional development in both advanced and developing economies.[115] Michael Porter of Harvard Business School, one of the leading theorists on economies of agglomeration, introduced the concept to business management theory, defining an economic cluster as, "A geographically proximate ground of interconnected companies and associated institutions in a particular field, linked by commonalities and complementarities."[116] Porter has since expanded and elaborated this definition of economic clusters and the considerable benefits they generate:

> Clusters consist of dense networks of interrelated firms that arise in a region because of powerful externalities and spillovers across firms (and various types of institutions) within a cluster. Clusters drive productivity and innovation. Firms that are located within a cluster can transact more efficiently, share

---

114 The original version of this analysis of the relationship between economies of agglomeration and persistent underdevelopment is generally credited to economist Paul Rosenstein-Rodan, who described it in his 1943 paper "Problems of Industrialization of Eastern and South- Eastern Europe" *Economic Journal* 53(210/211): 202-11.

115 See, e.g., Paul Krugman (1991) "Increasing Returns and Economic Geography" *Journal of Political Economy* (99)3: 483-499 ; Porter, Michael (2000) "Location, Competition and Economic Development: Local Clusters in a Global Economy" *Economic Development Quarterly* 14(1): 15-34; Solvell, O., G. Lindqvist, and C. Ketels (2006) "Cluster Initiatives in Developing and Transition Economies" www.cluster-research.org/dldevtra.htm; and Delgado M., M.E. Porter, and S. Stern (2010) "Clusters and Entrepreneurship," *Journal of Economic Geography* 10(4): 495-518

116 Porter, Michael (1998) "Clusters and the New Economics of Competition" *Harvard Business Review* November-December

technologies and knowledge more readily, operate more flexibly, start new businesses more easily, and perceive and implement innovations more rapidly. They can also efficiently access "public goods" such as pools of specialized skilled employees, specialized infrastructure, technological knowledge, and others. Clusters embody traditional notions such as input-output linkages, but much more.[117]

Due in part to the influential contributions Porter and other leading economic theorists the positive externalities produced by clusters are widely recognised as important elements of effective business management in a global economy, and understanding cluster dynamics is critical to effective economic policy in advanced and developing nations alike. The nature and impact of cluster formation has gained increasing attention from policymakers due to its implications for locational **comparative advantage**, especially in global export markets such as tourism.

Comparative advantage is the fundamental theory of international and interregional trade: it states that territories specialise in producing those tradable goods and services with the lowest opportunity cost of production relative to the opportunity costs of other territories. In other words, producers in each area focus on doing what they do best *relative to what producers in other areas do best*.[118] By each concentrating their productive efforts on goods and services with the lowest opportunity cost, and then trading with one another, different territories collectively

117 Porter, Michael (2007) "Clusters and Economic Policy: Aligning Public Policy with the New Economics of Competition" Harvard Business School, Institute for Strategy and Competitiveness White Paper, November 2007 (Revised October 2009) http://www.isc.hbs.edu/pdf/Clusters_and_Economic_Policy_White_Paper.pdf

118 The original version of this theory was set out by David Ricardo (1817) in On the Principles of Political Economy and Taxation London: John Murray, Albemarle-Street. Modern iterations can be found in any contemporary economics textbook; see, e.g., Parkin, Michael (2013) Economics, 11th Edition New Jersey: Pearson/Prentice-Hall.

maximise their efficiency. [119] The development of economies of agglomeration can accentuate regional comparative advantages, generating increasing aggregate welfare benefits over time. The cluster approach and its impact on regional comparative advantage have enormous consequences in determining economic geography, leading Porter to offer a provocative re-evaluation of how economic organisation is understood:

> The mix of clusters varies markedly across regions. Each regional economy normally has a relatively small number of traded clusters in which the region is truly competitive with other regions and countries. These clusters account for a major portion of the region's traded goods and services. *There is no national economy, then, but a series of regional economies that trade with each other and the rest of the world, each with its own particular pattern of cluster specialization.* Such regional specialization drives productivity and productivity growth in the national economy. There is growing statistical evidence that regions with stronger clusters achieve better economic performance and faster innovation.[120]

The pervasiveness and economic potential of clusters has not gone unnoticed by business management theorist, who have focused primarily on

---

119 Although the net benefits of comparative advantage as the basis for trade are mathematically demonstrable, this theory is notoriously difficult to understand. Economist Paul Samuelson was once challenged by mathematician and fellow Nobel Laureate Stanislaw Ulam to "name me one proposition in all of the social sciences which is both true and non-trivial." Samuelson responded with the theory of comparative advantage, saying in a letter "That it is logically true need not be argued before a mathematician; that it is not trivial is attested by the thousands of important and intelligent men who have never been able to grasp the doctrine for themselves or to believe it after it was explained to them." See Samuelson, Paul (1969) "The Way of an Economist" in International Economic Relations: Proceedings of the Third Congress of the International Economic Association London: Macmillan.

120 Porter, Michael (2007) "Clusters and Economic Policy: Aligning Public Policy with the New Economics of Competition" Harvard Business School, Institute for Strategy and Competitiveness White Paper, November 2007 (Revised October 2009) http://www.isc.hbs.edu/pdf/Clusters_and_Economic_Policy_White_Paper.pdf Emphasis added.

analysing the private economic benefits of clusters—the ability of firms to take advantage of the reduced transaction costs, mitigated risk, and technical innovation and knowledge spill-overs that clusters provide.[121] These private benefits of cluster development increase the **competitive advantage** of local firms, the sum of the macro and microeconomic conditions that influence a company's productive potential relative to that of its competitors. Competitive advantage is an elaboration on the theory of comparative advantage that stresses firm-level competitiveness, and especially the dynamic impact of knowledge and skill, as the basis of production efficiency; having a competitive advantage allows a firm to produce a greater quantity of goods or services for the same cost as its competitors, or the same quantity at a lower cost.

The concept of competitive advantage was originated by Michael Porter,[122] whose interest in economies of agglomeration and cluster development is not coincidental. Unlike comparative advantage, which is based on the relative opportunity cost of production at the regional or national level, competitive advantage is determined not only by firms' access to resources, but also by their individual capacity to use those resources effectively. Although the impact of competitive advantage on firm behaviour varies according to the characteristics of the market in which the firm operates, in most cases competitive advantage should generate higher profits for the firm and/or lower the cost of its goods or services to the consumer. Economies of agglomeration can boost the competitive advantage of all firms in the same location, giving them both an individual and collective edge over competitors in other locations.

Because of the enormous public and private benefits offered by cluster formation the principles behind economies of agglomeration have

---

121 See: http://data.isc.hbs.edu/cp/index.jsp

122 See Porter, Michael (1980) <u>Competitive Strategy: Techniques for Analyzing Industries and Competitors</u> New York: Free Press; and Porter, Michael (1985) <u>Competitive Advantage: Creating and Sustaining Superior Performance</u> New York: Free Press.

provided the basis for both broad economic development strategies and locally specific programs. These efforts have aimed at promoting income, employment and productivity growth by encouraging the formation of specific commercial and industrial clusters, in some cases involving the use of fiscal incentives to spur the growth of favoured sectors. These efforts are not without controversy, as many economists contend that using public policy to facilitate cluster development distorts economic incentives, shifting and realigning productive resources that would otherwise be employed elsewhere and squandering public funds in the process.[123]

However, there are many ways in which policymakers can support cluster development that do not involve distortive subsidies. Public investment in knowledge, workforce skills and sector-specific infrastructure can greatly facilitate the emergence of clusters without propping-up artificially profitable firms or creating a subsidy-dependent interest group.[124] And while economic interventions always involve drawbacks, it is clear that a targeted strategy of public support can help to overcome market failures that inhibit cluster formation. These include obstacles that are inherent in economies of agglomeration (i.e. that the first firms to enter an area generate unremunerated benefits for later entrants, systematically discouraging greenfield investment and rewarding a "wait and see" strategy) as well as those that are specific to developing countries (i.e. their relatively small consumer markets and limited reserves of domestic capital, which reinforce a low-supply/low-demand equilibrium, and the inaccurate price-signalling mechanisms of imperfectly competitive markets).[125] However, it is crucial to note that there is no guarantee

---

123 See, e.g., Desrochers, Pierre and Frederic Sautet (2004) "Cluster-Based Economic Strategy, Facilitation Policy and the Market Process" *Review of Austrian Economics* 17(2/3): 233-245

124 For more on the potentially damaging political-economic effects of subsidies and tax incentives see Chapter 4.

125 See Paul Rosenstein-Rodan (1943) "Problems of Industrialization of Eastern and South- Eastern Europe" *Economic Journal* 53(210/211): 202-11 and Scitovsky, Tibor (1954) "Two Concepts of External Economies" *The Journal of Political Economy* 62(2): 143-151

that public support will be sufficient to offset the structural disincentives faced by early investors or the other market failures that may inhibit cluster development.[126]

In terms of the distributive effects of cluster development policies there is little concrete evidence[127] that the promotion of tourism clusters in developing countries is likely to produce an inefficient allocation of resources. As international tourism in the developing world is capital intensive, and these capital costs overwhelmingly financed by foreign direct investment, encouraging tourism development should have only a limited impact on the distribution of domestic capital or the structure of factor prices. However, as noted in Chapter 3 any export-oriented industry funded by high levels of FDI may affect the exchange rate and influence consumer prices. These issues and their fiscal and monetary policy implications should be addressed at the national level.

An equally important concern is the fact that the present theory of cluster formation, particularly as it relates to the tourism industry, omits a number of key elements of sustainability. Given their demonstrable importance to the economic competitiveness of tourism destinations the principles of economies of agglomeration and cluster formation must be

---

126 In 2005 the government of Mozambique and the IFC invested over US$2 million dollars in the Mozambique Tourism Anchor Investment Program. This program aimed at attracting US$2 billion in private investments and generate over 25,000 jobs. Unfortunately the results of the initiative fell far short of expectations. In its post-analysis, the IFC identified the selection of tourism development sites as a major weakness: rather than capitalising on existing tourism clusters, most investment was directed to areas that were starting from scratch. The investment program was largely unsuccessful because the support it provided was not able to replace the positive externalities generated by a tourism cluster. See: http://www1. ifc.org/wps/wcm/connect/region__ext_content/regions/sub-saharan+africa/news/helping+attract+investment+in+mozambique

127 It should be noted that there is a general lack of empirical evidence on tourism cluster development. Of the 1.126 global cluster initiatives mapped by the Harvard Institute for Strategy and Competitiveness only 24 are from the tourism industry.

incorporated into sustainable tourism development and informed by its broader understanding of social, cultural and environmental value.

CLUSTER DEVELOPMENT AND SUSTAINABILITY

As we have seen, clusters of related companies—such as tourism firms—located in the same area produce economic externalities that benefit one another. But tourism clusters also produce **social, cultural and environmental externalities** with more complex and ambiguous effects, many of which are highly specific to the tourism industry and would not apply to the development of other commercial or industrial clusters. Although they are peripheral to the conventional understanding of economic value, these externalities may have a profound impact on a tourism cluster's economic viability.

Consider the first commercial hotel to open in an emerging tourism destination. As no other hotels are present in the area the management likely faces a number of serious problems. It may have difficulty finding skilled workers, particularly highly specialised professionals; it may have access to few upstream suppliers and consequently face high input costs; it may have difficulty finding appropriate lenders to finance additional investments; it will have to attract most or all of its customers itself and provide them with a wide range of services, as it cannot benefit from demand spill-overs produced by neighbouring hotels and other tourism firms; it will likely suffer from a lack of basic infrastructure or from deficiencies in sector-specific public goods, or both; and it may face an institutional and regulatory climate that is not well-suited to its business type, which increases the administrative cost of doing business. As more hotels move to the area their presence alleviates these conditions, generating positive economic externalities that encourage and accelerate the formation of a tourism cluster. However, each new hotel also imposes negative social, cultural and environmental externalities on the others, which generate a countervailing **diseconomy of agglomeration** that can have equally crucial implications for the sustainability of the cluster as a whole.

Although the first hotel faces a number of adverse economic conditions, it also enjoys significant advantages stemming directly from its novelty and isolation. The first hotel enjoys a local environment that is relatively pristine in terms of its physical beauty, ecological integrity and biodiversity; it may also offer its guests a high degree of cultural 'authenticity', in the sense that the local population remains largely unaffected by the tourism industry ; relatedly, the low total number of tourists at a destination tends to increase its appeal, and the first hotel can offer its guests a fairly 'un-crowded' tourism experience; and when the first hotel opens local public opinion towards tourism is likely to be at its height, as the first few tourists generate income and employment with a minimal overall impact and few obviously negative consequences for the local society. All of these conditions enhance the destination's value to tourists, which translates directly into a price premium for the hotel.

There is a final benefit that accrues to the first hotel in a new tourism destination: the first entrant has enormous influence over the 'tone' of tourism development and can largely define the **corporate brand identity** of the destination. Every destination offers specific types of tourism service, and each type is directed to a certain type of consumer. Not all forms of tourism are consistent with one another, and the development of one market profile will come at the expense of other possibilities: A destination that attracts vacationing students looking for a party may have limited appeal to pensioners in search of peace and quiet; a family-friendly atmosphere may conflict with a romantic environment;[128] a paradise for backpackers and independent travellers may be undermined by the arrival of large package-tour groups, and so forth. The first hotel can determine how the destination is perceived by potential customers, and this ability to establish the 'character' of the destination has considerable economic value.

---

128 The international chain of Sandals Resorts, for example, famously bars children from its accommodations for exactly this reason.

As additional hotels open in the area these conditions gradually change. The arrival of multiple firms will likely mean multiple visions for how the destination should evolve and what type of tourists it should appeal to. These differing ideas about how best to utilise the economic, social, cultural and environmental capital of the destination may result in inconsistent marketing and the overproduction of negative economic externalities. In addition, even in a context of highly effective regulation new tourism development will have an increasingly severe impact on the natural beauty and environmental quality of the destination. Over time it will gradually cease to be perceived as 'pristine' and begin to be viewed as 'built-up', typically diminishing its appeal.[129] Valuable ecological resources may also be damaged by excessive tourist 'traffic'; coral reefs, for example, are highly vulnerable to degradation due to overuse.

Meanwhile, the local community will become more and more habituated to the tourism industry, and the local culture will change as a result. This may diminish the perceived cultural authenticity of the destination, which can negatively impact its value to tourists, especially in destinations where a vibrant local culture is an important tourist draw. Depending on the quality and focus of subsequent tourism development, and the relationship between the tourism industry and the local economy, a changing local culture may ultimately result in the destination taking on a seedy, stressful or even hostile atmosphere.

Cultural habituation goes hand-in-hand with tourist 'crowding': as each new hotel adds to the total tourist population, the tourists may begin to feel that the destination is overly congested, or that it has become too commercialised—that is to say, too 'touristy'. And because any type of economic change involves trade-offs and drawbacks, as the number of tourists increases the downside of a growing tourism industry will become

---

129 There are cases in which the extremely 'built up' nature of a tourism destination is central to its appeal—Las Vegas, Monaco and Dubai being prime examples—but such instances are rare and largely confined to high-income countries.

increasingly clear to the local population, and a political opposition to it may take root. This can negatively affect the local government's interactions with tourists and tourism firms, adding additional costs that further damage its economic viability.

In the worst case scenario an idyllic tourism destination in a welcoming community gradually transforms into a seamy, overcrowded 'tourist trap' with a host population that is highly dependent on tourism and at the same time increasingly resentful of it. This has obvious implications for the profitability of individual firms and for the competitiveness of the destination as a whole. The potential for multiple firms to generate diseconomies of agglomeration is much stronger and more immediate in tourism than in other industries. The social, cultural or environmental damage caused by multiple textile firms, for example, may have little or no impact on their profitability. However, the same is not true for tourism, and in this context the principles of sustainable development are vital in addressing these negative externalities before they permanently damage the economic potential of the sector.

Tourism industries are unique in the extent to which their profitability depends on the maintenance of intact social, cultural and environmental capital. A cursory review of tourist advertising will reveal these three elements being emphasised time and again: the destination's natural beauty and environmental resources, its unique culture and heritage, and the friendliness and hospitality of its people. Moreover, in many cases the success of the destination depends not just on one or two, but on all three forms of capital working together. If one of these three forms of capital is seriously degraded, its loss will undermine the value of the other two, and destination will suffer as a result. The negative impact of environmental damage is perhaps the most obvious, but the widespread perception that a tourism industry is culturally exploitative, or that the local population is becoming alienated or hostile to tourists can be equally devastating to the destination. For this reason and effective and sustainable cluster development policy must maintain or increase the destination's stock of social, cultural and environmental capital in addition to its more traditional forms of economic capital. This in turn requires a strong managerial role for destination policymakers.

THE ROLE OF GOVERNMENT

As we saw in Chapter 6, firms that focus exclusively on their interests as individuals, and that operate without adequate mechanisms for dialogue and collaboration, may severely undermine their interests as members of a group. A major economic purpose of government is to provide a forum in which multiple competing actors can come together to find joint solutions to common problems, often deferring their immediate personal objectives for the sake of long-term collective goals. Due to the complex and intimate relationships between firms in a tourism cluster and the importance of aligning incentives among these firms and diverse civil society groups, the government has a major part to play in managing the competing and collective interests of an emerging tourism cluster.

In addition to ensuring the private competitiveness of the sector, the cluster approach to tourism development can advance a range of important macroeconomic and public policy goals. Encouraging regular dialogue between tourism firms, their suppliers, their colleagues in related sector and especially potential partners (such as local farmers) with whom they might not otherwise have direct contact can minimise revenue **leakages** and enhance the local economic impact of tourist spending. The more contact between local firms, the more likely they are to discover and exploit opportunities to work together, forming linkages that keep tourism revenue in the local economy while improving the efficiency of their services. In some cases these linkages might be formed on their own, but due to the large number of small and medium enterprises (and self-employed individuals) operating in the tourism industry or its ancillary sectors, finding local partners can be a costly and difficult process.

Cluster organisations can reduce the information and search costs of finding new partners, which can not only help to curtail leakages by increasing the density of local economic connections but can also have important social equity and poverty reduction effects by incorporating a broader share of the local community, and especially poor and marginalised groups, into the tourism cluster. Governments whose stated policy objectives include broad-based growth and poverty alleviation should make special efforts to include representatives of these groups in tourism-sector organisations and facilitate their integration into the tourism cluster. As the Overseas Development Institute noted in a 2006 study, the pro-poor impact of even marginally denser local economic integration can be dramatic:

> Research in seven Caribbean all-inclusive resorts found just one (locally-owned Sandals Resort in Jamaica) which was actively supporting farmers' groups to produce to their needs. The difference it made was substantial – purchases of melons alone injected an extra US$7,200 per month into the local economy and were keeping 70 local farming families well above the poverty line – indicating how much potential is being missed where hotel-farmer communication is lacking.[130]

The development of tourism clusters typically involves establishing a mix of formal and informal organisations, both among private firms and between the public and private sectors; these organisations are crucial to realising both the economic spill-over effects described above and the benefits of **multi-stakeholder collaboration** described in the previous chapter. The government's impact on cluster organisations is most critical during their formative period. As a tourism cluster matures, the companies and institutions within it will typically come to recognise themselves as parts of a larger whole, a group with shared interests that balance

---

130 ODI (2006) "Tourism Businesses and the Local Economy: Increasing Impact through a Linkages Approach" *ODI Briefing Paper* London: ODI

and condition their competitive incentives as individuals. However, this understanding is the product of mutual familiarity, repeated interaction and trust, all of which are established over time; at the outset of cluster formation the various firms, institutions and other actors will tend to be myopically focused on their personal objectives and unwilling or unable to pursue collaborative solutions or abide by mutual agreements. This is when the government, as regulator of economic activity and guarantor of the public interest, must take a strong leadership role in the defining rules and structures for the emerging cluster.

The government's first and most fundamental task is to ensure that it possesses the institutional knowledge and administrative capacity necessary to regulate the tourism sector effectively, and this will require a candid assessment of its own limitations. Institutional knowledge and administrative capacity are critical to **policy continuity**, the importance of which was first discussed in Chapter 3. In order to establish its credibility not only as a regulator but also as a manager of competing interests the government must be able to formulate appropriate policies (knowledge) and to implement them swiftly, competently and impartially (capacity). A government whose policies are arbitrary, contradictory or erratic, or whose enforcement of them is weak, unreliable or capricious, will face enormous difficulty in gaining the trust of the diverse actors that comprise the tourism cluster. As developing-country governments often face serious systemic deficiencies in institutional knowledge and administrative capacity, these should be regarded as prime areas for collaboration with international aid agencies. Many international NGOs, bilateral and multilateral organisations have considerable cross-country experience in successful destination management, and their input may be especially valuable in the early stages of cluster formation.

Tourism industries are frequently overseen at the national level by executive agencies dedicated to the purpose (e.g. "the Ministry of Tourism"; "the National Tourism Authority", etc.), but because cluster formation is an inherently local activity and generally cannot be directed efficiently by a central authority, the role of local government is critical. Local governments must take the lead in defining the processes, forums and regulatory regimes for the tourism sector, actively liaising with the cluster's first tourism firms and organising collaborative multi-stakeholder groups to discuss important issues in the nascent tourism sector.

Zoning regulations and other land-use policies are likely to be among the most pressing matters, as the physical disposition of tourism firms (how they are designed and where they are located) has a major influence on both positive and negative externalities generated by the tourism industry. The related subject of tourism firms' impact on local infrastructure should also be accorded a high priority; hotels, restaurants, transportation companies and recreational service providers can have a major impact on the local electrical and water grids, the road network, the sanitation and solid-waste management systems and other forms of public infrastructure. Ensuring that local infrastructure can bear the load, and establishing mechanisms to ensure that the costs of maintaining and upgrading infrastructure are provided for by appropriate revenue streams and prevent excessive strain on public goods and services. Pollution standards and environmental impact assessment procedures should also be among the first subjects for the local government to address; environmental damage is a major source of negative externalities and poses an especially severe threat to the sustainability of tourism destinations. Pre-emptive action in this area is essential, as such damage, once done, may be difficult or impossible to repair.

This is by no means an exhaustive list of policy areas that will require the attention of local government, and public policy priorities will be different in each tourism cluster. However, all tourism destinations face the same challenges of maintaining their social, cultural and environmental capital. This requires that the government go beyond its traditional regulatory role to build a diverse set of public forums and collaborative structures capable of addressing the complex social equity, cultural integrity and environmental preservation goals of destination stakeholders. Policymakers can incorporate sustainability issues into cluster development by integrating multi-stakeholder cooperation into standard policy processes, as described in Chapter 6. Local ecology, including the relationship of local communities with their ecosystem, socioeconomic and cultural inclusion and participation by marginalised groups, transparency and good governance, and the equitable allocation of economic returns to local environmental, social and cultural capital are among the key issues that determine the success of cluster formation, allowing local government to leverage the full benefit of the positive externalities generated by tourism development, while obviating or minimising the negative ones.

While public policy can be a powerful tool for fostering cluster development and strengthening the advantages offered by economies of agglomeration, it is also critical to understand its limits. Cortright (2006) observes that:

> Although not impossible, it is extremely difficult for public policy to call clusters into existence; claims that one can create a new cluster should be treated with extreme skepticism. However, the underlying micro-foundations of clusters offer a range of strategies that economic developers can potentially apply to strengthen their existing industry clusters.[131]

The international experience shows that rather than attempting to initiate cluster development, governments should instead identify organic cluster as they form and provide support through appropriate policies.[132]

131 Cortright, Joseph (2006) "Making Sense of Clusters: Regional Competitiveness and Economic Development" *Discussion Paper,* Brookings Institution Metropolitan Policy Program, Washington DC: The Brookings Institution
132 *Ibid.* See also: Porter, Michael (2008) "Clusters, Innovation and Competitiveness: New Findings and Implications for Policy" *Harvard Business School Note* 456-490

Today it is possible to identify many different clusters around the globe that have emerged as organised units with a coordinated governance structure, formal members, a common brand identity and a well establish development plan based on shared goals. However, in nearly every instance these clusters formed spontaneously though the convergence of market forces, government support was not necessary to establish them, and in some cases excessively interventionist policies have inhibited cluster development.[133]

The popularity of cluster approaches to economic development has grown rapidly in recent years, both in the academic literature and as a matter of public policy; indeed, it is estimated that more scholarly articles on agglomeration economies were published between 2000 and 2005 than had been in the entire 20 years prior.[134] In their rush to capitalise of the considerable advantages offered by cluster development, governments and international organizations have sometimes pursued overzealous attempts to create specific clusters as a matter of economic policy. Though in a few cases these policies were successful, top-down cluster development has more often failed. As a general rule, economic intervention in cluster development should be minimal, and the government should not attempt to 'pick winners' by granting special treatment to politically favoured industries, and especially not to specific firms.[135]

Rather than creating artificial incentives designed to stimulate investments that would otherwise be unprofitable, policymakers should

133 Delgado, M., M.E. Porter, and S. Stern, (2010) "Clusters and Entrepreneurship" *Journal of Economic Geography* 10(4):495-518

134 Maskell, P., and L. Kebir (2005) "What Qualifies as a Cluster Theory?" Copenhagen: Danish Research Unit for Industrial Dynamics, cited in Cortright, Joseph (2006) "Making Sense of Clusters: Regional Competitiveness and Economic Development" Discussion Paper, Brookings Institution Metropolitan Policy Program, Washington DC: The Brookings Institution

135 Porter, Michael (2003) "The Economic Performance of Regions" *Regional Studies* 37: 549-578; Rodriguez-Clare, A. (2007) "Clusters and Comparative Advantage: Implications for Industrial Policy" *Journal of Development Economics* 82: 43-57.

instead identify emerging clusters that they wish to support and work to encourage coordination among companies and institution within the cluster, defining a role for government that best suits the interests of the economic cluster and the society in which it is located. The benefits of a collaborative approach to tourism development are detailed in Chapter 6, and highlighting the dense economic interdependence of firms that operate in the same economic cluster can help to establish the foundation for productive cooperation between firms, public institutions and civil society organisations.

Support to cluster development need not be active, and in many cases passive support will be most effective: the capacity of governments to boost cluster development is directly linked to the quality of their institutions, the efficiency of their tax and regulatory structures, and the appropriateness and efficacy of their overall policy framework. The determination of if, when and how the government should intervene to promote cluster development must be made on a case-by-case basis. This is another area in which local governments should consider drawing on the analytical resources and breadth of experience offered by bilateral and multilateral aid agencies and by certain specialised NGOs.

Clusters emerge as firms, institutions and workers identify the economic benefits of agglomeration in a particular area and gravitate towards it. National economic research agencies, public and private universities and other academic institutions, and private firms providing market intelligence and economic information can all play an important role in identifying incipient clusters and proposing tailored strategies to foster their growth. Mapping clusters and forming cluster-specific sustainability policies can allow local governments to leverage the benefits of cluster formation to advance key public policy goals. These extend beyond the economic benefits of a thriving tourism industry and include social, cultural and environmental objectives that are critical to both the value of the tourism experience and in the quality of life for the local population.[136] Any analysis of an emerging or prospective tourism cluster must take into account the limited resources of the public sector, identifying gaps in administrative capacity that could undermine its ability to effectively manage the destination's development and taking steps to address them.

In addition to conventional political-economic assets such as high-quality infrastructure, sophisticated private sector institutions, and an efficient public administration, the tourism industry is unusually dependent on non-traditional forms of local capital. These include social stability and affinity for tourism, cultural integrity and authenticity, environmental quality and biodiversity, and the overall capacity to provide the complex and varied forms of utility that tourists demand. The long-term sustainability of a tourism destination is directly related to its ability to maintain or increase these non-traditional capital assets, and the cluster approach offers an innovative perspective on how destinations can accomplish this difficult but vital task.

CONCLUSIONS

The close geographical concentration of economic actors focused on the same industry or targeting the same customer base creates a unique opportunity for firms to benefit from one another's presence and achieve superior economic performance as a result of their proximity. Whether clustered in a neighbourhood, a city, a region, or even an entire country, firms in closely related value chains produce positive externalities that enable them to rapidly expand and diversify their industry, greatly magnifying its economic impact. In an international development discourse that is often dominated by a focus on macroeconomic fundamentals and the relative size and growth rates of national-level sectors the cluster approach offers a perspective rooted in economic geography and locational advantage.

---

136 See Aldred, Jonathan (2009) <u>The Skeptical Economist: Revealing the Ethics Inside Economics</u> London: Earthscan. Aldred analyses why traditional economics has largely failed to recognise and appreciate the impact of quality-of-life indicators.

This analytical framework is especially relevant in sustainable tourism, which is always intimately location-specific. Tourism destinations are also unusually reliant on social, cultural and environmental capital, all of which are highly sensitive to the negative externalities produced by competing firms. The cluster approach can help firms, public agencies, and local communities to recognise the interdependent nature of economic actors in a tourism destination and promote collaborative strategies for building the destination's stock of both traditional and non-traditional capital. It can enhance complementarities between different stakeholders and obviate a wide range of negative externalities, from environmental degradation to crime and corruption to the deterioration of social integrity or the debasement of cultural heritage.

The cluster theory offers more than a new theoretical framework for understanding the economics of tourism development. It also demonstrates in clear, practical terms of one of the most widely agreed-upon principles in the literature on sustainable tourism: namely, that successful destination development is dependent on effective multi-stakeholder dialogue and coordination to ensure the responsible use of local capital.[137] Economic development policies often focus on expanding an economy's vertical linkages, increase the amount of local 'value added', and tourism is no exception—import dependence is a major cause of revenue leakage and local sourcing is essential to generating broad-based income and employment effects.[138] However, in the tourism industry horizontal linkages and complementarities between firms drive the creation of com-

137 See, e.g., Inskeep, Edward (1991) Tourism Planning: An Integrated and Sustainable Development Approach New York: Van Nostrand Reinhold; Russo, A. P. (1998) "Organizing Sustainable Tourism Development in Heritage Cities" in Technical Report no. 28, Proceedings of the International Seminar on Tourism Management in Heritage Cities Verona: Cierre Gráfica; UNWTO (2001) Compilation of Good Practices in the Sustainable Development of Ecotourism Madrid: UNWTO; and SNV (2006) "Pro-Poor Sustainable Tourism: Lessons Learned in Nepal" Kathmandu: SNV, among many others.
138 These dynamics are discussed in detail in Chapter 4. See also: Gollub, James et al (2005) "Using Cluster-Based Economic Strategy to Minimize Tourism Leakages" San Francisco: GEDP

petitive advantage to a far greater extent than in almost any other form of economic activity. Forging close and enduring connections among suppliers, consumers, local institutions and communities is not only vital to ensuring an equitable distribution of the benefits of tourism, it is also critical to the economic success of the tourism destination.

When organised properly, multi-stakeholder collaboration can greatly strengthen the horizontal connections between firms and other actors, increasing the information spill-over and innovation dimensions of an economy of agglomeration. However, it will not always be easy to convince a range of participants from the public and private sectors and from civil society—groups which often see their objectives as being in direct conflict with one another—that cooperative dialogue is worthwhile. In many cases the first step will be to demonstrate the practical value of regarding the destination as an economic cluster comprised of numerous actors with interconnected, consistent, even mutually dependent interests.

Stakeholders collaborating in tourism cluster development should begin by engaging with simple issues based on clearly shared concerns in order to strengthen their organisational capacity and build mutual trust as the basis for addressing more complex challenges. As firms, groups and individuals come to recognise and appreciate the advantages of collaborative cluster development these benefits justify the time and resources invested and encourage further joint action; conversely, if collaborative efforts are handled poorly, or gains are slow to materialise, the stakeholder group may fracture and fail despite its potential. Establishing a common appreciation among stakeholders for the nature of cluster development and its role in sustainable tourism can help to hold a multistakeholder group together through its difficult formative period.

Meanwhile, national and local policymakers can work to enhance the natural advantages of cluster development, speeding the growth of tourism clusters without excessively distorting economic incentives. Although cluster development policies must always be tailored to local conditions, interests and aspirations, prospective strategies include accelerating human capital formation by providing education and workforce training in skills specific to the cluster, bolstering physical-capital formation by investing in sector infrastructure, or enhancing the business climate by reforming outdated regulations and streamlining administrative procedures that directly or indirectly impact the cluster. Public and private research institutions have an especially strong role to play in cluster development, as identifying, analysing, mapping and contextualising the growth of tourism clusters is the first step in formulating effective policy.

EXERCISES

1. What is a "positive externality"? List three examples of positive externalities not mentioned in the chapter.
2. What externalities, both positive and negative, are most relevant for tourism clusters? How might these create economies of agglomeration in tourism? How might they create diseconomies of agglomeration?
3. What is the role of information and knowledge in cluster development? How can tourism clusters promote innovation?
4. What is the primary role of the public sector in the development of tourism clusters? What types of policies should a government consider when attempting to foster the growth of a tourism cluster? What policies should it be wary of?
5. What economic and non-economic benefits of tourism clusters are most relevant for sustainable development?

CASE 10 – COMMUNITY TOURISM TRAINING EXCHANGE PROJECT IN SAPA, VIETNAM

By - V. Dao Truong, University of Canterbury, NZ - email: vandao83@ yahoo.co.uk

1. Background

Vietnam is considered among the fastest growing international tourist markets. Between 2003 and 2013, international tourists to Vietnam grew from 2.4 million to 7.5 million (Vietnam National Administration of Tourism (VNAT) 2011, 2014a). Vietnam's total tourism receipts increased from US$830 million in 2000 to US$9.5 billion in 2013 (VNAT 2014b). The potential of tourism as a means of economic growth and poverty alleviation has been recognised by the Government of Vietnam (Truong 2013). This potential is particularly important in remote and disadvantaged areas, including Sapa where poor ethnic minorities have limited off-farm livelihood opportunities. Although tourism has been considered a spearhead sector in Sapa, most tourism profits have accrued to privately owned tour operators (Truong, Hall, & Garry 2014). A majority of the locals view tourism as the only income generator outside of the main rice crop but they are far from having access to the benefits of tourism. The main barriers, *inter alia*, are their low levels of education and lack of professional knowledge and skills. Ethnic women often chase tourists to sell handicrafts, driving them away from some destinations and hence threatening sustainable tourism (Truong et al. 2014). It is in this context that the Community Tourism Training Exchange Project, which is funded by the Pacific Asia Travel Association (PATA) Foundation, is implemented by Capilano University (Canada) and Hanoi Open University (Vietnam) in partnership with Sapa Department of Culture, Sports and Tourism. This project illustrates the roles of capacity building and stakeholder collaboration in promoting sustainable tourism.

2. Project description

This PATA Foundation/Capilano University initiative built on the success of a community tourism training project which was funded by the Canadian International Development Agency from 2002 to 2007. It was implemented in Ta Phin and Lao Chai villages that are among the main points of interest and trekking destinations in Sapa. Starting from 2010 to 2012, the project aimed to provide capacity training to local villagers so that the benefits of increased tourist visitation would be distributed widely in the villages and positive experiences could be improved for both tourists and host communities. The project had three main objectives. The first was to provide practical tourism training as a means to assist rural communities reduce poverty, improve their living conditions, and help provide sustainable, authentic cultural and nature based experiences for visitors to their communities. The second was to build local capacity through the exchange of knowledge and skills of community members, domestic and foreign educational institutions, and other stakeholders. The third objective was to broaden the product base from homestays and street handicrafts to guiding, food and beverage services, artisan products, a village market, spa and wellness products, events and festivals, as well as other products and services (Sandilands 2012).

PHOTOS COURTESY OF MERCOTUR.

3. Project activities

This project began with the analysis of community needs and the organisation of stakeholder meetings. These activities aimed to establish learning objectives and develop training modules, clarify project objectives and expected outcomes with local authority of Sapa, organise meetings with village leaders and local homestay and business owners to establish project goals, hold meetings with members of local Women's Union and Youth Union to clarify training objectives, and discuss with handicraft sellers to understand the challenges they faced and identify possible measures to stop them from chasing tourists.

The next step was to deliver training sessions in the villages. More than 40 training sessions were conducted over the course of six training visits. Trainers were lecturers of Capilano University and Hanoi Open University. Participants included over 100 residents of Ta Phin and Lao Chai villages and 20 government officials. These sessions focused on general tourism knowledge for community members; community tourism planning for local authority and community stakeholders; entrepreneurship for local young adults and women; business development, marketing, and network building for small business owners; environmental stewardship for children; improvement of selling skills, including English language training; and homestay development.

Besides the formal training sessions, practical learning workshops were organised with homestay owners, street vendors, local government, and business owners. These workshops were facilitated by representatives of Ta Phin village, resulting in the formulation of a mission statement for tourism development which is arguably the first of its kind in Vietnam. The statement states, *"Ta Phin commune is proud to have developed community-based tourism activities. We not only provide herbal bath and handicraft... but also homestays, cultural and culinary traditions, natural scenic caves, and rice terraces. We must be friendly to customers, maintain the product, and encourage local traditions. We must preserve environmental hygiene and not follow or annoy tourists…" (www.cbtvietnam.com)*

A variety of additional activities were also undertaken. For example, individual business support and development was provided, including such activities as consultations to small community business owners and improvements of washrooms and catering facilities in homestays. A Community-based Tourism Management Board was created. Board members, who were voted by local villagers at a community meeting, included a village chief, a representative of the village police, a homestay representative, a representative for local handicrafts, and a representative for the local youth.

An interesting part of the project was the organisation of familiarisation trips for tour operators in Sapa town to experience local homestays. These trips offered tour operators and homestay owners an open forum where they discussed possible partnership opportunities. Tour operators challenged homestay owners to improve service quality while homestay owners challenged tour operators regarding benefit sharing. Some consensus was reached and partnerships established. Attention was also paid to the development of a market where local sellers can trade their handicrafts. A plan to build a community house and a market was approved by the local authority. Furthermore, a collaborative relationship was developed with the local authority of Sapa who highly appreciated the outcomes of the project and expressed their interest in developing similar projects in other destinations in Sapa.

4. Project outcomes

A range of positive outcomes were achieved from this project. Most importantly, residents in Ta Phin and Lao Chai villages greatly enhanced their capacity in developing tourism-related businesses. Service quality was improved of existing homestays, artisan products, and other tourism-related ventures. At least eight new homestays were established in these villages. New tourist guiding and food service businesses also emerged.

A new marketplace was created in Ta Phin, providing a regular workplace for more than eight village members. A number of local women shifted from chasing tourists in the streets to selling handicrafts in local marketplace and hence improved their selling skills as well as sales of handicrafts. Improvements were seen in the experiences of foreign tourists to Sapa.

At the regional and national levels, communications and cooperation were strengthened amongst the community, local government, and the private sector in managing sustainable tourism development. The project closure meeting attracted the participation of three tour operators in Hanoi, three tour operators in Sapa, three tourist guides, one social enterprise leader, one Youth leader, seven homestay owners, and two government representatives. An important outcome was the positive and respectful relationship that was established between the leaders of Sapa and the local residents (Sadilands 2012).

5. Challenges ahead

Tourism is economically important to Sapa in that it generates employment and income for the local labour force. However, a large number of the local ethnic minorities lack knowledge, skills, and experiences needed to participate in and realise the economic potential of tourism. This case study has illustrated that providing practical skills training to local villagers is among the keys to breaking down the barriers that prevent them from getting involved in tourism, and this can be achieved through effective collaboration amongst various stakeholders. Nevertheless, several challenges need to be overcome if tourism is to develop sustainably in Sapa. It is necessary to stop local women from chasing foreign tourists down the streets as this selling practice has driven tourists away from some destinations (e.g. Ta Phin) where sellers even verbally abuse tourists who refuse to purchase handicrafts (Truong et al. 2014). This practice puts local homestays at risk and threatens sustainable tourism overall. For example, a woman in Ta Phin borrowed a loan of US$3,000 to upgrade her homestay and diversify her products and services. She estimated that it would take her three to 10 years to repay. While she was proud of her homestay, she was worried that it would be difficult to earn income if local sellers continued following tourists (Sadilands 2012). The marketplace offered by the local authority, although necessary, did not have enough space for all sellers. It was also located at the edge of Ta Phin village where very few tourists visited. However, this is also a long-lasting practice of local women, many of whom already have over 10 years of experience as street vendors (Truong et al. 2014). Therefore, while an alternative that is at least equally beneficial is required to reduce the number of street vendors, measures are also needed to promote voluntary behaviour change in handicraft sellers. In short, the case of Sapa suggests that sustainable tourism cannot be achieved by chance. Instead, it requires not only meaningful collaborative relationships amongst relevant stakeholders in the private and public sectors but also positive cooperation and, to some extent, voluntary behaviour change in members of the host communities.

REFERENCES

Sandilands, K. (2012). *Ta Phin and Lao Chai Vietnam: Community tourism training exchange project final report*. Retrieved from www.cbtvietnam.com.

Truong, V.D. (2013). Tourism policy development in Vietnam: A pro-poor perspective. *Journal of Policy Research in Tourism, Leisure and Events, 5*(1), 28-45.

Truong, V.D., Hall, C.M., & Garry, T. (2014). Tourism and poverty alleviation: Perceptions and experiences of poor people in Sapa, Vietnam. *Journal of Sustainable Tourism*, DOI: 10.1080/09669582.2013.871019.

Vietnam National Administration of Tourism (VNAT). (2011). *Tourism statistics 2011*. Retrieved from www.vietnamtourism.gov.vn.

Vietnam National Administration of Tourism (VNAT). (2014a). *International tourist arrivals to Vietnam 2013*. Retrieved from www.vietnamtourism. gov.vn.

Vietnam National Administration of Tourism (VNAT). (2014b). *Tourism receipts 2000-2013*. Retrieved from www.vietnamtourism.gov.vn.

Eight

The Role of Information, Research and Analysis

"If we were running a business with the biosphere as our major asset, we would not allow it to depreciate. We would ensure that all necessary repairs and maintenance were carried out on a regular basis." Prof.

Alan Malcolm, Chief Scientific Advisor, Institute of Biology, IUPAC

OBJECTIVES OF THE CHAPTER:

- Expand the definition of economic, social, cultural and environmental capital and examine methods for measuring each type of local capital.
- Explore the various types of information required for effective destination management and how this information may be acquired.
- Review the key role of subjective assessments and qualitative data in sustainable tourism development.

INTRODUCTION

As in other areas of development policy, effective tourism destination management requires a constant flow of high-quality information. Sustainability goes beyond immediate economic viability, and its fundamental imperative, to maintain capital intact, greatly increases the informational demands of destination management. Sustainability broadens the scope of relevant data and adds much-needed complexity and nuance to complement more traditional forms of economic analysis. The market intelligence generated by the private sector is no less important in tourism than it is in other industries, but as tourism is more sensitive than other industries to the impact of **negative externalities**, more prone to conflicts over **common-pool resources**, and more dependent on a broad range of actors with diverse and often competing interests, sustainable tourism policy requires information of greater scope and detail than what the market typically provides.

Understanding trends in exchange rate dynamics, the composition of local factor prices, the administrative costs, regulatory compliance issues, and other aspects of the business climate relevant to tourism, and the relative market position and forecasts for competing destinations are all essential to formulating effective destination policy. However, these data do not tell the whole story, and policies based solely upon them cannot be expected to ensure the long-term sustainability of the destination. As described in previous chapters, sustainability is predicated on maintaining or increasing the local stock of economic, social, cultural and environmental capital in order to guarantee **intergenerational equity**: constant returns across indefinite future generations.[139] To accomplish this, policymakers and other stakeholders must be able to assess the current value of these local capital stocks and evaluate changes over time. As these forms of capital extend beyond traditional economic assets, so too must the analysis on which tourism policy is based.

---

139 See the discussion of intergenerational equity presented in Chapter 2.

As sustainability has gradually moved towards the mainstream of development policy, experts in monitoring and evaluation methodology have increasingly turned their attention to measuring these forms of non-traditional capital, and a number of different estimation techniques are now available. Much like other forms of data that inform public policy, there is in many cases a trade-off between the sophistication of the technique and the transparency of the findings. While more complex forms of research can yield more precise data, they are also more opaque to the public and may be more easily distorted or manipulated to serve specific interests. The objectivity and trustworthiness of tourism information is essential to **multi-stakeholder collaboration**; policymakers, entrepreneurs and local stakeholders must share an accurate and consistent analytical framework as the foundation for cooperative problem-solving. Information gathering and analysis consequently presents an important avenue for partnerships with international organisations, many of which offer both strong analytical capacity and credible impartiality.

Successful tourism destinations continuously expand their capacity to understand the needs, values and aspirations of local stakeholders and work to design policies that reflect evolving attitudes towards tourism and its role in local development. Achieving a comprehensive accounting of local capital and ensuring flexibility and responsiveness in tourism policy requires multiple forms of information-gathering. Routine data collection on a range of tourism-specific indicators must be augmented by carefully designed surveys targeting individuals and groups from multiple sectors of society. Preliminary analysis used to ground policies and programs must be complemented by ex post evaluations their costs and impacts. Quantitative data much be matched by qualitative assessments. In order to design an information management structure capable of underpinning sustainable tourism policies, it is essential to understand the types of information required and the methodologies available for acquiring them.

ASSESSING LOCAL CAPITAL STOCKS

There a two possible approaches to measuring local capital stocks. Each form of capital—economic, social, cultural and environmental—may be defined and assessed individually according to its own discreet methodology, or all forms may be assessed under a single integrated framework. Each approach has its own advantages and drawbacks. Using different assessment techniques may yield more precise results for each capital type, but an individual may require more work and raises the possibility duplicative or otherwise unnecessary efforts. An integrated approach can greatly simplify information gathering, but its interdisciplinary nature may result in the use of inappropriate or outdated methods for assessing some capital types. Policymakers should consider which approach is best suited to their research and assessment capabilities, but whichever is chosen consistency over time is always the most important element. Methodological changes, even those designed to enhance the accuracy of the information produced, introduce the possibility of data incompatibility, systematic error, or even intentional manipulation. Once data collection processes and analytical methodologies are established they should be changed rarely, if ever.

In terms of individual indicators, methods for valuing traditional **economic capital** and identifying trends in the capital stock over time are very well developed. Assessing economic capital is a relatively a straightforward process involving easily identifiable assets (bridges, factories, ports) that have a clear monetary value. The adjusted net savings method used by the World Bank[140] is among the most widely accepted techniques and encompasses measures of human capital (education) and environmental capital (see below) in addition to physical capital. Although it is typically used at the national level, adjusted savings can also be calculated at the regional or local level. However, it should be noted that accurately determining the adjusted savings rate and measuring changes in the underlying capital stock require a high degree of analytical capacity that may not always be available at the sub-national level. Local governments should

---

140 See Chapter 2, Box 2.

consider seeking assistance from international agencies in this and other areas of information-gathering and analysis.

Methods for gauging **social capital** have received considerable attention in development literature, and there is now a growing consensus regarding both the value of social capital in sustainable development and the criteria for precisely measuring it. Social capital describes the fundamental cohesiveness and unity of a society and its resilience to division and conflict. The most easily quantifiable forms of social capital relate to membership in civil society organisations and their influence in local decision-making, which can have an enormous impact on individual satisfaction and community integrity.[141]

Other, related dimensions of social capital are more difficult to measure but no less important. These include the extent to which members of society share a single identity and a common set of values and aspirations, which influences their ability to identify and overcome problems collectively and to use shared resources efficiently. Thanks in part to the World Bank's ground-breaking Social Capital Initiative (1996-2001) there is now a substantial literature on techniques for assessing the strength of social connections and progressive integration (or disintegration) over time as well as methods for analysing their impact on social and economic development.[142]

Social capital is both directly and indirectly important to the tourism industry. As illustrated in Chapter 2, instability, violence and conflict can

141 This was the focus area of XXXX, whose seminal work, Bowling Alone, is a cornerstone of modern sociology.

142 This project encompassed two dozen working papers from prominent economists, sociologists and technical specialists from a range of disciplines. For an overview of its findings see Grootaert, C. and T. van Bastelaer (2001) "Understanding and Measuring Social Capital: A Synthesis of Findings and Recommendations from the Social Capital Initiative" Social Capital Initiative Working Paper No.24 Washington DC: The World Bank. The entire series was later consolidated and operationalized in Understanding and Measuring Social Capital: A Multidisciplinary Tool for Practitioners (2002) Grootaert, C. and T. van Bastelaer (Eds.) World Bank Directions in Development Series, Washington DC: The World Bank

have an especially devastating—and remarkably lasting—impact on the tourism industry. A destination that develops a reputation for any type of dangerous unpredictability will have an extremely difficult time overcoming it. Strong social cohesion is necessary (though not sufficient) to ensure that a peaceful socio-political environment is maintained, both locally and nationally. Yet even in the absence of significant systemic insecurity social cohesion can greatly affect the quality of tourism services, though the strength of its impact depends in large part on the specific type of tourism development.

In the controlled environment of an all-inclusive resort the destination's relative degree of social cohesion may be largely irrelevant, as most interactions between tourists and local citizens will be closely monitored and involve paid hospitality staff. However, in an environment where interactions between tourists and local society are common and spontaneous—e.g. in contexts where a **tourism cluster** has formed and tourists move freely between many different firms, or where cultural tourism, ethno-tourism, or any form of community-based tourism is a major element of the industry—social cohesion is extremely important. If tourists sense dissatisfaction, tension, or hostility in the destination community, whether directed towards the ruling government, towards rival political parties or social groups, or especially towards the tourism industry itself, these negative perceptions can exert a significant dampening effect on tourism demand. Given the often disruptive social impact of tourism development it is vital that local policymakers actively monitor changes in social capital and take steps to reinforce social cohesion—for example, by addressing equity concerns regarding the distribution of tourism revenues, a common source of tourism-related discord. Assessing and strengthening social capital may not be as simple or direct a process as monitoring and building economic capital, but it is equally vital to the sustainability of the tourism industry.

Measuring **cultural capital** is an even more complex and ambiguous process. In one sense the worth of cultural capital can be understood as a matter of economic calculus applied to cultural assets; yet in another, perhaps more meaningful sense is an abstract value of cultural achievement on which no monetary figure can be placed. For example, one might ask how much is the Taj Mahal worth? On the one hand it is worth the amount of revenue it generates, both directly through visitor fees and indirectly through tourism-related transportation, accommodations, food and other services. Its "cultural value" distinguishes it from any comparable building, but it is still an economic asset with a value expressible in currency. On the other hand, however, it is a unique cultural artefact, a peerless expression of the power of human endeavour and an inspirational vision of what mankind can accomplish. It is incomparable, inimitable, and irreplaceable. Its value is incalculable.

Further complicating matters is the fact that cultural capital extends beyond historical sites and other tangible cultural products, encompassing traditions, practices, attitudes and ways of life that are the products of a singular history and the essential elements of a communal identity. The value of these cultural assets is even more abstract, and damage done to cultural integrity is far harder to calculate. In 2003 UNESCO launched a ground-breaking initiative aimed at preserving these forms of cultural capital, which it terms "intangible cultural heritage". The centrepiece of these efforts is the International Convention on the Safeguarding of Intangible Cultural Heritage, to which over 150 countries are now signatory. In 2009 UNESCO published a "kit" on intangible cultural heritage as a "basic reference and pedagogical instrument for promoting and ensuring an effective understanding of intangible cultural heritage and the 2003 Convention by governments, communities, experts, concerned UN agencies, NGOs and interested individuals."[143] In 2011 the kit was updated to include a manual for assessing intangible cultural capital.[144]

---

143 UNESCO (2009) Kit of the Convention for the Safeguarding of Intangible Cultural Heritage Available online with later additions at http://www.unesco.org/culture/ich/index.php?lg=en&pg=00451#1
144 UNESCO (2011) Identifying and Inventorying Intangible Cultural Heritage Available online at http://www.unesco.org/culture/ich/doc/src/01856-EN.pdf

Due to the near impossibility of fixing a meaningful monetary value on cultural forms and practices, UNECO recommends establishing a comprehensive local inventory of cultural assets comprising five basic types of intangible culture: "(a.) Oral traditions and expressions including language as a vehicle of intangible cultural heritage; (b.) Performing arts; (c.) Social practices, rituals and festive events; (d.) Knowledge and practices about nature and the universe; [and] (e.) Traditional craftsmanship."[145] Once this list is compiled it must be regularly updated and modified in order to reflect the on-going evolution of cultural forms and address the emergence of new threats. While it may not be practical to place monetary value on local cultural assets, and assessing success in cultural preservation may be more art than science, following the UNESCO methodology for identifying and protecting intangible cultural heritage can adequately serve the sustainability imperative to maintain cultural capital intact.

The importance of **environmental capital** continues to receive much attention in the international development literature. This emphasis reflects two underlying trends: (i) a growing awareness among policymakers and the public regarding the implications of transnational pollution and especially the threat posed by climate change, and (ii) an emerging, and related, consensus among economists that previous growth models did not adequately account for the economic value of environmental

---

145 *Ibid.* Compiling a national inventory is part of the requirements of the Convention, but UNESCO procedures for doing so are recommendations, not mandates. See also UNESCO's 2012 *List of Intangible Cultural Heritage in Need of Urgent Safeguarding* (http://www.unesco.org/culture/ich/doc/src/20435-EN.pdf), which encompasses 298 forms of cultural capital that are in danger of disappearing, ranging from traditional Zafimaniry woodcrafts in Madagascar to the Ride of the Kings festival in the Czech Republic to the Sbek Thom shadow theatre of Cambodia. It should also be noted that endangered forms of cultural capital are not restricted to developing or transitional countries; France, for example, has nine forms of intangible cultural heritage listed as in need of urgent safeguarding, including Alancon needlework and even "gastronomic meals of the French".

assets, both local and global.[146] Currently there are a number of different methodologies for assessing changes in natural capital, at least two of which have gained widespread acceptance.

The environmental cost component of the net national savings calculation used by the World Bank (see Chapter 2) provides an excellent example of one common technique for valuing environmental capital. This may be thought of as the "negative approach", as it involves assessing the economic costs incurred through the depletion of three types of natural capital (energy, mineral, and forest resources) and two types of pollution damage (carbon dioxide and particulate matter), but does not include a positive assessment of the value of the underlying environmental capital stock. In other words, it measures costs of environmental degradation rather than the value of environmental assets. Each type of environmental cost is determined according to a methodology appropriate to its circumstances. To learn more, visit: http://siteresources.worldbank.org/ENVIRONMENT/Resources/Calculating_Adjusted_Net_Saving.pdf

An alternate method for determining changes in the environmental capital stock is to assess the total value of all natural capital assets, and then compare that value with the results of subsequent assessments. Constanza et al. (1997) propose a methodology for gauging the economic value of an impressive range of "ecosystem goods and services". This technique estimates how much different types of ecosystem are "worth", per unit area, based on the market-determined prices of the goods and services produced by those ecosystems or their nearest manmade substitutes. For example, one hectare of rainforest provides an estimated US$1,900 per year by providing services ranging from preventing soil erosion (US$245) to facilitating recreational activities (US$112) and goods

146 These two trends are closely linked, and the recognition of climate change prompted a radical rethinking of how environmental capital is assessed in economic terms. See, e.g., Nordhaus, William D. (1993) "Reflections on the Economics of Climate Change" *The Journal of Economic Perspectives* 7(4):11-25 http://www.jstor.org/stable/2138498

ranging from raw materials (US$315) to foodstuffs (US$32), along with many others.[147]

Among the advantages of this "positive approach" is that it allows for much greater comprehensiveness in terms of the types and extent of environmental damage measured. It also provides a compelling look at the economic value of environmental resources, which can be used as a basis for policies that take these values into account. It is also easily scalable: because it is based on value per unit area (hectare) the assessment can be tailored to fit any geographic territory. However, there are also significant downsides. Performing this type of assessment is an even more complex process than the World Bank methodology, and it must be done repeatedly in order to identify changes over time. This is another instance in which local policymakers and other stakeholders may wish to partner with international organisations

Finally, one of the most innovative **integrated approaches** to assessing the value of all local capital stocks was devised by Choi and Sirakaya (2006). This methodology was designed specifically for the tourism sector and is based on the principles of sustainable, community-based tourism development.[148] It comprises 125 indicators used to measure six dimensions of local capital, which include the four dimensions described above—economic, social, cultural and environmental capital—as well as the two additional dimensions of political and technological capital. The assessment is based on a modified version of the Delphi technique, which uses expert consensus to set values for indicators that would otherwise be difficult to quantify.

---

147 Constanza et al. (1997) "The Value of the World's Ecosystem Services and Natural Capital" *Nature* 387(May) http://www.esd.ornl.gov/benefits_conference/nature_paper.pdf All US$ values are for 1997.
148 Choi, H.C. and E. Sirakaya (2006) "Sustainability Indicators for Managing Community Tourism" *Tourism Management* 27: 1274-1289 http://www.sciencedirect.com/science/article/pii/S0261517705000737

This approach can greatly simplify the assessment process; instead of performing complex calculations for each indicator, those performing the assessment simply solicit expert opinions from a variety of sources with intimate knowledge of the relevant subjects and then aggregate those opinions. However, the low analytical capacity demands of the modified Delphi technique are offset by its significant drawbacks in accuracy and comparability. Expert consensus is a valuable tool for predicting future events, but it is less useful in defining present conditions, when more precise methods are available. Moreover, the estimates made for any one time and place are inherently subjective and conditioned by contemporary expectations, limiting the possibilities for comparisons over time or between cases. Nevertheless, the simplicity of this approach can make it a viable option when resource constraints prevent extensive data collection or complex forms of analysis.

LOCAL CAPITAL AND THE TOURISM INDUSTRY

An accurate and up-to-date assessment of local capital—and an evolving strategy for protecting it—should form the foundation of tourism policy, but a great deal of additional information may also be required by destination policymakers. Regular surveys are an integral part of local information gathering, and can generate critical data that would otherwise be unavailable. Unfortunately, in the tourism sector these efforts have too often focused exclusively on understanding the experience of tourists and have failed to account for local perceptions of tourism development or take advantage of local knowledge as a policy tool.

Local knowledge is valuable maintaining or enhancing all forms of capital, and surveys should solicit information on local economic, social, cultural and environmental conditions. **Economic information** may be classed into two categories, efficiency and equity.[149] Efficiency informa-

---

149 It should be recalled that these categories are not mutually exclusive and in fact often reinforce one another. See Chapter 2.

tion includes conducting market research and identifying potential competitive advantages, analysing constraints faced by the both the local private sector and international investors, and defining priorities for improving the business climate. Efficiency information is concerned solely with the competitiveness of the destination, and in many cases it has been the primary, if not the exclusive, focus of policymakers.

Yet from a public policy perspective, and recognising the sustainability implications of social cohesion, equity information is equally important. Equity information is about how the benefits of tourism are distributed; it describes the participation of the local community in the tourism industry and the extent to which they add value to tourism services. Conversely, it can be regarded as a measuring revenue **leakages**—the extent to which tourism value is added by imports rather than by the local community. Expanding the integration of the tourism industry into the local economy can have important benefits in terms of how the industry is viewed and received by the destination community (with important implications for social cohesion) as well as its net economic value, both for public sector revenues and private incomes.

When designing tourism surveys it should be born in mind that although private sector representatives can be extremely useful sources of local knowledge, economic information is not solely the province of formal private firms. Everyday citizens who operate in a particular economic environment will have important information about local market conditions, information which may explain why seemingly obvious opportunities go unexploited and why interventions that appear clearly beneficial will in fact fail. In gathering economic information, as in the other subject areas described below, surveys and other informational tool should not focus myopically on a single group, but rather balance expert opinions with broad-based local knowledge. Asking direct questions about local participation in the tourism sector (e.g. "Do you work with tourists or tourism firms?" or "Do you benefit personally from the tourism industry?") can help illuminate the extent of untapped potential in the local economy, while questions about why this might or might not be the case (e.g. "If you don't work with the tourism industry, why not?" or "What would allow you to take advantage greater of the tourism industry?") can help to identify binding constraints on local participation.

In terms of **social information**, tourism destinations have a clear interest in monitoring the local community's changing perceptions of, and attitudes towards, the tourism industry. Less obvious but no less important is the extent to which the general satisfaction of the local community impacts tourist perceptions and, consequently, the competitiveness of the industry. Asking general questions about the respondent's overall happiness and impressions of community wellbeing (e.g. "Are you better off now than you were a year ago?" or "Do you feel that your community is heading in the right direction?") can help to gauge general satisfaction, while questions about social empowerment and resilience ("Do you feel that community leaders listen to your opinions?" or "Can you influence the direction of your community?" or "If you were in trouble, would others in your community come to your aid?") can serve as a proxy for social capital. Finally, specific questions about the actual or potential impact of the tourism industry on local society (e.g. "Do you feel that the tourism industry benefits the community or harms it?" or "How could the tourism industry do more to benefit your community?") can inform policies that respect the economic impact of local perceptions.

Similarly, important **cultural information** can be obtained from surveys, but acquiring and interpreting it can be a difficult because cultural value is subjective and situational. Cultural capital is not restricted to local perceptions and values: the worth that outsiders place on cultural forms and expressions is just as real as the local value, and there need not be a clear distinction between the two. Defining and safeguarding what tourists or other foreign observers view as valuable elements of local culture can be as meaningful as identifying and protecting locally recognised cultural assets. The value of cultural capital depends on current information, perceptions and market linkages. Consequently, cultural value shifts over time, and decisions about what to preserve may suffer from **discounting** based on imperfect information.

Discounting is a term used in economics to describe the exchange of future value for present value. For example, consider a farmer harvesting grain: he or she can consume all of the harvest now (maximizing its present value) or save it all as seed to replant for the next year (maximising it future value). The farmer's "discount rate" is the proportion of grain he or she consumers now relative to what he or she replants for future consumption. As in farming, decisions involving cultural capital depend on the information available at the time, which determine the expectation of something's future value relative to its current value. Since the value of cultural capital changes unpredictably over time, its owners cannot always accurately estimate the discount rate involved in preserving cultural artefacts.

Moreover, there is often a significant disparity between the **private opportunity cost** and the **social opportunity cost** of cultural preservation: cultural patrimony has an abstract social value that extends beyond its private value to its owner. In cases where cultural property is privately owned, the opportunity cost of preserving it (rather than selling it or putting it to some economically useful purpose) is borne entirely by the owner. Society benefits from its preservation, but society cannot compensate the owner for those benefits. As a result, economic incentives to preserve cultural heritage cannot accurately reflect its value to society. Poverty and insecurity compound the incentive to discount cultural heritage, maximising its current value at the expense of its value in the future. All too often the loss of cultural is noticed only after it has already happened.

BOX 9 - CULTURAL VALUE: COINS, PYRAMIDS, GATES AND BUDDHAS

In Ethiopia, on the islands of Lake Tana near Bahir Dar, it is common for artisans to melt down antique silver coins in order to make small religious talismans and pieces of jewellery. While some of these are worn by local people, many are sold to tourists for a modest price. Yet the coins being melted down, Austrian Maria Theresa Thalers, have considerable cultural and economic value, both of which are growing over time.

Maria Theresa Thalers have a special place in Ethiopian history dating back to the 18th Century, when they were among the first forms of European currency used in East Africa. Most Maria Theresa Thalers currently in Ethiopia date to the early 20th Century, as do the even rarer "Tallero XE" introduced by the Italians during the Second World War, and both are currently appreciating on international numismatic ("coin collecting") markets. However, local silversmiths may lack information about international numismatic markets or access to them, they may be unaware that the coins are appreciating or that they constitute cultural artefacts, and their ability to preserve these coins as a matter of cultural heritage may be undermined by Ethiopia's widespread poverty and economic insecurity. The cost of keeping these coins falls entirely on the owner, who must forego the value of selling them, but is not compensated for that cost.

In many instances cultural value is different to different people. Consider the case of the Nohmul Mayan pyramid in Belize, which was demolished in 2013 to provide gravel for a new road. In the estimation of the international community of archaeologists and, potentially, tourists, the pyramid was an invaluable example of Toltec architecture. Yet in the estimation of the

Belizean road construction company, the pyramid had a very definite and limited value as a source of gravel. These two values were mutually incompatible, and now the road exists, while the pyramid does not. This can be seen as a conflict between economic and cultural values, or between the immediate economic value of the road and the longer-term economic value of the pyramid as a cultural site and tourist attraction. However, there are also instances in which two competing cultural values are intrinsically at odds and cannot be reconciled.

Extreme cases such as the levelling of the Babri Masjid by Hindu fundamentalists in 1992, the Taliban's dynamiting of the Bamiyan Buddhas in 2001, or the more recent demolition of the "End of the World" Gate in Timbuktu by Islamist insurgents serve to illustrate the power of radically different, fundamentally incompatible visions of cultural value. However, in most circumstances the destruction of objects, practices and local forms of knowledge is not the result of a deliberate attempt to change (or impoverish) the culture of a society, but is simply a consequence of prevailing economic circumstances: unplanned, undirected and unmotivated except by economic calculus. When considering how to alter this calculus, it should be borne in mind that tourism is one of the most effective mechanisms available for translating cultural value into economic value, and it offers a crucial means to offset the market imperfections and distorted incentives that too often result in the destruction of irreplaceable cultural heritage.

Understanding cultural value, identifying what cultural forms, artefacts, traditions and practices can and should be protected and determining how to preserve them in a rapidly evolving modern world requires soliciting input from a wide range of stakeholders and reconciling complex competing interests. Though local communities must be recognised as the primary repositories of living cultural heritage, efforts to gather information on cultural value must also include private sector representatives, especially from the tourism industry, who are often in a superior position to accurately estimate the value of culture as an economic resource. Broad-based surveys should be supplemented by interviews with academics and socialised experts who can shed light on both the current and prospective future value of cultural patrimony from an international perspective and in an appropriate historical context.

Collecting **environmental information** is a similarly complex process. Much like cultural capital, environmental capital is often subject to severe discount rates and significant disparities between private and social costs. The unsustainable harvesting of ecological resources, the destruction of biodiversity and the pollution or degradation of both natural and manmade environments are textbook products of market failures and distorted incentives. Resolving these problems often requires extensive dialogue and active **multi-stakeholder collaboration**; but in order for environmental capital to be effectively protected, it must first be understood.

Assessing the worth of environmental assets and gathering information about how communities interact with local ecosystems requires ongoing input from a diversity of sources. Local communities often have an intimate, multifaceted, and constantly evolving relationship with their environment, one which may be difficult for outsiders to fully understand. Ecosystems are a source of basic services such as food, water, clean air and shelter; it provides income both in cash and in kind; and in many cases it is central to individual history, social identity and cultural meaning. Consequently, the worth of environmental assets can be very different to different parties, and the private economic value assigned to them through the allocation of property rights may greatly underestimate their value to society.

The quality of the ambient environment, both natural and manmade, has a profound influence on the fundamental happiness and wellbeing of the people who inhabit it. It also has a clear economic value that can be realised through tourism. However, as described in previous chapters a portion of this value derives from the **positive externalities** of environmental quality, the extent to which it benefits (or harms) people and firms who have only a limited ability to influence it. Researchers have developed a number of techniques for estimating the value of environmental resources in the tourism industry, such as "contingent valuation," the "hedonic travel cost method" and "choice modelling".[150] However, all currently available econometric techniques suffer from significant limitations, and none is able to adequately account for the value of natural resources and its ecosystem services to the local community, or assess how tourism development may affect that value.

Achieving a comprehensive understanding of environmental resources and how they are valued by the tourism industry, the local community and other stakeholders requires an interdisciplinary approach. Traditional socio-economic data collection designed to assess the market value of property and commodities, the income and employment effects of resource development and ecological damage, and the public health and economic productivity implications of toxic pollutants must be supplemented by qualitative information designed to address the subjective experience of the local environment and its impact on overall happiness and wellbeing. This is not an ancillary policy matter or an optional field of research. The subjective experience of environmental quality is linked to the competitiveness of a tourism destination directly through its impact on the value of tourism services, and indirectly through its effect on how the industry is perceived by the community, with all attendant social and political implications.

---

150 Tisdell, Clem (2003) "Valuation of Tourism's Natural Resources" *Economics, Ecology and the Environment Working Papers* No. 81 Brisbane: University of Queensland

Understanding and evaluating ecosystem services is also fundamental for tourism destinations as a growing need to mitigate and adapt to climate change rise. For example, investing in 'ecological infrastructure' makes economic sense in terms of cost effectiveness and rates of return, once the whole range of benefits provided by maintained, restored or increased ecological services are taken into account. Well-documented examples include investing in mangroves or other wetland ecosystems as well as watersheds, instead of man-made infrastructure like dykes or waste water treatment plants, in order to sustain or enhance the provision of ecosystem services. Experience shows that it is usually much cheaper to avoid degradation than to pay for ecological restoration. This is particularly true for biodiversity: species that go extinct can not be brought back. Nonetheless, there are many cases where the expected benefits from restoration far exceed the costs. If transformation of ecosystems is severe, true restoration of pre-existing species assemblages, ecological processes and the delivery rates of services may well be impossible. However, some ecosystem services may often be recovered by restoring simplified but well-functioning ecosystems modelled on the pre-existing local system. This and other critical natural capital and ecosystem services critical thinking should be mainstreamed in tourism destinations policy and public management practice. To learn more about ecosyste services assessments, I recommend to visit the Convention on Biological Biodiversity web page.

BOX 10 – CELL PHONES FOR ELEPHANTS
Lewas wildlife Conservancy has become a model for African conservation, demonstrating how the tourism that wildlife attracts can benefit neighboring communities, providing them with employment and business opportunities. Since 2000, Iain Douglas-Hamilton, who founded the organization Save the Elephants, had pioneered the use of GPS and satellite communications to study the movements of elephants. At Lewa,

Douglas-Hamilton outfitted elephants with tracking collars that connect to the Safaricom mobile networks easily as any local cell phone did. These connections allow Lewa's researchers to effectively call the tracking collars of the conservancy's elephants and download their location data on demand, all the while plotting their migration between Lewa and the forest flanking Mount Kenya.

Today Lewa uses collars for more than research, piloting a program to reduce human-elephant conflict that results when elephants raid crops and to provide safes passage for elephants when they move through agricultural and other settled areas. Using accumulated data on elephant migration routes, the conservancy identified and protected ideal migration corridors. It even constructed a highway underpass to reduce the risk of elephants colliding with cars. Lewa also straps tracking collars on problem elephants with history of raiding crops. If one of the elephants approaches a farm or village, its collar sends a text message to wildlife rangers, who can quickly locate the animal and move it away in order to prevent any damage. True to their reputation for intelligence, the elephants quickly learn to mind such virtual fences and keep clear of farms.

The Lewa project shows how a relatively simple, low-cost tracking device can transform wildlife conservation. Using data from such devices, conservationists can shape protected areas around predictable migratory patterns – avoiding needless, often fatal confrontations between endangered species and human civilization.

Source: Jon Hoekstra, Chief Scientist at WWF

CONCLUSION

Gathering information on subjective experiences is an inherently difficult process, but it is indispensable to understanding on the economic, social, cultural and environmental impacts of tourism. The sustainability imperative to preserve all local capital stocks intact requires that these impacts must be included in the analytical foundation used to inform tourism policies and underpin multi-stakeholder dialogue. Without an accurate assessment of the nature, and its ecosystem services type and extent of local economic, social, cultural and environmental resources it may be impossible to fully appreciate what is at stake in tourism development until it is already lost.

Examining evolving perceptions of how the tourism industry is affecting the destination—including those of tourism operators, local community members, and specialised experts—requires a mix of quantitative and qualitative research methods. While a detailed description of these methods and their specific advantages and limitations is beyond the scope of this chapter, considerable academic resources are available to help guide the research process. Regular surveys, whether undertaken by a public authority or contracted to a private firm or international organisation can provide invaluable information on public attitudes and can enable policymakers to identify and address issues that might not be revealed by statistical data. However, it should be borne in mind that while subjective, qualitative information is essential to sustainable tourism policy it is a compliment to statistical data, not a substitute for it.

EXERCISES

1. Discuss the concept of "cultural capital". How is the value of cultural resources determined, and by whom?
2. How can policymakers use information on the distribution of tourism-sector income to achieve public policy goals?

3. What is "discounting"? How does it affect decisions about social, cultural and environmental value?
4. In what circumstances might the private value of a good, service or asset differ from its social value?
5. How can differences in private and social values affect the sustainability of tourism development?
6. List several possible perceptions by community members of a tourism industry's impact on the destination society, both positive and negative. How can these perceptions affect the destination's competitiveness?
7. Ellaborate a one page essay based on - TEEB for National and Internacional Policy Markers –" Chapter 8 – Recognizing the value of protected areas".

CASE 11 - BRANDING DESTINATIONS: THE CASE OF THE MPIKA, BANGWEULU AND KASANKA - ZAMBIA
By Chola Mfula, SNV – Netherlands Development Organization.

INTRODUCTION
Zambia is truly an interesting case; a country brimming of tourism potential and yet much of it remains untapped and unknown not only to the international tourism market but to the domestic market as well. Zambia as a tourism destination is primarily known for 2 destinations, namely Victoria Falls in Livingstone and South Luangwa National park in Eastern Zambia. There is however more to Zambia than these two areas.

Northern Zambia is well endowed with tourism features and is considered an emerging destination. The government of Zambia has recognized this and is spending considerable resources to develop tourism in the Northern Province. Most of the resources as targeted at the Kasaba Bay Area on the South tip of Lake Tanganyika which shall be a high end and exclusive tourist destination. While this government effort is commendable its focus is only on one area and it's debatable if it will stimulate widespread participation of local communities or create viable opportunities for them in the tourism industry in Northern Province.

SNV has partnered with destinations in Mpika, Bangweulu and Kasanka areas, these emerging tourism destinations seem to offer more opportunities for local participation. Generally these destinations have abundant tourism features but are little known, poor marketed and uncoordinated. SNV has been working with these areas to enhance their destination management operations, tourism product development, destination branding and marketing.

BRIEF DESCRIPTION OF THE DESTINATIONS

KASANKA

Kasanka is located in Central Province in Serenje District. The area is accessible by road and is located on the off Tuta Road which links Mansa and Luapula province to the Great North Road. The population in this area is quite sparse. There is little or no economic activities in this area with few employment opportunities. Subsistence agriculture, fishing and natural resources utilization are the predominate livelihoods in this area. The people in this area are extremely poor. In spite of this poor economic and social status in Kasanka, the area is well endowed with Natural Resources which could be harnessed for tourism and economic development. The main attractions in this area are; the Kasanka and Lavushi Manda national-al Parks, the Bangweulu wetlands, Chitambo Mission Hospital where Dr David Livingstone heart was buried and Kundalila Falls. The area is also a birders paradise and has many scenic areas.

The Kasanka ecosystem supports unique flora and fauna which include the Sitatunga, a shy aquatic antelope which spends its days in thick papyrus swamps. Kasanka also hosts the largest known concentration of straw-colored fruit bats from October to December every year. Around 5 million bats migrate to the Mushitu Forest to roost and feed for 2–3 months at the end of every year.

About 50 km to the North of Kasanka National Park is the vast Bangweulu Wetlands which is of significant ecological global importance.

BANGWEULU WETLANDS

The Bangweulu wetlands systems is a vast complex located in the Northern and Luapula provinces in Northern Zambia. It stretches northwards encompassing Lake Bangweulu, other adjoining smaller lakes, its swamps, floodplains, islands and adjoining woodlands and further extends into southern parts of the Democratic Republic of the Congo (DRC). Most of the Bangweulu swamps is lake, swamps, flooded grasslands and pristine Miombo woodlands. The Chambishi and Lualaba rivers which drain the Bangweulu wetlands form the southern tributaries of the Congo River. The Bangweulu wetlands are of great ecological importance not only to Zambia but globally as well. Because of this, it has been designated as an Important Bird Area by Birdlife International and is a recognised Ramsar site. Ramsar sites are wetlands gazetted under the Ramsar convention which are considered highly important conservation areas that have to be sustainably managed to maintain economic, social and ecologic balance. This wetland supports amazing bird life including the rare Shoebill stock and wildlife species such as Tsessebe, Sitatunga and the largest concentration Black Lechwe in Africa.

MPIKA AND SURROUNDING AREAS

Mpika is rural town in Northern Province at the junction of the Great North Road to Kasama and the Tanzania- Zambia highway to Dar Es Salaam. Mpika and Surrounding areas consist of the Mutinondo Wilderness area, Mpika town, Shiwa Ngandu, North Luangwa National Park, Nachikufu Caves and Kapisha Hot Springs as its main attractions. The area covers part of Mpika district, extending from Luangwa valley in the east to the Bangweulu swamps in the west. It shares boundaries with North and South Luangwa National Park in the valley areas in the Muchinga Escarpment and with Lavushi Manda National Park on the plateau areas on the western borders. Mpika is fairly accessible by rail using TAZARA, by good road using the Great North Road and some areas in North Luangwa have air strips.

Though Mpika is not a tourist destination, it does attract nearly 16,000 tourists who spend an estimated US$ 3.7 million annually, however the bulk of these people are business tourists, either transiting to or from Tanzania and also the fishing areas around Lake Tanganyika in Northern Zambia. Generally business tourists do not stay longer than a day and do not spend much money because their primary interest is not tourism but their business profit margin. Consequently opportunities for the poor to participate in tourism are low, this is evidenced by the fact that only 3% of tourism money spent in Mpika ends up with the poor.

BRANDING AND MARKETING

Open Africa, a pan African project aimed at linking the splendors of Africa in continuous route networks from Cape to Cairo has partnered with SNV to promote and market these destinations. Prior to SNV/ Open Africa involvement these destinations struggled with branding. Kasanka and Bangweulu had an idea about branding and therefore used either the species such as the Shoe Bill or Sitatunga, though it was not is a package that could easily be communicated to the tourism market. For Mpika the whole concept of branding is new. While its recognized that some private operators in Mpika have used certain unique features to brand their respective products, branding was never done at destination level. It became apparent however that if the destinations are to be marketed especially via the internet, they need to take branding more seriously and distinguish themselves from the competition. Below are the logos and destination brand names that have been developed by the areas.

The Kasanka Area has been branded "Nsobe-Sitatunga Experience-Where the water meets the sky!" The brand has two elements to it; a) the Nsobe-Sitatunga which is a water antelope commonly seen in the areas and b) where the water meets the sky, which is the English translation of Bangweulu.

Mpika and Surrounding Areas have been dubbed **"the Munjili Wilderness Experience: Home of the Muchinga Walking Safaris".** The slogan selected has two prominent features a) **Munjili** –which is the local name for Warthog and b) **Muchinga** which refers to the escarpment which forms part of the Great Rift Valley. This areas also has the North Luangwa National Park, the only park in Zambia with Black Rhino.

It was important for the destinations to understand that a growing number of tourists are using internet search engines to get information on destinations. It is therefore imperative to include better know features in there branding. For instance, the brand for Mpika**"the Munjili Wilderness Experience: Home of the Muchinga Walking Safaris"**, the distinguishing feature is the Muchinga escarpment because its more probable that a tourist would search for Muchinga Escarpment than for Mpika. Mpika would however come up in the search because it's closely associated to the Muchinga Escarpment.

Lastly as part of the market efforts these destinations areas were officially launched at the Zambia International Tourism Expo held in Lusaka in March 2010 and were also showcased at the Tourism Indaba held in Durban South Africa in May 2010.

PROMOTING LINKAGES AND INTEGRATING DESTINATIONS
Individually these destinations are not strong but collective the form a very strong tourism destination. The tourism packages that can be developed when the three areas are better linked and collaborated will be more attractive, more interesting and easier to market. A tourist for instance, would have a wetlands experience in the Bangweulu, visit South or North Luangwa National Parks in Mpika, sample the culture diversity of local tribes in the destinations and also visit the archeological sites. The scope and combination for the tourism packages is immerse. When this is done tourists stays and expenditure shall increase and impact positively on the local economies in respective destinations. Through Multi-stakeholder Workshops facilitated by SNV, the process of strengthening the linkages between the destinations has began.

The immediate collaborative actions areas agreed upon by the destinations included ; Improved tourism data collection- Product performance and market performance, Lobbying for an enabling tourism environment, developing of strategic plans/ tourism action plans (vision-objectives-strategies-actions), marketing and promotion, training, improved signposting, jointly sourcing for additional investors/ partnerships, Biodiversity protection, Alternative livelihoods development and Tourism awareness. These action areas are all aimed at strengthening the Mpika/ Kasanka/ Bangweulu destination as a whole.

CONCLUSION
With individual destinations being strengthened and with branding and marketing underway, there is a genuine promise that the emerging and little know destinations in Northern Zambia shall become tourist destinations of choice. Since the routes were launched on the Open Africa website in March 2010, there have been nearly 100 enquires over a period of 3 months and some have translated into actual visits. However, the journey has only began and more resources need to be invested for this transformation to occur. SNV shall continue to play it role of providing

capacity building services and also help to coordinate and synergies the actors in these destinations. SNV shall additionally also help to stimulate increased private sector and local participation in tourism in Northern Province, because without them growth in this sector will be too slow and not provide the benefits to the local economies that this sector could potentially provide.

Nine

Marketing Strategies and Special Interest Tourism

Everything is worth what its purchaser will pay for it.

– Publilius Syrus, Roman Writer, 1ˢᵗ Century BCE

OBJECTIVES OF THE CHAPTER:

- Introduce the main concepts and instruments involved in marketing tourism destinations.
- Describe some of the principles on which differentiation strategies for tourism destinations are commonly based.
- Analyse how marketing strategies are applied at each phase in the development of the tourism destination.

INTRODUCTION

As international tourism continues to expand as part of the on-going process of economic globalisation, the nature of competition between destinations is evolving. Marketing strategies are becoming increasingly sophisticated, both conceptually and strategically, and the ability of destinations to adopt innovative strategies for tourism marketing and to capitalise on non-traditional assets is proving to be just as important as more conventional advantages. Large-scale, mainstream tourism will always occupy a major place in the global industry, but the radical diversification of tourism offerings and the robust development of unlikely destinations is a testament to the power of marketing to broaden the appeal of destinations and extend the benefits of the tourism industry.

In the 1960s and 70s, at the dawn of the modern age of mass tourism, destination offerings were most often focused a hospitable climate and abundance of leisure activities—the 'sun-and-sand' model. The Riviera in southern France, the Costa del Sol in Mediterranean Spain, and the Copacabana in Rio de Janeiro were all prime examples of traditional 'sun-and-sand' tourism. Many European destinations also offered some of the luxury prestige appeal of previous ages, when tourism was solely the province of the wealthy—before the dramatic growth of the Western economies in the mid-20th Century, coupled with the global expansion of affordable air travel, put international tourism within reach of the Western middle class. In many established destinations. However, for many of these destinations the contradictions inherent in relying on a reputation for refinement and exclusivity as the basis for mass tourism came to define their development in the post-war period.

This period also saw the development of an early form of cultural tourism, with the rise of 'exotic' destinations in the South Pacific, Latin America and parts of Asia and Africa. Tourist advertisements from this period reveal the combination of exoticism, adventure, romance and luxury that marketers were striving to impress as key features of destinations in French Indochina, British India and colonial Africa, among others. Elements of this marketing style persist, and in some cases a destination's historical reputation for these features may be central theme in its advertising strategy.

In earlier eras tourism marketing tended to focus primarily on the obvious natural advantages of the destination, while cultural, historical or unique environmental assets were often commoditised in a way that many modern consumers of tourism services would consider hopelessly crass. In many cases the marketing of these forms of tourism capital proved to be tragically unsustainable. By the 1980s a number of once-competitive destinations had become ugly, overpriced, and seedy 'tourist traps', and saw their local tourism industries go into a protracted decline. Brazil's Copacabana Beach, for example, had once been among the world's premier sun-and-sand destinations, but its inadequate governance mechanisms failed to prevent the rise of illicit activity, particularly the sex trade, earning it a reputation for tawdriness and violence and pushing the destination into a lasting slump from which it has only recently begun to show signs of recovering.[151] This experience and others like it spurred the growth of contemporary theories of tourism management, including the basic principles of sustainable tourism development described in the preceding chapters. But it had an equally profound impact on tourism consumers, many of whom began to turn away from mainstream, commercial mass tourism and helped to create the increasingly diverse modern market for special interests tourism services.

The global tourism industry now presents an incredibly broad range of offerings tailored to highly specific consumer types. In this new market social, cultural, and environmental assets are used to differentiate the services on offer, presenting a comprehensive experience unique to the destination. According to recent studies differentiation of tourism services can greatly boost the attractiveness of a destination to consumers, which this means that destination competitiveness is highly dependent on effective marketing.

In the new, globalised tourism industry destination managers are increasingly using marketing techniques to develop commercial strategies that enhance the appeal of the destination by defining its unique identity.

---

151 Vignati, Federico (2011) "Tourism and Prostitution in Copacabana Beach: A Demand Analysis." UMA: Malaga.

This chapter will examine some of the most important marketing techniques used to strategically position a tourism destination in an ever more diverse and competitive international market.

THE ROLE OF MARKET RESEARCH IN TOURISM DEVELOPMENT

The starting point for creating a successful marketing strategy is consumer research. Policymakers must understand the characteristics of the consumers they are attempting to reach and the specific nature of the services those consumers demand. Consumer research focuses on two groups: (i) current tourists, the consumers the destination is presently serving, and (ii) potential tourists, the consumers it could attract if it appealed to them more effectively.

The objective of research into current tourists is to help destination managers better appreciate the present state of the destination and understand how it is perceived in international markets. Research on current tourists can help to shed light on the destination's present **brand identity**, define **reputational effects** that may impact its appeal, and determine how best it might expand its current customer base. It can also inform research on potential tourists by identifying potential synergies or conflicts between the existing consumer base and new segments of the consumer market.

The objective of research into both current and potential tourism demand is to help destination managers define specific consumer groups to target. Tourism consumers are remarkably diverse, and have many narrow, highly specialised interests. Moreover, different consumer groups are frequently incompatible with one another (see Chapter 8) and certain groups, though desirable from the destination's perspective, may not be attainable. Research on current and potential tourists can also serve to identify the major competitors that the destination is likely to face in its efforts to attract these groups, and recognise how it might expand its market share among new customers by altering its image in international markets.

In determining a marketing strategy destination managers must begin by deciding which **market segments** to reach, whether to expand the current consumer base, reach out to new consumer groups, or pursue some mix of both. Prospective market segments can range from consumers of conventional mass tourism provided by large-scale tour operators to highly specialised **niche tourism**, or **special interest tourism (SIT)**, models, appealing to particular groups and capitalising on very specific and often non-traditional assets. The unique target groups of SIT differ wildly from one another: bird watchers, scuba divers, golfers, ice climbers, kayakers, spelunkers, sport fishers, cyclists, yoga practitioners and enthusiasts for every type of art, architecture, craftwork, history and cuisine are all highly specific market segments that provide potential opportunities for SIT.[152] Some of these market segments are intuitively compatible with one another—often falling under rubrics such as 'extreme sports' or 'ecotourism'—while others have little or nothing in common.

Understanding this great diversity of market segments and the potential synergies (or discordances) between them is the foundation of a successful tourism marketing strategy. In order to appeal to specific target groups destination managers must determine what types of tourists are already attracted to the destination, how it might further develop its appeal to these current market segments, and explore what new types of tourists might be interested in the unique social, cultural, or environmental assets the destination offers. There are at least three major objectives of market research in the tourism industry: (i) assessing the available stocks of local capital, (ii) identifying the current consumers that the destination attracts and the potential consumers that it could attract, and (iii) evaluating the effectiveness of the destination's efforts to reach those consumers

---

152 One of the world's most intensely specific forms of niche tourism is found in Tunisia, where scenes from five of the six "Star Wars" films where shot. Largely intact film sets and props remain in towns such as Tatouine (the inspiration for the fictional planet "Tatooine"), and every year these extremely non-traditional forms of tourism capital draw large numbers of visitors to places that might otherwise have little or no tourism industry at all. For more, see: http://goafrica.about.com/od/peopleandculture/ss/Star-Wars-Tours-In-Tunisia.htm.

through advertising and other forms of outreach. Understanding current weaknesses in destination marketing and the missed opportunities that result from them is a first and necessary step in improving a marketing strategy. Moreover, building new niche markets from scratch has in many cases proven to be extremely difficult and expensive. While niche tourism offers significant opportunities, it also entails considerable risks.

The first objective, assessing local capital stocks, is discussed in Chapter 8. Non-traditional forms of social, cultural and environmental capital are especially important to niche tourism, and these are often far less obvious than sandy beaches and a warm climate. It may be difficult for outsiders to observe these assets because doing so requires a high degree of local knowledge and experience. Meanwhile, entrepreneurs and policymakers who are from the destination may tend to take its non-traditional assets for granted: strong social resources, peculiar cultural forms and rare environmental attractions that could potentially be of great value to the tourism industry may be overlooked by local people who are used to them and do not regard them as special or think they would be of interest to outsiders. Moreover, the most valuable forms of tourism capital are often the rarest and most intimately specific to the destination. Consequently, discovering which local assets may appeal to prospective tourists may require significant effort and involve the use of innovative research methods. Destination managers should pursue creative strategies for assessing local capital that are suited to the peculiarities of the destination's social, cultural and environmental context. As always, actively soliciting feedback from current and recent tourists can help to identify new opportunities and areas for improvement.

Once the destination's marketable assets have been thoroughly assessed, the second research objective is determining which consumer groups it should market those assets to. International tourism consumers are a highly complex customer base. Tourism consumers come from a wide range of economic classes and cultural backgrounds, and as noted above, they have widely varied interest and demand highly specific tourism services. Understanding this incredibly diverse group may seem daunting, but fortunately tourism consumers have been, and continue to be, the subject of considerable academic research, which destination managers can and should draw upon as they lay the groundwork for a marketing strategy.

In conducting tourism research it is essential to recall that even in the developing world destinations may have unexploited potential for domestic or regional tourism and need not rely solely on developed-world source markets. Growing middle-income countries such as Brazil and Thailand have thriving domestic tourism industries, and regional economic leaders such as South Africa draw a large share of tourists from surrounding countries. These domestic and regional tourism industries can provide an important compliment to international tourism, yet may be overlooked by business interests and policymakers focused on seemingly more lucrative source markets in advanced economies. Destination managers should bear in mind that new marketing opportunities may be closer to home than they initially appear.

The third objective of tourism research has to do with the effectiveness of communications. Taking advantage of these highly specific SIT assets requires raising awareness among the market segments that demand them. Once destination managers recognise the various types of tourism capital their destination has to offer and identifies the specific market segments that demand those assets, they can tailor their marketing strategy to meet the specific needs of their particular target group or groups. Consumer research can help to determine how effectively the destination is reaching customers from both its current and potential market segments.

It should be noted that achieving these research objectives is always an on-going process. Over time, a destination's social, cultural and environmental resources will inevitably change. Older forms of tourism capital will become altered or degraded, or even disappear altogether, while at the same time new and different assets will emerge. A successful destination must stay abreast of these development and continuously re-evaluate its tourism capital. Meanwhile, consumer groups will also continue to evolve. The trend towards greater specificity in tourism demand has been dramatic, and the internet, with its remarkable ability to collate information on diverse interests and link disparate individuals into groups that share those interests, will continue to accelerate the diversification of the tourism consumer base. Finally, the effectiveness of tourism outreach must also be periodically reassessed, as older marketing strategies become outmoded and new outreach techniques emerge.

SPECIAL INTEREST TOURISM

In many ways the defining characteristic of modern tourism is the search for authentic and personalized experiences, marking a dramatic shift away from the mass tourism model of earlier eras. Generally speaking this trend has been an enormously positive development for the global tourism industry, benefitting both tourists and destinations alike. Consumers typically derive greater enjoyment from specialised services that suit their personality and interests than they would from more homogenised forms of tourism. **Differentiation** is the process of developing a set of meaningful differences that distinguish the offerings of a particular tourism destination; this is especially important for emerging destinations looking to establish their identity. **Positioning** means ensuring that the particular image cultivated through differentiation comes to occupy a prominent place in the market and that it effectively reaches both current and potential customers. Both differentiation and positioning require that the reality of the services offered by the destination remain closely aligned with the marketing strategy.

Differentiation and positioning both help to establish the destination's distinctive character, its **brand identity**, as discussed in Chapter 7.

However, a strong sense of individuality not only accelerates the growth of tourism clusters, it also increases the destination's resilience to shifting market conditions by reducing its **substitutability** as an economic good. "Substitutability", in this context, refers to the extent to which one good can be used in place of another to meet the same basic demand. Butter and margarine, for example, are very close substitutes, and changes in the price of one good will have a strong impact on demand for the other. Tourism destinations are much the same: the more generic a destination, the more easily consumers can substitute other, similar destinations for it. This leaves undifferentiated destinations vulnerable to unpredictable changes in market conditions, since an increase in local prices, a decrease in prices among its competitors, or any type of shock that adversely affects its competitiveness will have deeply negative impact on demand for its services.

Differentiation and positioning also play critical roles in the sustainability of the local tourism industry. The cultivation of a special and distinctive identity not only allows destinations to broaden their appeal beyond their traditional tourism assets, it also enables them to more closely engage tourists in the conservation and protection of the unique forms of social, cultural and environmental capital that the latter demand as consumers. Often the traditions, customs, natural assets and ways of life that attract tourists are highly valued by local communities, yet these communities may face great difficulties preserving them in the face of modern social and economic pressures. Special interest tourism can align the values of domestic and international tourists with those of local residents, creating strong monetary incentives to maintain unique forms of social, cultural and environmental capital that might otherwise vanish. SIT can consequently make a major contribution to the sustainability of the destination by helping to preserve its cultural and environmental capital. Because of the numerous interests from the private sector and civil society involved in this type of tourism, SIT is a key area for **multi-stakeholder collaboration**.

In many cases there are also significant economic and overall competitiveness advantages to fostering the growth of a robust SIT sector. Tourists with the most highly specialised interests also tend to come from demand segments with the most buying power, for the simple reason that cultivating a highly specialised interest tends to require a considerable amount of leisure time and disposable income. For example, developing an appreciation for fine wines involves substantial expense, and consequently oenophiles ('wine enthusiasts') come almost exclusively from upper income groups. Tourism operators in renowned wine-growing regions are well aware of this, and tend to cater to upmarket clientele.

France's Loire Valley, for example, is home to countless luxury tourism establishments supported by the regional wine industry. But even oenophiles are not a homogeneous group; they reflect a diversity of tastes, regional interests, income levels and countries of origin, leaving opportunities for winemakers in California, Chile, Australia, South Africa, and elsewhere to attract tourists looking for experiences that are more expansive, more specific, more affordable, or closer to home. And because of their greater purchasing power, a budget destination for wine enthusiasts is still typically considered a luxury destination by global standards.

The paradox of special interest tourism is that the interests of SIT consumers tend to be remarkably diverse within their narrow areas of focus. Many tourists with highly specialised interests will seek out a wide range of experience across numerous potential destinations. Bird watchers may find Romania as attractive as South Africa or Costa Rica simply for its variety of rare birds, while for avid golfers the Seychelles may hold as much interest as Scotland, despite these destinations having essentially nothing else in common. Moreover, for many tourists it is not simply a choice of one or the other, as individuals will often visit a number of different destinations in widely divergent countries in order to satisfy the same fundamental interest. Consequently, shifting from mass tourism to SIT can be a smart choice for destination managers looking to tap in to lucrative market segments, provided that they know what assets their destination has to offer, which consumers demand those assets, and how they can reach their target segment (or segments) with effective marketing and outreach efforts.

Although many forms of SIT present possibilities for emerging destinations in the developing world to access existing market segments by cultivating their appeal to various types of special interest tourists, the SIT model can also be used to establish or develop a unique, destination-specific identity and promote the growth of a dedicated and loyal customer base that is focused on the unique special interests the destination provides. Sometimes these interests originate with a particular culture and, while they may be replicated elsewhere, there is nevertheless a considerable 'authenticity' value associated with experiencing them in their home country. For example, Brazilian capoeira, Thai kickboxing and Indian yoga are all important international tourist draws in their respective countries. While capoeira, kickboxing and yoga classes are now widely available throughout much of the developed world, thousands of people continue to travel every year to experience the 'original', 'authentic' version of these activities in their native land.

In other cases the cultural experience may be unique and inimitable. Watching a traditional wrestling match in Niger, betting on a camel race in the United Arab Emirates, running with the bulls in Pamplona, Spain, or shopping in the medina of Marrakesh are all examples of non-reproducible tourism draws. They also reflect the widely varying extent to which different destinations are able to capitalise on their peculiar cultural forms. Running with the bulls in Pamplona is a major international tourism event, while traditional wrestling in Niger is barely on the tourism radar. This disparity is of course not only a matter of publicity, and reflects the numerous dimensions of effective tourism marketing described in this chapter.

BOX 11 - HOME AWAY FROM HOME

In recent years many emerging destinations have developed thriving 'homestay' tourism industries, in which visitors stay for one or more nights in the home of a local family rather than at traditional hotels or guesthouses. Host families are often members of ethnic minorities or groups that practice traditional lifestyles, and in many cases homestays are included in a broader cultural experience that may involve trekking in nearby wilderness areas, observing or participating in the daily activities of the host community, or taking part in some form of unusual, locally specific experience, be it riding an elephant or sampling local food and drink.

In other cases homestays may simply provide an inexpensive addition to the range of available accommodations, especially in remote areas that cannot sustain a professional hospitality industry. The experience provided by a homestay is typically unique to its host community and presents the destination with an opportunity to develop its own unique SIT tourism segment. It also has enormous potential to positively impact the livelihoods and local economies of marginalised and disadvantaged groups, while also attaching a clear monetary incentive to the maintenance of traditional practices and unique ways of life.

Southeast Asia has been a global leader in this trend, and a growing number of destinations in Thailand, Laos, Cambodia, Vietnam, Malaysia and elsewhere now include homestay tourism as a major component of their local tourism industries. Moreover, there appears to be considerable potential to export this model to other regions; though safety concerns and regulatory hurdles may currently inhibit its growth in some areas, destination managers should consider exploring this option as a way to both broaden and deepen their appeal to prospective tourists, while extending the economic impact of tourism to communities that might otherwise be unable to benefit from it.

In some cases it is not a cultural form but rather a specific place or unusual artefact that proves to be a powerful, and in many cases unexpected, tourism draw. In 2011 the government of the Ukraine opened the Chernobyl nuclear disaster site to tourists. Long a symbol of calamity and of the legacy of Soviet domination the Chernobyl site is now proving to be a lucrative, albeit divisive, attraction, and one which is absolutely unique to Ukraine. It not only provides a frozen-in-time window into a Cold War world that is rapidly receding from living memory, but has also become an unlikely hotspot for biodiversity. The quarantine area around the site has effectively become a national wildlife park, and Chernobyl is now home to some of the last wild wolves in Eastern Europe. The peculiar appeal of Chernobyl has given rise to so-called 'nuclear disaster tourism', a highly unusual SIT market that has allowed the Ukraine to finally derive some measure of benefit from the site of one of its worst national tragedies.

Understanding the interests of actual and potential market segments allows destinations to both broaden and specialise their services, focusing investments and policies on meeting the demands of particular SIT market segments in order to expand their overall market share and diversify their consumer base. Undifferentiated destinations offering only generic 'sun-and-sand' experiences often command little loyalty among their customers, and as a result they are highly susceptible to external pressures and shifting competitive advantages. SIT destinations, however, cater specifically to the interests and desires of particular groups, offering distinctive services and experiences for which there are no easy substitutes. The uniqueness of SIT destinations is an essential element in tourist satisfaction and greatly contributes to building a loyal and resilient consumer base.

The rapid growth of SIT is a remarkable and exciting development. It represents one of the greatest opportunities currently available for marketing new tourism products and boosting the growth of emerging destinations in developing countries. The challenge lies in discovering, marketing, and sustainably exploiting these rare forms of tourism capital. The only limit to the possibilities of SIT is the capacity of destination managers, entrepreneurs and local communities to identify niche markets and exploit their own peculiar and non-traditional tourism assets to differentiate their destination from more run-of-the-mill alternatives.

BOX 12 - UNLIKELY OPPORTUNITIES: CAMBODIA'S NORRY TRAINS

During its brief but horrific rule the Khmer Rouge thoroughly destroyed Cambodia's railway system. Hundreds of kilometres of French-era rail lay unused, much of it in remote areas with little other transport infrastructure, until resourceful locals began to build and operate their own makeshift trains. These so-called "norry" trains (an approximation of the British term "lorry") are constructed out of bamboo and a few spare machine parts. Most consist of just two simple metal axles joined by a wooden raft and powered by an engine repurposed from a motorcycle or a piece of farming equipment. When two norries approach each other on the same track, the train with the lighter load is dismantled, removed from the track, and then reassembled once the other train has passed.

After the Khmer Rouge was ousted from power and conditions in the countryside began to stabilise, norry trains gradually fell out of use. In some cases they were supplanted by more conventional forms of transportation, and in other cases the government attempted to discourage their use. The authorities tended to view norry trains as unsafe and anachronistic—symbols of a dark period in the country's history from which it was struggling to recover. Over time the use of norry trains would almost certainly have ceased altogether, had it not been for a remarkable discovery: the last working norry line, operating between the city of Battambang and a nearby brick factory, was swiftly becoming an important local tourist draw, with visitors offering considerable sums in exchange for a ride on the bizarre and unique norries.

Today, Battambang's norry trains are among the city's leading attractions; not only are they a source of local pride, but they provide a significant flow of revenue for tour guides and norry train operators, along with vendors of "bamboo train" t-shirts and other souvenirs. They have even proved to appeal to domestic tourists, for whom their historical content is especially important. Cambodia's norry trains are a prime illustration of the value of highly specific, non-replicable experiences, and of the extraordinary value that the tourism industry can confer on the unlikeliest of things. Destination managers, entrepreneurs and local communities should be on the lookout for opportunities offered by rare and unusual assets, and should be mindful that the way that these assets are viewed by tourists may be very different from how they are regarded by their home society.

THE MARKETING STRATEGY

A destination's marketing strategy is the sum of all methods and means used by the destination's public sector to communicate its offerings and identity to current and potential consumers. The marketing strategy may attempt to set the tone for the private sector's marketing efforts, leading by example and influence, but it is rarely if ever able to control all aspects of the message that the local tourism industry sends to the consumer market. The ability of destination managers to define the image of the destination and communicate its offerings to consumers is limited both by the autonomy of private firms and the unpredictability of impressions that may be communicated by news or social media; and these constraints must be borne in mind.

In designing a marketing strategy destination managers should begin by identifying the basic characteristics of the local tourism industry and determining what the destination can and should mean to consumers. As they address these questions destination managers may wish to use the "4 Ps" basic marketing framework, which organises a destination's attributes according to four dimensions: **product**, **price**, **promotion**, and **place**. This frame allows destination managers to systematically assess the particular services that the destination offers its current and prospective customers ("product"), its cost-competitiveness in providing these services in the international marketplace ("price"), the extent to which information about these services reaches—or fails to reach—its target audience ("promotion"), and the technical feasibility of customers' access to those services ("place").

In other words, destination managers should be absolutely clear about the services they intend to offer consumers and how those services—and the destination's overall **brand identity**—will be presented to the domestic and international tourism market. Those in charge of destination marketing must be able to provide accurate answers for a number of fundamental questions about the destination.

These include:

- **Product**. What are the specific experiences that the destination is attempting to provide, and what are the actual experiences of tourists that visit the destination? What steps can be taken to improve the overall quality of tourism services, and what assets might the destination possess that are not being exploited? Is the current set of offerings sustainable over the long term, and how will the destination respond to inevitable changes in the services it provides?

- **Price**. What is the destination's effective price range, and how are services distributed within it? How wide is the difference between the most expensive and least expensive offering, and are offerings weighted towards one end of the scale or the other? Are high- and low-cost options compatible with one another, and will they remain so as differently priced options continue to develop? What are the effects of seasonal price fluctuations on both the supply and demand of tourism services?

- **Promotion**. How is information about the destination transmitted to current and prospective customers? Is tourism information centralised and easy to access? Is it accurate and up-to-date? Does information communicated through independent sources (news reports, consumer reviews, guidebooks, social media, etc.) conflict with the image that the destination is attempting to present? Are new opportunities to develop non-traditional tourism assets being revealed through independent media? What are public sector agencies doing to shape positive perceptions of the destination? Are private sector firms and local communities regarded as partners in promoting tourism?

- **Place**. How accessible is the destination to tourists from different source markets? What can be done to make visiting the destination easier and less expensive? Are visa costs too high? Are procedures for obtaining visas too difficult? How accessible are different locations and attractions within the destination? What is the quality of transportation infrastructure and services? Are opportunities to broaden the destination's appeal, or cultivate particular niche markets, inhibited by a lack of transportation infrastructure or by costly, inconvenient services? These issues are among the most severe obstacles to the growth of tourism in the developing world, and taking steps to alleviate them, while potentially costly, can generate enormous returns.

Answering these questions will enable destination managers to formulate—and regularly update—a marketing strategy suited to their specific needs and policy objectives. Effective outreach efforts have numerous benefits. A sound marketing strategy can help to expand the destination's market share and diversify its consumer base, mitigating its vulnerability to demand shocks in its source markets; it can help to develop a varied and competitive set of offerings that appeal to target groups and encourage customer loyalty, reducing its substitutability with similar destinations; and it can lessen the destination's dependence on a limited number of large-scale mass-tourism providers, over-reliance on which may result in a range of market imperfections described in Chapter 4. Finally, a well-deigned and effective marketing strategy can promote a healthy appreciation for the destination's social, cultural and environmental uniqueness, which can encourage conservation of these forms of capital both by tourism firms and the local community. This remains a central challenge for building sustainable tourism industries in the developing world.

CONCLUSIONS

Marketing strategies and special interest tourism have the potential to accomplish a wide range of objectives that promote the competitiveness, resiliency and sustainability of the tourism industry. Differentiating the destination from its competitors and advantageously positioning it in the international market can help to build a strong brand identity and generate positive reputational effects, while promoting special interest tourism can diversify the destination's customer base and exploit the economic potential of unique social, cultural and environmental assets. Moreover, these efforts tend to reinforce each other: an effective marketing strategy can publicise the unusual, specific, non-traditional forms of tourism capital on offer in the destination, while cultivating an industry based around rare and individualised experiences boosts the destination's market visibility, further differentiating its identity and enhancing its positioning. This process can accelerate the growth of the tourism industry while reducing its vulnerability to shocks and, perhaps most importantly, giving destination managers, entrepreneurs and local communities a shared stake in conserving the destination's most distinctive forms of social, cultural and environmental capital.

EXERCISES

1. Define the term "marketing strategy" and describe its relationship to brand identity, differentiation, and positioning in the tourism industry.
2. List some of the potential benefits of special interest tourism. What are some specific advantages to attracting tourists from existing interest groups, such as bird watchers or wine enthusiasts?
3. Why should a destination attempt cultivate an interest in—and a market demand for—its own unique forms of social, cultural and environmental capital? How might it begin this process?
4. Can you think of two unique social, cultural or environmental assets that draw tourists to your home city, region or country? Can you think of any similar assets that might become a tourist draw if they were better publicised?

CASE 12 - LAIKIPIA BRANDING CASE-STUDY - KENYA
By. Dr. Chris Thouless, SNV - Netherlands Development Organization.

BRANDING AND DESTINATION MANAGEMENT

Branding is an important part of destination management. In order for destinations to attract visitors they need to be able to differentiate themselves from each other, highlighting their appeal to different types of visitors. Destination management organisations need to be able to communicate these distinguishing features in a consistent and coherent manner. They must also reflect this unique appeal throughout a wide variety of marketing channels in a way that promotes the destination's strengths and reinforces people's image of it. Today there are many destinations competing for the attention of potential visitors and successful marketing depends on engaging their interest in a few seconds so that they will be motivated to investigate further and ideally translate this interest into a visit. In order to do this the destination needs to have a clear identity. The branding process helps to clarify this identity and to find ways of communicating the key features of the identity through brand values.

THE LAIKIPIA DESTINATION

Laikipia District in northern Kenya has gained a reputation in the last few years as a leading sustainable safari tourism destination. It is characterised by small exclusive owner-managed accommodation facilities on private and community land. Laikipia is the only district in Kenya where wildlife numbers (particularly lions and wild dogs) have increased over the last twenty years. Laikipia is now only second to the Masai Mara in the quality of the game viewing experience, but this occurs under much more private conditions. It has the great advantage over national parks that a much wider range of activities beyond the conventional 'game drive' can take place, including walking, riding horses and camels, mountain biking, night drives and so on.

The majority of tourism facilities in Laikipia have a strong emphasis on ecological sustainability and supporting local development. They employ mostly local staff, purchase local food and support local development projects such as mobile health clinics and schools. Some of the lodges support major private conservation areas. Laikipia is also well known for the development of some of Kenya's first community owned tourism facilities. The majority of these are managed and marketed with the support of nearby private operators.

The development of tourism in Laikipia has been coordinated by the Laikipia Wildlife Forum. LWF is a local organisation that brings together private and communal land-owners with other interested parties such as tourism operators to address common concerns and to promote sustainable development in the district. SNV supports LWF in developing Laikipia as a tourism destination, through increasing the volume of tourism and increasing pro-poor benefits. This work has been part funded by the Embassy of the Kingdom of Netherlands. During the course of the development of the Laikipia tourism strategy in 2008 one of the key issues that emerged was the need to distinguish Laikipia from rest of Kenya, which has a reputation for over-crowded, exploitative tourism.

THE BRANDING PROCESS

The Laikipia Wildlife Forum commissioned Tom Buncle to lead the branding process for Laikipia. He had previously worked as Chief Executive of the Scottish Tourism Board and had led the rebranding process for Namibia. Since time and resources were limited it was not possible to engage with overseas focus groups. Therefore the branding process was limited to a 10 day inspection visit in September 2008 combined with interviews with the major tourism operators. There were 4 one day workshops for operators from the different sub-regions, and a final meeting at which the proposed brand values were presented and fine-tuned.

There was a great deal of interest from the operators in this process. They tend to operate very independently and it was interesting to see competing operators from different backgrounds interacting over such issues as developing brand values.

One of the main issues that was discussed was whether 'Laikipia' was a suitable name for the destination. It is the name of an administrative district, which used to be reserved for European settlers, and hence has somewhat negative connotations for some Kenyans. The western part of the district has been the scene of ethnic clashes, and it is these troubles that have dominated local news coverage of the area. Some people were in favour of a more general destination name, such as *North Kenya or the Northern Frontier*, because of these issues and the close linkage between tourism in Laikipia and in adjoining areas, particularly Mt Kenya and Samburu. However, the majority was in favour of sticking with the current name, because it is distinctive (no confusion on 'Google) and the geography of Laikipia – cool dry high altitude rangeland – sets it apart from nearby areas.

There was also much discussion about what areas compete with Laikipia both nationally and internationally, and what images most conjure up the essence of Laikipia.

THE LAIKIPIA BRAND

Following the consultative process, the Laikipia brand was developed. This consisted of a series of components as described in the following sections:

- **Key attributes**

This describes how Laikipia differs from other destinations. It was recognized that abundant wildlife, attractive scenery, and interesting culture are shared with many other African destinations, but what makes Laikipia stand apart is the combination of these with a more personal experience. This description is not something that would be shared with journalists and agents, but more used internally to ensure that the other components of the brand are used in a coherent way.

A sense of freedom and space that is related to the quite "untouristed" and tranquil landscape; and an intensely personal experience, which reflects both the level of personal hosting in lodges as well as the exhilaration of experiencing nature close up by, for instance walking, cycling or riding in relative solitude in this expansive landscape.

The animals and culture which are visible and accessible within this setting, while not themselves unique to Laikipia, are very important elements too. The combination of these four elements (space, personal experience, wildlife and culture) combine to define the Laikipia experience, which makes it different from most other destinations.

• **Positioning statement**

The positioning statement is a brief description of the destination's personality and how it appeals to visitors. This is for external circulation, and can be used to brief advertising agencies, and as a yardstick for Laikipia tourism operators to gauge the extent to which their own marketing messages reflect the Laikipia brand.

> **"Laikipia is Kenya's high country. It offers wildlife, solitude, freedom and space in a wild landscape, with diverse landscapes ranging from the snow-capped peaks of Mt Kenya to the edge of the Great Rift Valley and the deserts of the north.**
>
> It has an abundant variety of wildlife and diverse cultures. Yet it is a genuine working environment, where you can engage with people on a personal level – with guides, hosts and the local people, who are working together for a sustainable future for Laikipia.
>
> It offers genuine intimacy and adventure: whether experiencing its wildlife, scenery and solitude on horseback, foot, bicycle, balloon or flying safari.
>
> It is warm, friendly and stylish, in the way guests are personally hosted in architecturally unique and comfortable lodges.
>
> Laikipia's crisp clear air, boundless vistas and unrestricted access to the landscape and wildlife offer an invigorating and exhilarating experience in an astonishingly comfortable climate for an equatorial destination.
>
> Its expanding eco-system reflects one of Africa's most successful attempts to restore the balance that used to exist between people, wildlife and the land. It is a place where people treasure the resources they have inherited and are committed to securing them for future generations.

- **Brand Values**

Laikpia's brand essence (or brand values), are a small number of words that distil the region's personality. It is not expected that these words will be used directly in marketing materials, but that pictures and words will capture the spirit of these ideas.

- **Expansive.** This captures the idea of wide open spaces with relatively few other visitors.
- **Engaging.** This relates to the fact that safaris in Laikipia are likely to lead to more direct personal interactions than the relatively impersonal experiences in National Parks, because of the small groups involved and the more personal style of hosting and guiding.
- **Exhilarating.** This refers to the opportunities for activities such as riding and the opportunity to see wildlife close-up on foot, again in contrast to the National Parks where most of Kenya's safari tourism takes place.
- **Stylish.** This captures the idea that the majority of accommodation facilities in Laikipia have interesting and unique architecture, making innovative and striking use of local materials.

These brand values need to be backed up by presentation of a consistent message through the use of words and particularly visual characteristics. The most significant visual element that serves to identify Laikipia is the background of Mt Kenya, since this is a distinctive snow-capped landmark that can be seen from most of the tourism properties in the district. The sort of image that most encapsulates the Laikipia brand values and clearly identifies the location would be of tourists engaged in the kind of activity such as walking or riding horses or camels, that cannot be carried out inside National Parks, with Mt Kenya in the background. Ideally they would be accompanied by distinctively dressed local guides, emphasising the engagement of local people in Laikipia's tourism and to be set in an expansive landscape with wildlife visible.

LOGO

A new logo was designed to highlight the new brand. It was clearly not practical to include all the elements described, so the key elements of wildlife in front of Mt Kenya were maintained. The logo is deliberately simplified, and slightly 'funky' to give the impression of Laikipia as a youthful, energetic destination.

STRAP LINE

A great deal of effort often goes into coming up with a single line description of a destination, and these often fail to capture what is unique about a destination, and are often even rather ludicrous. In this case there was also much debate, but there was a good degree of consensus around the final version, which was:

Laikipia – Kenya's High Country

The reason for this strap line is that it combines the association of the word 'high' with 'exhilarating' with the geographic description of Laikipia as a high altitude plateau. It reinforces the link between Laikipia and Mt Kenya and points to the fact that Laikipia is relatively cool and malaria free.

Results

Monitoring the specific effectiveness of a branding process would be very difficult. It might be possible to analyse images and words used by local tourism operators before and after the branding process to see whether these had changing in accordance with the brand values. It might also be possible to use Google to search associations between the destination name and brand values – for instance in this case to find out if the strap line is being picked up by external agents, or whether the words encapsulating the brand values are being used in association with the destination name. However, it is difficult to imagine that any destination management organisation will go to these lengths, and one will have to simply take on trust the importance of the branding process. In any case in Laikipia, the general feeling was that the main importance of the branding process was not the actual output in terms of the brand but getting the rather independent-minded operators together to think about their destination as collaborators rather than competitors.

In any case the branding process has gone hand in hand with a larger destination marketing campaign. which has been extremely effective in getting Laikipia recognised as a distinct destination associated with sustainable tourism. Ten years ago tourism facilities in the Laikipia area were included in guide books and brochures as part of 'Northern Kenya' or 'the Mt Kenya Area'. Now almost all the guidebooks to Kenya have specific chapters on Laikipia, referring to its role in conservation and social development. The success of the strategy has been shown by the way that

Laikipia's tourism has been sustained and grown even during a very difficult time for Kenya's tourism. In early 2008 the industry came almost to a complete standstill in the wake of post-election violence, and a partial recovery late in the year was halted by the global economic crisis. Although tourism development in the rest of Kenya has come to a standstill, there are 7 new accommodation facilities developed or under construction in Laikipia in the two years since the election violence, creating at least 200 new full-time jobs for local residents.

Bibliography

Adler, M. and E. Posner (eds) (2001) Cost-Benefit Analysis: Legal, Economic and Philosophical Perspectives. Chicago, Chicago University Press.

Alcacer, J and W. Chung, (2010), "Location Strategies for Agglomeration Economies, Harvard Business School Working Paper, No. 10-064.

Ashley, C. and Haysom, G. (2009), Bringing local entrepreneurs into the supply chain: the experience of Spier, ODI Project Briefing 20, ODI, London

Ashley, C. and Haysom, G. (2008) 'The Development Impacts of Tourism Supply Chains: Increasing Impact on Poverty and Decreasing Our Ignorance', in: Spenceley, A. (ed.) Responsible Tourism: Critical Issues for Conservation and Development, Earthscan, London

Ashley, C. (2006), How can governments boost the local economic impacts of tourism? SNV and ODI, The Hague/London.

Ashley, C., H. Goodwin, and D. Roe, (2001) Pro-Poor Tourism Strategies: Expanding Opportunities for the Poor. Pro- Poor Tourism Briefing No.1. London: Overseas Development Institute.

Balaguer, L., & Cantavella-Jorda, M. (2002). Tourism as a long-run economic growth factor: The Spanish case. Applied Economics, 34, 877–884.

Barney, J. B. (1996) "The Resource-Based Theory of the Firm" *Organization Science* 7(5): 469–470.

Barney, J.B. (1991), Firm resources and sustained competitive advantage, Journal of Management, Vol. 17 No. 1, pp. 99-120.

Beckerman, W. and J. Pasek (2001) Justice, Posterity and the Environment. Oxford, OUP.

Birmingham University (2002), Urban Governance, Partnership and Poverty: ESCOR-funded Research in Ten Cities: 1998-2001, Birmingham, UK.

Blackburn, James (et al.) 2000), Mainstreaming Participation in Development, The World Bank, Washington D.C.

Black, J. (1999) Development in Theory and Practice Boulder, Colorado: Westview Press.

Buhalis, D., 2000, Marketing the competitive destination of the future, Tourism Management, Vol.21 (1), pp.97-116.

Burns, P. (2004) "Tourism Planning: A Third Way?" Annals of Tourism Research 31: 24-43

Burns, P. (1999) Paradoxes in Planning Tourism: Elitism or Brutalism. Annals of Tourism Research 26:329–348.

Clancy, M. (1999) "Tourism and Development: Evidence from Mexico" Annals of Tourism Research 26:1–20

Crouch, G., and B. Ritchie (1999) "Tourism, Competitiveness and Social Prosperity" Journal of Business Research 44:137–152

Capra, Fritjof. O ponto de mutação. São Paulo: Cultrix, 1982.

_____. A teia da vida. 4.ed. São Paulo: Cultrix, 1996.

CMMAD. Nosso futuro comum. 2.ed. Rio de Janeiro: FGV, 1991.

CREA-RJ. *Projeto Brasil 21: Uma nova ética para o desenvolvimento*. Rio de Janeiro: CREA–RJ, 1999.

Constanza, R., R. D'Arge and 11 others (1997) 'The value of the world's ecosystem services and natural capital.' Nature 387: 253-260.

Connelly, G. (2007). Testing governance—A research agenda for exploring urban tourism competitiveness policy: The case of Liverpool 1980–2000. Tourism Geographies, 9(1), 84–114.

Conyers, D. (1983), "Decentralization: The latest fashion in development administration?", Public Administration and Development, No. 3.

David J. Telfer; Geoffrey Wall.(1996) LINKAGES BETWEEN TOURISM AND FOOD PRODUCTION. Annals of Tourism Research, Vol. 23, No. 3, pp. 635-653

Daly, H. E. "On economics as a life science". London: Journal of Political Economy, 1968.

De Franco, Augusto. Além da renda: a pobreza brasileira como insuficiência de desenvolvimento.

Brasília: Millennium–Instituto de Política, 2000.

Delgado M., M.E. Porter, and S. Stern, (2010) "Clusters and Entrepreneurship," Journal of Economic Geography, 10 (4), pp. 495-518.

Feldman, M.P. and Audretsch, D., (1999) "Innovation in cities: Science-based diversity, specialization and localized competition," European Economic Review, 43, pp. 409-429

Fluvia, Modest et al. *Politica turistica: entre la sustentabilidad y el desarrollo económico*. Barcelona:

Esade-Cedit, n. 3, pp. 34-41, 1998.

Frey, B. and A. Stutzer (2002) Happiness and Economics. Princeton, Princeton University Press.

Fujita, Masahisa, Krugman, Paul and Venable, Anthony (1999): The Spatial Economy: Cities, Regions and International Trade. Cambridge, MA: MIT Press.

Hawkins, D. E. and Calnan, L. (2009), Comparative Study of the Sustainability of Donor-Supported Tourism Clusters in Developing Economies, Tourism Recreation Research, Volume 34 (3).

Hjalager, A. (2002) Repairing Innovation Defectiveness in Tourism. *Tourism Management*, 23 (5), 465-474.

Ketel, Christian. (2003)The development of the cluster concept: present experiences and further developments.

NWR Conference on clusters, Duisburg.

Goeymen, K. (2000), Tourism and governance in Turkey, Annals of Tourism Research, Vol. 27, No. 4, pp. 1025±1048, 2000

Gollub, James et al (2005). Using cluster-based economic strategy to minimize tourism leakages. San Francisco: GEDP.

Gossling, S. and Hall, C M (eds.) (2006): Tourism and Global Environmental Change: Ecological, Social and Political Interrelationships. Routledge, London.

Hall, C. M. (2011). Framing governance theory: A typology of governance and its implications for tourism policy analysis. Journal of Sustainable Tourism.

Haugland S. et.al. (2011) Development of Tourism Destinations: An Integrated Multilevel Perspective. Annals of Tourism Research, Vol. 38, No. 1, pp. 268–290.

Hamel, G. and Prahalad, C.K. (1994). "Competing for the Future", Harvard Business School Press.

Kozak, M. (2002). Destination benchmarking. Annals of Tourism Research, 29(2), 497–519.

IADB (2001), Summary of Findings: Decentralization and Effective Citizen Participation: Six Cautionary Tales. OVE. WP1/01. April.

ILO 2011: Promoting decent work in the green economy. ILO background note to Towards a Green Economy. Geneva 2001, International Labour Office

ILO 2008: Guide for Social Dialogue in the Tourism Industry. Working paper 265 by Dain Bolwell and Wolfgang Weinz. Geneva 2008, International Labour Office.

ILO 2010: Developments and challenges in the hospitality and tourism sector. Issues paper for discussion at the Global Dialogue Forum for the Hotels, Catering, Tourism Sector (23–24 November 2010). Geneva 2010, International Labour Organization.

ILO 2011: Measuring Employment in the Tourism Industries beyond a Tourism Satellite Account: A Case Study of Indonesia/International Labour Office. Jakarta

Inglehart R. and H.D. Klingemann (2000) Genes, culture, democracy and happiness. Cambridge, MIT Press.

Ivars, Josep et al. "Planificación y gestión del desarrollo turístico sostenible: Propuesta para la creación de un sistema de indicadores". Documento de Trabajo Numero 1. Universidad de Alicante, 2001.

MARSHALL, A. (1920) "Principles of Economics," Macmillan, London.

MD. AL-AMIN ; MD. NAZRUL ISLAM; TOFAYEL AHMED (2007) Local Governance and Sustainable Development in Bangladesh. Asian Affairs, Vol. 29, No. 4 : 5-28, October-December, 2007

Mann, S; Hayat A. Development Impacts in the Tourism Sector through the Lens of Two IFC Hotel Investments: What They Show and What We Can Learn. IFC.

Mathieson, A., & Wall, G. (1982). Tourism: Economic, physical, and social impacts.London, England: Longman.

Marchena, Manuel. "El desarrollo sostenible del turismo: El papel del municipio". Seminario sobredesarrollo sostenible del turismo. Havana: OMT, 1996.

Ministerio de Medio Ambiente. Sistema español de indicadores ambientales de turismo. Madri: Ministerio de Medio Ambiente, 2003.

MORGAN, G. (1986) "Images of Organization", Sage, Beverly Hills, CA

OECD (2004), Supporting decentralization and local governance: Lessons Learned on Donor Support to Decentralization and Local Governance, OECD, Paris.

OECD.(2000) "OECD core set of indicators for environmental performance reviews". Environmental Monographs, 83, Organization for Economic Cooperation and Development.

ODI (2006). Tourism businesses and the local economy: increasing impact through a linkages approach. ODI Briefing Paper, March, London.

OMT. Previsiones del turismo mundial hasta el año 2006 y después. Madri: OMT Publications, 2005.

Positive Psychology?", Psychtalk, 56, 17-20.

Pearce, D. (1989). Tourism development. Harlow, Essex: Longman.

Porter, M; Kramer, M. (2011) The Big Idea: Creating Shared Value - Harvard Business Review 1/13/11 5:09 AM http://hbr.org/2011/01/the-big-idea-creating-shared-value/ar/pr Page 9 of 12

Porter, Michael (2008) Clusters, innovation and competitiveness: new findings and implications for policy. Harvard Business School Note 456-490.

-------------------- (2003) The economic performance of regions. Regional Studies, 37, pp 549-578.

-------------------- (2001) Regions and the new economics of competition. In A.J Scott (Ed), Global City-Regions. Trends, Theory and Policy, New York: Oxford University Press, pp.145-151.

-------------------- . (1998) "Clusters and the New Economics of Competition". Harvard Business Review. November-December

Prahalad, C.K. and Hamel, G.(1990). "The Core Competence of the Corporation", Harvard Business Review, May–June.

Prahalad, C.K. and Hamel, G. (1990), ªThe core competence of the corporation°, Harvard Business

Review, May/June, pp. 79-91.

Roriguez-Clare, A., (2007), "Clusters and Comparative Advantage: Implications for Industrial Policy," Journal of Development Economics, 82, pp. 43-57.

Rosenthal, Stuart S. and STRANGE, William C. (2001): .The Determinants of Agglomeration. Journal of Urban Economics, 50, 191.229.

Rosenfield, S. (2002) Creating smart systems: a guide to cluster strategies in less favored regions. Brussels:

European Commission.

_____. Overachievers: business clusters that work, regional tech-nology strategies. New York: Inc, 1995.

RUSSO, A. P. "Organizing sustainable tourism development in heritage cities". In Technical Report n. 28. Proceedings of the international seminar: tourism management in heritage cities. Verona:

Cierre Gráfica, 1998.

UNDP (2004), Decentralized Governance for Development, (http.//www.updp.org/governance/local.htm

UNDP (2008) Human Development Report - Fighting climate change: human solidarity in a divided world.

UNDP (2011) Human Development Report: Sustainability and Equity - A Better Future for All.

UNEP (2011) Tourism: investing in energy and resource efficiency.

UNEP & UNWTO (2005) Making tourism more sustainable: a guide for policy makers.

UNEP &WTO. Final report of the International Conference on Sustainable Tourism in small island developing states and other islands. Lanzarote: Unep-WTO, 1998.

UN International Labour Organization (2008) "Guide for social dialogue in the tourism industry. Sectoral Activities Programme" Working Paper 265 prepared by Dain Bolwell and Wolfgang Weinz.

Schilcher, D. (2007). Growth versus equity: The continuum of pro-poor tourism and neoliberal

SNV. Tourism Destinations Governance: enhancing equity and inclusive development. SNV Concept Papers - Regional Knowledge Network East & Southern Africa, Nairobi, 2011.

SNV & UNWTO (2010). Manual on Tourism and Poverty Alleviation: practical steps for destinations. Madrid.

SNV; ODI (2009), Making success work for the poor: Package tourism in Northern Tanzania, SNV and ODI, London.

SNV (2006), Pro-poor Sustainable Tourism Lessons Learned in Nepal, SNV, Kathmandu.

governance. Current Issues in Tourism, 10, 166–193.

Solvelli, O., G. Lindqvist, and Ketels. C. (2006) Clusters Initiatives in Developing and Transition Economies. Report, Ivory Tower AB, Stockholm, www.cluster-research.org/dldevtra.htm

Torres. E (2005) Review of Tourism Market Trends. Economic Policy Papers (p61-69): Malaga University.

Trousdale, W. (1999). Governance in context—Boracay Island, Phillipines. Annals of Tourism Research, 26(4), 840–867.

Yuksel, F., Bramwell, B., & Yuksel, A. (2005). Centralized and decentralized governance in Turkey. Annals of Tourism Research, 32(4), 859–886.

Vera, Fernando; IVARS, J. A. (2000) "Una propuesta de indicadores para la planificación y gestión del turismo sostenible". Comunicación al congreso nacional de medio ambiente, Universidad de Alicante.

Vignati, Federico (2012). Value Chain Analysis as a Kick Off for SME's Development in Maputo City. SNV.

Vignati, Federico (2008). Gestão de Destinos Turísticos: como atrair pessoas para polos, cidades e paises. SENAC-Rio.

Wang, Y. (2008). Collaborative destination marketing: Understanding the dynamic process. Journal of Travel Research, 47, 151–166.

Williamson, Oliver (1998).Transaction Cost Economics: How It Works; Where It Is Headed, The Economist, 146: 23–58.

White, A (2007), „A Global Projection of Subjective Well-being: A Challenge to

World Bank (1994), Governance: the World Bank's Experience. Washington D.C.

carbon
neutral

The printing of 3000 copies of *Sustainable Tourism: promoting shared prosperity in emerging and fast growing economies*, have generated 1.8 tons of carbon emissions (CO2e). The carbon footprint has been offset through REDD+ conservation initiative in the Amazon Rain Forest (Tambopata - Peru). The acquired bonds are verified and validated under the VCS international standard and registered at Markit Registry. To learn more, visit: www.iniciativaverde.com.pe